£ 70·58
11½ 91
£ 1500

OIL, DEBT AND DEVELOPMENT: OPEC IN THE THIRD WORLD

Oil, Debt and Development: OPEC in the Third World

PAUL HALLWOOD
Lecturer in Political Economy, University of Aberdeen

and

STUART W. SINCLAIR
Formerly Lecturer in Economics, University of Reading

London
GEORGE ALLEN & UNWIN
Boston   Sydney

First published in 1981

GEORGE ALLEN & UNWIN LTD
40 Museum Street, London WC1A 1LU

© Paul Hallwood and Stuart W. Sinclair, 1981

British Library Cataloguing in Publication Data

Hallwood, Paul
   Oil, debt and development.
   1. Underdeveloped areas — Economic conditions
   2. Petroleum — Prices
   I. Title   II. Sinclair, Stuart W
   330.9′172′4   HC59.7   80-41132

ISBN 0-04-382027-1

Typeset at the Alden Press, Oxford, London and Northampton in 10 on 11 point Press Roman and printed in Great Britain by Billing and Sons Ltd., Guildford, London and Worcester

Contents

Tables

Figures

Abbreviations

b/d	barrels per day
c.i.f.	cost insurance freight
dc	developed country
f.o.b.	free on board
ldc	less developed country
lldc	least less developed country
NOPEC	non-oil exporting less developed country
OPEC	Organisation of Petroleum Exporting Countries
UNCTAD	United Nations Conference on Trade and Development

Preface

OPEC has seldom been out of the news in the last decade. Although its formal existence dates from 1960, and its antecedents can be traced back further still, it remains to most people an enigma. Even to specialists in academia, policy analysis and the serious press, its nature is unclear and its interests are opaque. But nowhere is this lack of clarity more apparent, perhaps, than in discussions of the relationships which have sprung up between OPEC member states and the other developing countries, what we call the 'non-oil ldcs' or 'NOPECs'. It is the aim of this book to investigate this last topic.

Immediately after the spectacular oil price rises in late 1973 commentators tended to the view that the world had witnessed the first of a series of developing country manoeuvres. There was talk of OPEC being replicated in a number of other commodities – in bauxite, copper, rubber, tin. If they could do it with oil, why not with everything else? Initially the OPEC countries themselves encouraged this view. At a special United Nations session hastily convened in the spring of 1974, Algeria, the host nation, took exactly this line. What OPEC had done, it proposed, was just the first strike for the developing world. Taken with the other measures long sought in other areas (notably in trade relationships, debt, aid) OPEC had taken the first step towards the new international economic order. Seen in this light, what OPEC had done could only be good for the non-oil ldcs.

Having raised hopes and obscured truths, however, the OPEC members found disillusion came all the harder. Within months grumblings came from black African statesmen about the huge rise in their import bill the oil price rises had caused. It became apparent, therefore, that just as OPEC had not blazed a trail which other ldcs could easily follow, so had OPEC not been the catalyst in creating new allegiances in the north–south debate. Indeed, we find that while there are elements of both co-operation and competition in the economic relationships between OPEC members and the non-oil exporting ldcs, it is competition which tends to dominate, a factor that cannot be disguised by 'Third World' rhetoric.

London, February 1980

C. Paul Hallwood
Stuart W. Sinclair

Introduction: Oil, Debt and the Developing World

> October 1973 was a turning point in the history of international relations . . . the point when the Third World countries became aware, not of their rights, but of their power. (Amin, 1979)

This dramatic statement by a well-known radical Egyptian social scientist sums up what many people thought initially about the oil 'crisis' of 1973–4. In Japan a word was specially invented: 'oilshock'. Elsewhere in the developed world groups of eminent scholars met and issued documents replete with dire warnings. Typical of the essays which the oil price rise prompted was 'A turning point in north–south economic relations'. Written in early 1974, this was full of references to a 'critical turning-point in history', and to OPEC having 'detonated an explosion in north–south economic relations that has been building up for years' (Gardner *et al*, 1974). Similarly, another collection of essays on energy and US foreign policy claimed that the OPEC price rises 'threatened little short of unmitigated disaster for many of the ldcs' (Dunn, 1974, p. 165). Even in 1978 apocalyptic views were still common: for instance, it was argued that the advent of 'expensive energy' had led to 'nothing short of a fundamental shift in the international economic power configuration' (Cohen, 1978). With the benefit of a few years' hindsight, though, it is possible to see that most of these views were too stark. The substantial rise in oil prices announced by the Shah of Iran on 23 December 1973, contrary to expectations, did not plunge all the less developed countries into irremediable crisis: there were in fact ten loan reschedulings and overall their growth rates were not severely affected. Nor indeed was the oil price rise the only important event of that year: other commodity prices, notably of copper, sugar, tin and rubber, were booming, and inflation was moving upwards in the developed countries (dcs), the ldcs' main trade partners.

During this period, economists, observing what was going on, were beginning to pose development questions differently. By the early 1970s emphasis on the 'growing gap' in living standards between developed and developing countries was being dropped in favour of a more selective perspective in which the differential growth rates and markedly varying experiences of the 1960s – the first United Nations Development Decade – were recognised. Separate groupings of countries came to be distinguished much more boldly than before: one read of the 'middle income fast growers' (eventually to become the NICS, or 'newly industrialising countries'), the 'least developed', and others. But the two sets which perhaps became the most clearly differentiated from the mass of ldcs after 1973 were the members of OPEC, the oil exporters' organisation, on the one hand, and the 'most seriously affected' group on the other. The latter – the forty-five countries of the world stuck in the most hopeless poverty – were largely distinguished by the success of the former; that is, by the blow their prospects were thought to have suffered from the oil price rise of late 1973.[1]

The concern of this book is not however primarily with the relationship between these last two sub-sets of countries or between the developed and developing countries in aggregate. Rather, the concern is to investigate the results of one group of developing countries' successful effort to improve their welfare *vis-à-vis* the rest. The specialist literature contains many discussions of the feasibility of setting up a bauxite cartel or a joint tea and coffee producers' group, but none of these has come to fruition. There is also a lot of discussion of the ways in which ldcs' manufactured exports might enjoy better terms of access to dc markets – that is, be subject to fewer and less intensive protectionist barriers. In these and other cases the clear aim of policy deliberation is to better the welfare of the inhabitants of certain groups of ldcs. Despite the success that the manufactures exporting ldcs have enjoyed (as Chapter 1 will show, they increased their exports to dcs from $3 billion in 1960 to $32 billion by 1974), the group which has beyond question enjoyed the most spectacular boom is OPEC – a group of thirteen ldcs, seven of them Arab, with 320 million inhabitants and an income per head by 1978 of over $15,000 for the best-off, the Kuwaitis. In 1974 OPEC exports of 29.6 million barrels per day (b/d) were generating $90.5 billion in revenue; by 1978 a slightly lower volume (27.7 million b/d) was yielding $119.2 billion.

It is immediately apparent that revenue of this magnitude could not be collected by one group of countries without constraints being imposed elsewhere in the world, and a substantial portion of this book is devoted to showing the welfare effects on the rest of the developing world of this rise in the price of oil. Before embarking on this task, however, the rest of this introduction presents a short *tour d'horizon* of the type of issues to be dealt with later.

A not surprising consequence of the success of OPEC in raising the price of oil has been a series of rifts in the negotiating stances of the developing world itself, most noticeably at the meetings of UNCTAD (the UN standing conference which deals with trade, financial and commodity issues) and other international fora. By 1979 these rifts had become plain, and before the fifth session of UNCTAD in that year, Costa Rica had been active in assembling a new grouping calling itself OPIC, the Organisation of Oil Importing Countries. OPIC argued that Venezuela as the regional OPEC member should sell crude at concessional prices to its poorer Latin American and Caribbean neighbours, although Venezuelan ministers had in fact long been calling for more OPEC aid, suggesting that its scope be extended so that more than just Bolivia, El Salvador, Honduras and Haiti in that part of the world be recipients. Indeed, the Venezuelan energy minister had made a two week tour of North Africa and the Middle East drumming up support, or at least attention, for his plans earlier in 1979. At UNCTAD V Iraq was also censured on these grounds, particularly in the second week of the conference when patience with the OPEC position was beginning to wear thin.

In the event a few accommodating moves were made. The Iraqi deputy trade minister proposed a new fund to compensate the poorest oil importing nations, but the idea was felt to lack conviction. A characteristically robust retort came some five weeks later from the OPEC meeting in Geneva on 26–8 June when it was recommended that its member governments add $800 million to the OPEC Special Fund. Apart from this they proposed that a long-run OPEC-OECD facility to compensate ldcs for rising oil and manufactured goods prices be studied. A communiqué then reiterated their fundamental position – by now familiar to non-oil ldcs – that no dialogue on energy could be undertaken unless it also embraced a full discussion of all north–south development questions. Nor did the Special Fund's announcement of a few days earlier that a selection of non-Arab African countries (including Cameroon, Lesotho, Mali and Zambia) were to share in a further $38.5 million of project assistance assuage ldc disappointment.

By mid 1979, then, many ldc governments were apparently asking whether the generous – if arbitrary – aid packages they stood a good chance of receiving were sufficient compensation for the oil price rises they supported – implicitly or explicitly – at so many conferences. OPEC had lost some of its early support and few ldc leaders retained a vision of overnight wealth on the coat-tails of this particular commodity cartel.

Just as important as this type of conflict within the developing countries, however, is the further fact that most OPEC members' planners are intent on having their countries undergo a second transformation. Having already substantially augmented their export earnings from crude oil, most of them desire now to become industrial economies as well, and thus eventually purveyors to the world of refined oil products, petrochemicals, plastics, rubber, steel, aluminium, and more. To take only the simplest example, OPEC states were still by 1978 able to refine before export only 13% of their crude oil output – equivalent to 2.59 million b/d *(OPEC Bulletin,* April 1979, p. 26). To raise this proportion is as much a matter of prestige as of economic calculus.

The rate at which these OPEC members intend to force themselves through the costly initial stages of industrialisation has undoubtedly slowed since the halcyon days of 1973—4 but there is no doubting their conviction. Policy statements have often been strident, for some audiences at least, with hints of curtailed crude oil supplies for those countries which attempt to obstruct the OPEC industrialisation effort. In a speech dealing with the need for industrial diversification in his country, for example, the Saudi minister for industry, Dr Ghazi Al-Ghosaibi, claimed that 'industrialisation is as ferocious a battle as war . . . but we will finally triumph' *(MEED*, August 1978, p. 13).

Initially many OPEC states exhibited an eagerness bordering on panic to use their burgeoning oil revenues to build up an industrial base. Intent on making his country the world's fifth power, the Shah of Iran doubled the expenditure ceilings of the fifth national plan halfway through. It was the beginning of a brief exercise in forcefeeding, a gesture aptly described as 'unashamedly grandiose' (Graham, 1978, p. 18).

Given that many of these projects are intended to create goods for export, it follows that as they enter the 1980s the non-oil ldcs will be facing not just a world with higher oil prices but a world containing another clutch of newly industrialising countries, some of whom have the power to subsidise the energy and capital components of their costs of production if they so wish. For the foreseeable future the range and volume of OPEC manufactured exports is likely to be slim; but the creation of this capacity will none the less be in the minds of planners in the non-oil ldcs.

During the 1960s, while the oil price was low and stable, a number of non-oil ldcs were building up their own industrial capacity across a wide range of sectors. In 1960 ldcs as a whole produced only 6.9% of the world's industrial value added (or net output). But this grew to reach 8.6% by 1975, after a 280% increase in their value added in manufacturing, expressed in 1970 prices. Part of this growth in output was itself a direct consequence of the 1973 price rise, since an early reaction by many ldcs to mitigate the worst consequences was an effort to build more oil refineries, so that crude oil rather than (more expensive) refined oil products could be imported. In general, the countries with the largest domestic market for refined products (India, Egypt, Brazil, Argentina) were able to secure favourable deals with oil companies, who were awarded marketing concessions in return for assistance in establishing refineries (Odell, 1979, p. 168). The smaller ldcs, on the other hand, were less well placed; many of those which did go ahead found their excess capacity a perennial problem. In aggregate, there are now more oil refineries in developing countries outside OPEC than sited in OPEC members: in 1978 there were 149 refineries in non-OPEC ldcs as against 57 in OPEC member states (the world total was 843) *(Oil and Gas Journal,* 25 December 1978).

Among the ldcs which have refineries but no domestic oil productions are some of the world's poorest. Ethiopia, Ghana, Ivory Coast, Liberia, Madagascar, Mozambique and Senegal each have a refinery; so do Sudan, Tanzania, Togo and Zambia. A further 101 are under construction or expansion in ldcs at present *(Petroleum Economist,* September 1978). It might be argued that these refineries are essential components of an industrialisation strategy in any case, and that their construction implies no misallocation of resources. But apart from the fact that the capital start-up costs are vast — now perhaps $500 million — it is also known that the multiplier effects (that is, the stimulus received by other parts of the economy) from the construction of an oil refinery are meagre (Yotopoulos and Nugent, 1973). Here, then, is another instance in which interests appear to clash; in this case many very poor ldcs have been obliged to build themselves expensive refineries in the hope of conserving some of the foreign exchange costs of importing crude-based products. It is to a full consideration of these and other conflicts of interest that attention is now turned.

Chapter 1 begins by presenting an overview of the main changes that have emerged in the economies of the ldcs since 1960, first to facilitate the subsequent analysis of changes in their prospects, and second to emphasise the extent to which they had diverged by around 1973. In terms of economic structure, considerable progress was made in diversification in the 1960s. The share of unprocessed raw materials in ldcs' export earnings fell from 86% in 1960 to 57% in 1976 (excluding crude petroleum). Correspondingly, the share of fully manufactured goods in their exports rose from 13% in 1960 to 43% in 1976.[2]

Chapter 2 then describes the main changes in the international economy witnessed in the 1960s and early 1970s. Again, the intention here is not to provide a definitive account of the economic environment but to set out briefly the background against which the ldcs' progress as just described can be understood and against which the impact of the oil price rises in late 1973 must be judged. The chapter begins by describing the performance of the world economy in the 1960s and then moves on to explain why these patterns faltered and changed in the 1970s. The significance of higher oil prices, the collapse of the international monetary system and governments' policy reactions to higher inflation and unemployment than had hitherto been normal are assessed in turn.

Surprisingly, in view of all the attention that has been paid to the effects of OPEC's oil policy, there has been relatively little effort expended on understanding more fully the nature of OPEC as an organisation. It is commonly referred to as a cartel, but a moment's reflection shows that in practice it fulfils only one of the three prerequisites of a cartel in economic theory. Furthermore, by implicitly or explicitly viewing the organisation as a cartel, and thus akin to oligopolistic industries in certain periods in dcs' history, analysts are frequently drawn into predicting its demise. In 1974 the conventional wisdom, as expressed in this typical example from a conference on energy and US foreign policy, was that 'present prices of $9 per barrel are likely to fall substantially' (Fried, 1974, p. 269). Clearly, then, there is a need to deliberate on the nature of OPEC, and Chapter 3 performs this task.

One of the findings of Chapter 3 is that the notion of 'swing producers' in the organisation (countries whose actions in the oil market can alone underwrite or undermine the desires of the organisation's other members) is insightful. It is also suggested that precisely because of the absence of the formal or centralised prorationing scheme essential in a true cartel, the more radical member states have been unable to exert leverage over the members whose political inclinations are towards continuity of production and relatively stable prices.

The tensions which exist within OPEC, of which the latter point about continuity of production is merely one example, will naturally be significant in determining the nature and scope of the organisation's relations with non-member states. For OPEC countries' success in raising the oil price in the 1970s has presented them with a number of difficult new questions, as well as intensified the need to ponder some old and familiar, and largely unresolved, ones too. OPEC members have been made acutely aware that their new income has posed many worrying problems in diplomacy.

There can be little doubt that whatever happens there is great concern to identify OPEC countries as loyal members of the 'Group of 77'. Official statements by OPEC spokesmen are invariably peppered with references to the organisation's members' being 'full members of the Third World',[3] and there are frequent statements to the effect that 'OPEC members have in the past proved their strong solidarity with the Third World' *(OPEC Press Release, 1979)*.

A relatively unobtrusive foreign policy tool much used by OPEC in the 1970s is aid. Although there have always been grumblings about the regional dispersion of OPEC aid — it was initially heavily weighted by Arab recipients — there is no doubting its scale. OPEC concessional aid (that is, resources offered at less than prevailing market rates of interest) has rapidly built up from its 1973 level of $1.3 billion to $5.3–$5.5 billion annually during the 1975–7 period. In 1977 this was equivalent to some 3% of OPEC combined GNP: a substantially higher figure than the 0.3% achieved by the members of the OECD Development Assistance Committee in that year. Some individual country cases are even more startling: in 1976 the United Arab Emirates allocated in excess of 10% of its GNP to aid, while Saudi Arabia managed 6% and Qatar over 7%. Moreover, the grant (or gift) element in each loan is increasing, and — unlike a substantial portion of Western aid — OPEC aid is not 'tied'. In addition, the share of OPEC aid going to the least developed countries has been increasing. This is in accordance with the spirit of most of the major aid donors, who in the 1970s expressed their intention of concentrating aid on the poorest countries and on the poorest groups of people in those countries. From $23.7 million of aid to the least developed in 1973 (2% of total OPEC aid) OPEC donors' contributions rose enormously to $858 billion, or 6% of the total, by 1977 (UNCTAD, 1979a).

It would be easy to regard the OPEC aid institutions' efforts as a placebo for other ldcs' having to put up with higher oil prices. However, neither group would be willing to see these transfers in that light. On the one hand, the ldc recipients rarely see the disbursements as sufficient to offset their higher import bills for fuel (Chapter 6 here examines the justification of their claim); and on the other, their OPEC patrons refuse to accept the implication that their oil policy necessarily damages poorer ldcs. Arab spokesmen in particular are adamant on this point. In a paper presented in London in July 1977 at a conference organised by the Islamic Council of Europe, one speaker repeatedly made the point that 'the oil weapon was not forged by the Arabs: it was forged by Gulf, Shell and BP'. Moreover, he set the energy 'problems' of the ldcs, whatever they may be, firmly in the context of developed countries' policy: 'the causes of the economic deprivation of the third world lie not in the oil wells of Arabia but in the prevailing economic system' (Islamic Council of Europe, 1979). It can, then, be easily seen that the motives of OPEC's aid institutions' policies are complex and subtle, and in addition to the elucidation offered in Chapter 6, Chapter 4 looks at the net payments impact for non-oil ldcs of their oil imports since 1973 and Chapter 10 again returns to these topics in its summing up of the relationship.

A major consequence of the changed world economic circumstances after 1974 was a dramatic worsening of the non-oil ldcs' balance of payments position. While the value of the oil-exporters' exports soared from $42 billion in 1973 (fob) to $115 billion a year later – a 174% rise – the import bill facing non-oil ldcs rose from $78 billion to $124 billion. The non-oil ldcs' current account deficit rose to $24 billion in 1974, reached $38 billion in 1975 and fell away somewhat to $25 billion in 1976. As has already been suggested, these and other trends form the basis of the analysis in Chapter 4, in which various measures of the balance of payments and terms of trade experience of the ldcs *vis-à-vis* both OPEC and dcs are judged.

The fact that most ldcs were unable to cope at once with these increases in their import bill meant that they resorted to borrowing on an unprecedented scale in addition to using the foreign exchange reserves they had been accumulating for some years. Chapter 5 deals with the resulting problem of debt, and in assessing the extent to which there exists a serious likelihood of widespread default, attempts to identify that proportion of the growth of ldc debt in the 1970s that can reasonably be attributed to the actions of OPEC.

Western observers have persistently been surprised at the ability of OPEC countries to spend the money they have earned from oil exports.

The OPEC surplus of export earnings over import disbursements was projected to increase spectacularly each year after 1973, and in the early years Sheikh Yamani frequently cited an estimate which predicted that the OPEC current account surplus would reach $250 billion by 1978. But in the event it has never exceeded the $64.2 billion which was its 1974 peak. It fell steadily from that level to reach $23 billion by 1978,[4] with only Saudi Arabia and the small Gulf states in consistent surplus. In its 1978/9 financial year even the Saudi Arabian government managed to overspend its official budget by SR 196 million ($57.6 million), drew from reserves and cut back public spending by 2% in real terms for 1979/80.

It follows from this that exporters to OPEC have been doing well, and certainly ldc exporters have not been slow to take a share in this import boom. Apart from the export of temporary labour dealt with in Chapter 8, many ldcs have been successful in exporting processed and semi-processed goods, as well as services such as consortia teams and consultancy. India alone secured $1.2 billion-worth of projects over 1974–7, and became second only to South Korea as a purveyor of contracts from ldcs to the Middle East *(FT,* 18 April 1979). In aggregate terms, non-oil ldcs managed to increase by nearly 50% their share of world exports to OPEC by value over the period 1973–6, from 4.3% to 6.1% (UNCTAD, 1979b, p. 61). A number of interesting questions about this penetration by ldc companies present themselves. For instance, to what extent is their success due to preferential treatment by OPEC clients? Do ldcs generally present lower tenders than dc firms or consortia? And if so, does this reflect an element of government subsidy? These and similar topics are dealt with in Chapter 7.

The various 'employment problems' of ldcs have been the subject of exhaustive analysis by economists. Recently difficulties anticipated in sustaining employment levels despite higher fuel prices have given rise to serious fears of 'oil-induced' unemployment. But at the same time the advent of higher oil revenues in the Middle East and in other OPEC member states raised the possibility that demand for labour might boom. Chapter 8 therefore looks at labour, migration and remittances as they affect OPEC countries. It begins with an overview of the Middle Eastern countries' influx of labour from neighbouring ldcs, but also assesses a rather different case. For by no means all OPEC members are sparsely populated labour-scarce countries. Indonesia, Nigeria and Iran, which between them have three-quarters of the population within OPEC, have severe employment difficulties, and special mention is made of these.

Finally, before beginning it must be mentioned that while OPEC and other ldcs are distinguished throughout this book and are so distinguished in almost all discussions, it would be wrong to imagine that no ldcs outside OPEC produce or export crude oil. In fact there are few countries that do not produce some crude oil: even some of the twenty-five 'least developed countries' (those judged by the UN to have been hardest hit in 1974) possess reserves of crude oil. In 1975 these countries exported $212 million-worth of oil products, equivalent to 7.52% of all their exports.

There is oil exploration in most ldcs, and naturally each increase in the OPEC oil price enhances the possible benefits from the search. In 1978 even Ivory Coast, Chad, Niger, Gambia and Tanzania, not likely-sounding oil sources and among the world's poorest countries, drilled for oil (*World Oil*, 15 August 1978; *Oil and Gas Journal*, 25 December 1978). Hardly any Central or Latin American states failed to drill and in mid-1979 Peru became Latin America's fifth net oil exporter. One of these, Mexico, remains an enigma in some respects. An exporter of 750,000 b/d by late 1979, her price is set just above that of Saudi marker crude, and while keen to deny she is in any sense a 'blackleg', Mexico sees no reason for joining OPEC (*FT*, 26 January 1979). She is thus in a position to straddle the two sets of countries whose sometimes divergent and sometimes congruent interests are the concern of this book.

Notes

1 This group, which includes twenty-four members of another UN category, 'the least developed countries', was recognised officially in May 1974.

The original twenty-five 'least developed' identified by the UN General Assembly in December 1971 were: Afghanistan, Benin, Bhutan, Botswana, Burundi, Chad, Ethiopia, Guinea, Haiti, Lao People's Democratic Republic, Lesotho, Malawi, Maldives, Mali, Nepal, Niger, Rwanda, Sikkim, Somalia, Sudan, Uganda, Tanzania, Upper Volta, Samoa, Yemen Arab Republic. Six more have since been added: Bangladesh, Central African Empire, Democratic Yemen and Gambia in 1975, and Cape Verde and the Comoros in 1977. The group now comprises 257.7 million people, or 12.3% of the population of all ldcs. See UNCTAD (1979a).

2 'Total exports' is defined here to exclude crude petroleum. If petroleum is included, the share of manufactures in total export value stood at 17.2% in 1976.

3 See, for example, the address of Rene G. Ortiz, Secretary General of OPEC, to UNCTAD V in May 1979.

4 OECD figures; surplus defined as balance on goods, services and private transfers, excluding official transfers.

1

Economic Divergences between Developing Countries

This chapter discusses the growth and development experience of the less developed countries from *circa* 1960, the beginning of the first United Nations Development Decade, through to about 1973. Its purpose is to show how, through various channels and at various times, certain ldcs or groups of ldcs became differentiated from the mass so that by the end of this period a number of them had made considerable progress towards raising the average income of their inhabitants. Since this would later have an important influence on these countries' response to the oil price rises of the 1970s, it is important to set out this background before proceeding.

The following sections deal with growth patterns in the First Development Decade of the United Nations and continues up to 1973. Initially the discussion is couched in terms of aggregative growth; that is, in terms of gross national product and industrial output. But it is widely recognised by now that these terms provide only one perspective on ldcs' development, and that while they are helpful in pointing up overall patterns they do not reveal everything about the nature of the growth experience for those who live through it. For this reason the final section of this chapter discusses different measures of economic and social development.

The development experience, 1960–73

As the first United Nations Development Decade opened, the prospects for most ldcs were coloured by the position of primary commodity prices. For in 1960, 86% of all ldcs' foreign exchange earnings were obtained through the exports of raw materials in unprocessed forms.[1] The preceding decade had seen growing dissatisfaction with primary commodity specialisation, and the influence of economists such as Lewis, Prebisch and Singer led to greater interest in import substitution, or the setting up of an indigenous manufacturing base to replace dependence on imports of finished goods in exchange for primary commodity exports. Of special significance here was the decline in the terms of trade (that is, the relationship between a country's export price index and import price index) that

Table 1.1   *Growth rates in GNP, 1960−7*

Growth rates per annum	Number of ldcs	Share of total ldc population %
6% or over	18	15
4% − 6%	25	31
under 4%	37	48

Source: UN (1967).

ldcs had suffered during the 1950s.[2] From an index of 100 in 1950, ldcs' terms of trade *vis-à-vis* dcs fell to 86 by 1961.

The objective of the First Development Decade was, quite naturally, to 'accelerate progress towards self-sustaining growth of the economy of the individual nations and their social advancement so as to attain in each under-developed country a substantial increase in the rate of growth' (UN, 1962). The growth rate of GNP specified as the minimum objective was 5%, to be attained by the end of the decade. This was sufficient to double per capita living standards within 25−30 years.

It became apparent as early as 1967, however, that the 5% goal was not being attained throughout the developing world and furthermore that the gap in per capita incomes between 'rich' and 'poor' countries' inhabitants was widening both relatively and absolutely. Population growth was the major contributor to the failure to achieve growth objectives, for although 'total real product' as calculated by the UN rose by 4.5% annually over 1960−5 in ldcs − a figure close to the 5.1% achieved in developed countries − in per capita terms, the improvement in ldcs was about 2%. This was barely better than half the developed countries' per capita rate of 3.6% (UN, 1967).

These growth rates were not, of course, shared by all ldcs, still less by all regions or sectors within each ldc. In a sample of eighty ldcs whose data was collected by the UN over the years 1960−7, the mode growth rate was less than 4% per annum but a number of countries achieved growth in excess of 6% and even up to 20% (see Table 1.1).

The spread of growth rates for the longer period 1951−76 is shown in Table 1.2. This indicates how the groups of ldcs that have now come to be termed 'lower', 'middle', 'upper middle' and 'higher' exhibited throughout that period annual average growth rates that were consistently different. For all ldcs the decade of the 1960s was, by a small margin, the period of fastest GNP growth. For certain ldcs it was the growth of manufacturing output (and, later, exports of manufactures) that generated the major part of the observed GNP growth. Their experience in this respect is discussed here and then by way of contrast the trends in raw materials output are assessed.

Table 1.2 *Annual growth rate of per capita GNP by country group, 1951–76*

	1951–60 %	1961–70 %	1971–6 %	1951–76 %
Developed market economies	3.0	4.1	2.3	3.2
Developing countries[a]	2.8	3.2	3.0	3.1
of which:				
lower income	1.4	1.6	0.1	1.1
middle income	2.2	2.0	2.9	2.4
upper middle income	2.4	3.2	4.6	3.4
higher income	3.2	5.8	5.4	5.1

[a] Grouped by 1975 GNP per capita. Groups are: up to $265; $266–$520; $521–$1,075 and $1,075 and over, respectively.
Source: IBRD, *World Bank Atlas,* various issues.

Ldcs and world manufacturing

Over the period 1960–75 the value of world manufacturing value added more than doubled. In 1960 the world's manufacturing value added totalled $468 billion (expressed in 1970 prices) and by 1976 it had grown to $1,056 billion. Yet ldcs' output grew faster than this and nearly trebled in value, rising from $32.4 billion worth in 1960 to $91.3 billion at the end of the period. Their share in the world total did not begin rising significantly until midway through the 1960s, however, and in 1966 was actually 0.1% lower than its 1960 level of 6.9%. But by 1976 it had reached 8.6% (UNIDO, 1979a). What helped give ldcs this boost in their share was the recession that most dcs suffered from in 1974–5, when GNP actually fell in the OECD region. During these two years ldcs' output continued to increase, rising by nearly $7 billion, to raise their share of world output from 7.9% to 8.6% in two years.

This increase in ldcs' manufacturing value added turns out to have been shared reasonably equitably between regions. Analysis of the figures when arranged in four geographical categories (Africa, Latin America, East Asia and West Asia) shows that over the period 1960–75 the growth trends were surprisingly close, at 7.3%, 7.2%, 7.5% and 9.2% respectively (UNIDO, 1979a). The African countries showed no net rise in their share of world manufacturing (it remained at 0.8%) during the post-1973 period; while by contrast the Latin American group managed to increase its share of world manufacturing output at 4.8% in 1975 from 4.5% in 1973 despite only a 1.1% rise in output in 1975. The East Asians' share rose slightly from 2.2% to 2.5% over 1973–5 and that of the West Asians remained unchanged at 0.5%. This was despite annual increases of 10.8%, 8.2% and 8.0% in the years 1973 to 1975 respectively.

This discussion of the regional experience can be supplemented by groupings based on income levels expressed in 1975 prices. This shows

Table 1.3 *Growth of manufacturing value added in ldcs, arranged by income levels, 1960–75*

Group	GNP per capita ($) 1975	Constant growth rates per annum %	Standard error
Low income	up to 265	5.2	0.03
Lower middle income	265–520	7.1	0.03
Intermediate middle income	521–1,075	8.6	0.05
Upper middle income	1,076–2,000	7.3	0.03
High income	greater than 2,000	8.3	0.04

Notes

Low income: Egypt, Ethiopia, Zaire, Tanzania, Kenya, Uganda, Mozambique, Madagascar, Upper Volta, Mali, Malawi, Niger, Guinea, Rwanda, Chad, Burundi, Somalia, Benin, Sierra Leone, Central African Empire, Mauritania, Lesotho, Gambia, Comoros, Cape Verde, India, Bangladesh, Pakistan, Vietnam, Burma, Afghanistan, Sri Lanka, Nepal, Yemen Arab Republic, Yemen (People's DR), Haiti, Indonesia.

Lower middle income: Nigeria, Morocco, Sudan, Ghana, Cameroon, Angola, Senegal, Zambia, Togo, Liberia, Botswana, Swaziland, Equatorial Guinea, Sao Tome, China, Philippines, Thailand, Jordan, El Salvador, Honduras, Grenada, Bolivia, Papua New Guinea.

Intermediate middle income: Algeria, Ivory Coast, Rhodesia-Zimbabwe, Tunisia, Congo, Mauritius, Republic of Korea, Republic of China, North Korea, Malaysia, Syria, Mongolia, Cuba, Guatemala, Dominican Republic, Nicaragua, Costa Rica, Peru, Colombia, Ecuador, Chile, Paraguay, Guyana.

Upper middle income: Iran, Iraq, Hong Kong, Panama, Trinidad and Tobago, Barbados, Brazil, Argentina, Uruguay, Surinam, Fiji.

High income: Libya, Gabon, Israel, Saudi Arabia, Singapore, Oman, Puerto Rico, Bahamas, Venezuela.

Source: UNIDO (1979a).

very clearly the extent to which the increases just discussed were in fact concentrated in relatively few countries. Table 1.3 summarises the data. This table suggests that it is the middle income group, with income per capita lying between $521 and $1,075 (in 1975 prices), that accounted for most of the ldcs' rising share of world manufacturing. Between them this group increased their manufacturing value added (expressed in 1970 prices) from $10.8 billion in 1960 to $36 billion in 1975 – a rise of 230%. This exceeds the percentage rise of any other income group, especially those during the years 1966–75. For before 1966, when ldcs as a whole were not successful in increasing their share of world manufacturing value added, the middle income group's annual increase in this term, at 6.9%, fell below that of the high income ldcs, who managed 8.3%, and was in turn no better than the performances of the lower and upper middle income groups. After 1966, however, a clear opening up of the field became apparent, with the middle income ldcs exhibiting average annual

Table 1.4   *Contribution of individual ldcs to the total increase in ldcs'
share in world manufacturing value added, 1966–75 ($ million at 1970
prices)*

Country	Increase in manufacturing value added	Per cent contribution	Cumulative percentage
Brazil	6,642.5	34.2	34.2
South Korea	3,124.6	16.1	50.3
Mexico	1,926.5	9.9	60.2
Turkey	1,303.2	6.7	66.9
Iran	1,003.2	5.2	72.1
Argentina	843.5	4.3	76.4
Hong Kong	773.8	4.0	80.4
Indonesia	767.8	4.0	84.4
Thailand	649.2	3.3	87.7
Singapore	379.1	2.0	89.7
			89.7%

Source: UNIDO (1979a).

rates of increase far in excess of the others. Over the 1966–75 period, this
group's average annual increase in manufacturing value added was 9.6%,
and in six of those years it was in double figures. In 1973 it reached 14.1%.
The other groups, in contrast, did manage some bursts of rapid growth –
notably the 13.7% rise in output recorded by the lower middle income
group in 1973 and the 12.9% rise in 1968 by the high income group –
but failed to sustain them. Overall their mean annual increase of manufacturing value added ranged from 4.5% for the low income countries
to 7.2% for the high income countries.

Focusing now upon countries within these groups, it transpires that
only ten ldcs between them accounted for nearly nine-tenths of the entire
increase in ldcs' share of world manufacturing over the 1966–75 period.
Indeed, over one-third of the entire increase was accounted for by one
ldc – Brazil. As Table 1.4 shows, Brazil and South Korea together produced over half the total rise, with the other eight together contributing
around four-tenths.

Judging from this, the geographic spread of industrialisation in the
period under consideration might appear to have been restricted. However,
these semi-industrialised ldcs (which can be defined as those with between
40% and 60% of value added in commodity production coming from
manufacturing) contain a substantial proportion of the population of ldcs.
If China and India are included in this category, the semi-industrialised
ldcs have a total population of 1,881 million, or 62% of the 1976 developing world total. It would, however, be completely wrong to imagine that
because a country is classified as semi-industrialised the majority of its
economically active population are primarily engaged in industry. It is

typical to find that only a small share of the workforce is permanently
and formally engaged upon industrial tasks. For the others, work outside
the rural areas is likely to be seasonal, fitful or temporary. (This is a theme
of importance in Chapter 8, where labour flows from non-oil ldcs to OPEC
countries are discussed.)

The initial impulse behind much of this industrialisation was a persistent shortage of finished goods from dcs. In the 1940s most ldcs found
their primary product exports in high demand but because of the excess
demand for goods within dcs themselves during and after the Second
World War, ldcs were unable to import all they wanted, and their foreign
exchange reserves accumulated (Little, Scitovsky and Scott, 1970, p. 32).
Many policy makers in ldcs therefore decided to have processing and
manufacturing begin in their own countries. The case of Brazil is particularly well documented, and data from there indicate that after the war
the value of industrial output grew by 250% between 1947 and 1961,
far faster than any other sector's output. As an assessment of Brazilian
development has put it, 'the single-minded objective of Brazilian economic
policy in the 1950s was industrialisation . . . All the economic ideologies
of the day pointed to industrialisation as the solution to Brazil's economic
needs' (Syvrud, 1974, p. 12).

Yet as soon as the initial stage of import substitution – that in which
the extant market had been satisfied – was exhausted, manufacturers
needed to resort to other markets for expansion (Alexander, 1967). For
most of the 'early' industries that had been set up in import substitution
programmes featured substantial economies of scale that dictated high
rates of capacity utilisation if unit costs were ever to be internationally
competitive. One possibility lay in expanding domestic sales by lowering
prices and selling other than merely to the domestic élite. Another possibility, however, and one which did not rely so much upon the income
distribution of the country changing appreciably, lay in exporting surplus
production. In many countries this policy came to be accompanied by
comprehensive or *ad hoc* export subsidies. In India in particular there
grew up much concern about the fiscal cost of these subsidies, about their
efficiency implications, and also about the distributional aspects of this
type of state and central government expenditure. A critic concluded
that 'while government export subsidy schemes have been effective in
increasing exports of new manufactured goods, these schemes are subject
to serious criticism on grounds of efficiency . . . it is important that the
government adopt policies which minimise the domestic resource cost of
net foreign exchange earned by exports' (Frankena, 1975, p. 137). In
other countries a range of policies designed to assist exporters (for
example, remissions of tariffs paid on imported components needed to
produce export goods) were used (Donges, 1977), Hong Kong, Taiwan and
Singapore were among the countries where high rates of manufactures
export growth were encouraged by policy.

Frequently, however, what generated the interest in export markets was not so much the need to obtain high capacity utilisation rates from plants as the *raison d'être* of the firm itself. Many plants were set up specifically to manufacture for export: to export either to other ldcs or to re-export some components back to the country which had established the foreign subsidy in the first place.

Indeed, one of the most important characteristics of the set of fast-industrialising ldcs just identified is the substantial involvement in their sectors of foreign, typically multinational, firms. In value, direct foreign investment in ldcs has risen from $32.8 billion in 1967 to $68.2 billion in 1975. The fast-industrialising ldcs (Brazil, Mexico, India, Malaysia, Argentina, Singapore, Peru, Hong Kong, Philippines) together accounted for 34% of this in 1967 and 39% in 1975 (UN, 1978, p. 254). In all of these ldcs except Philippines, this foreign investment is concentrated in the manufacturing sector: in each country at least 59% of total foreign direct investment in 1975 was found in manufacturing.

Developing country exports

This growth of exports from ldcs was not of course common to all types of output. By far the biggest increase was in SITC groups 5 to 8; that is, chemicals, machinery and other manufactures. From a volume index in 1970 of 100 they rose to 205 by 1976 but this by no means covered all categories within those classifications. Other increases were recorded by fuels (123) and food (122); the weighted average index of exports rose to 140. This disproportionate weighting of manufactures and chemicals applied to both trade with developed countries and to intra-ldc trade, with the indices increasing to 194 and 236 respectively (UNCTAD, 1978a).

However, only a small set of countries contributed the bulk of the increase in manufactures exports from the Third World. In 1965, ten ldcs – those which have recently been called the 'power-house' middle-income exporters by Keesing – accounted for 65.7% of all ldcs' exports of manufactures by value. Ten years later these same ten accounted for slightly more: 69.2%. Within the total, the importance of Hong Kong and Singapore, the earliest mass exporters of many products, waned a little, and their places were taken by Taiwan and South Korea. Both of these increased their share within the ldc total more than threefold, and ended up in 1975 accounting for nearly 24% of ldc manufactures exports.

Despite this dominance by a few leading ldcs in the growth of manufactures export earnings, some other countries have also managed to take up a share. Between 1965 and 1974 the number of ldcs exporting over $25 million worth of manufactures grew from 36 to 51 and the number exporting over $100 million worth annually grew from 14 to 30 (IBRD, 1979a).

Taking a more restrictive definition of both manufactures and of ldcs does, however, dramatically reduce the impressiveness of these trends, and serves to show up the comparatively weak performances of areas such as the sub-Saharan African ldcs. In their case, manufactures exports in current dollars arose from only $90 million in 1965 to $500 million by 1976 (IBRD, 1979a). Moreover, if all those ldcs with GNP per capita over $1,300 in 1975, plus Brazil, Mexico, Taiwan and Korea (which fall below that threshold but are building up industrial structures), are excluded from the country register and Africa's exports of uncut diamonds (not truly manufactured goods at all, but usually appearing in the statistics) are also excluded, the picture changes. It is found that exports of manufactures grew from $1.59 billion in 1965 to only $8.5 billion in 1976 – against the $35.3 billion figure for 1975 for all those countries normally classified as 'developing'. What this analysis suggests is that by the mid 1970s there had grown up a clear group of industrialising ldcs which dominated a large and growing portion of ldcs' processed goods trade with the rest of the world. Referring to the 'ranks of the developed countries', the World Bank has suggested that the 'power-house' exporters are among the leading candidates to join these ranks next (IBRD, 1979a, p. 30). By contrast, the low-income ldcs, whose export growth – not just in manufactures, but typically in all goods – has been slow, 'still have most of the features that characterised the Third World in the 1950s' (IBRD, 1979b, p. 2).

The counterpart of these fast-industrialising countries is the group which by 1973 remained virtually unindustrialised. Those ldcs with less than 20% of their value added from commodity production coming from manufacturing tend to be small, and twenty-six of the thirty defined this way in 1976 are in Africa (Hughes, 1979).

The raw material exporters

Foreign markets for raw materials have generally expanded rather slowly. Competition from synthetic materials has been severe in some cases; technological developments have economised on raw material input requirements to manufactures in other cases and tariffs and other barriers to trade have restricted (sometimes severely) the growth of foreign markets.

The poor export performance of the raw material-dependent exporters is highlighted if, following UNCTAD's classification, the ldcs are divided into four groups: the major petroleum exporters, the fast-growing exporters of manufactures, the least developed countries and the remaining ldcs (UNCTAD, 1979b). The members of the third and fourth groups here are those that are largely dependent upon slowly expanding raw material markets. Thus, between 1960 and 1970, while the value of exports from the first and second groups increased at 7.7% and 7.6% per annum respectively, those of the other two groups increased at only 4.5%

Table 1.5 *Commodity structure of less developed countries' exports, 1955 and 1970 (percentages)*

	1955	1970
Food[a]	36.7	26.5
Agricultural raw materials[b]	20.5	10.0
Ores and metals[c]	10.1	13.3
Fuels[d]	24.9	32.9
Manufactures[e]	7.6	16.7

[a] SITC 0 + 1 + 22 + 4
[b] SITC 2 - 22 - 27 - 28
[c] SITC 27 + 28 + 67 + 68
[d] SITC 3
[e] SITC 5 to 8 less 67 + 68
Source: UNCTAD (1979b), p. 102.

and 6.3% per annum respectively. Both volume and price factors worked against the latter two groups of exporters. For over the rather longer period 1955—73, the volume of the least developed countries' exports increased by only 38% and their export price index by only 41%, the respective figures for the fast-growing exporters of manufactures were 165% and 82%. The remaining ldcs also compared unfavourably in this period. Looked at another way, the purchasing power of exports (that is, an export value index divided by an import value index) increased by only 21% between 1960 and 1973 in the case of the least developed countries and by 92% in that of the 'remaining' ldcs. These performances compare unfavourably with the more than 200% increase of the other two groups.

An implication of these trends is, of course, that the share of non-oil raw materials in the ldcs' export structures fell substantially while that of oil and manufactures increased markedly in the period up to 1970, as Table 1.5 shows.

The share of food, agricultural raw materials and ores and metals taken as a group fell from 67% in 1955 to 50% in 1970 (UNCTAD, 1979b). Thus, the counterpart to the small group of fast-growing exporters of manufactures (about ten in all) and oil exporters is a large mass of ldcs who remained largely dependent upon sluggishly growing raw material exports.

The oil exporting countries

In contrast with the mass of ldcs which remained dependent upon slowly growing non-oil raw material export markets, the oil exporting countries experienced rapid growth in their export markets even before the 1973

Table 1.6.   *Per capita incomes of OPEC members, 1974*

	$
UAE	14,000
Kuwait	11,300
Qatar	10,300
Libya	4,360
Saudi Arabia	3,100
Gabon	2,200
Venezuela	2,100
Iran	1,400
Iraq	950
Algeria	770
Ecuador	520
Nigeria	300
Indonesia	200
Memo. items	
USA	6,700
UK	3,500
Italy	2,700
Brazil	940
India	120

Source: IBRD (1977a).

oil price rise. The volume of their exports increased by 175% between 1960 and 1973, more than any other of the four ldc categories identified by UNCTAD. Even oil export prices increased on average in this period more than the prices received by the non-oil raw material exporting countries. As is pointed out in Chapter 3, oil prices began their sharp upward trend as early as 1971, when the Tehran Agreement was signed by certain oil exporting countries and oil companies. Discussion of the nature of OPEC, the development of its relationships with the oil companies, the behaviour of oil prices after 1973 and the prospective stability of that cartel is reserved for Chapter 3. Here, the objective is only to point out that a small group of oil exporting countries was able to differentiate itself from the mass of ldcs. It did so by taking control of the process of oil export pricing, something that had to be wrested from the oil companies.

Thus, by 1974 some OPEC members achieved per capita incomes greater than even the USA (see Table 1.6). Indeed, five Arab members of OPEC (the UAE, Kuwait, Qatar, Libya and Saudi Arabia) already had per capita incomes larger than that of several industrial countries. In fact, Libya's per capita income (ranked only fourth amongst OPEC members in 1974) was 1.6 times that of Italy. Amongst ldcs, all thirteen OPEC members, except Indonesia, Nigeria and Ecuador, have substantially higher per capita incomes than those of India and the mass of Asian and African

Table 1.7   *Net crude oil exports from non-OPEC ldcs*

	Net oil exports barrels per day, 1976 (000s)	% of total	Growth rate of exports, 1970–6 (% annually)
Angola	75	5.9	0.2
Bolivia	21	1.6	20.1
Brunei	207	16.4	9.4
Egypt	111	8.8	-5.5
Mexico	58	4.6	46.0
Oman	353	28.0	3.2
Syria	121	9.6	21.8
Trinidad and Tobago	171	13.6	4.3
Tunisia	40	3.2	-3.7
Others (4)	102	8.1	92.6
Total	1,259	100.0	5.2
Total as % of OPEC crude oil exports	4.12%		

Source: Petroleum Economist, October 1979, p. 427; own calculations.

countries. Even Brazil's per capita income compares unfavourably with most OPEC members and Brazil is one of the most economically successful newly industrialising countries.

Oil production in the NOPECs

Not all ldc oil exporters are members of OPEC, however. While OPEC member states' share of world crude oil output is around 60% there is a large number of ldcs each contributing a small share of the rest. Among these countries are Mexico, Trinidad and Tobago, Egypt, Morocco and many others. In 1977 there were twenty-five ldcs outside OPEC producing oil: even Taiwan was producing 4,400 barrels per day. Between them these same ldcs also accounted for some 2,200 wells being drilled out of the 1977 world total of 57,816 (*World Oil*, 15 August 1978, p. 43). Some of these countries were able also to export a surplus: thirteen non-OPEC members between them exported approximately 1.3 million barrels per day in 1976. Brunei and Oman together accounted for nearly half of this total, as Table 1.7 shows, but some other ldcs made significant progress in the first half of the 1970s towards raising their oil export volumes. The effect of the oil price rises engineered by OPEC during the 1970s on the ldcs as oil *exporters* has naturally been small for most of these countries, given the small extent of their involvement in the oil export trade. The exception is Mexico, which should by the early 1980s be a substantial net exporter with volumes at around 2.4 million barrels per day.

Synthesis: the ldcs posed in 1973

The preceding sections of this chapter have discussed the ldcs' experience of growth, structural transformation and trade involvement in strictly aggregate terms. Sufficient evidence has been assembled to illustrate how much the ldcs had fanned out from their positions of the early 1960s. Still by the 1970s there remained the hopelessly poor — now termed the least developed countries — whose population of 257 million in 1978 represented 12.3% of the ldc total. Similarly there existed the Croesus-rich: Kuwait, Qatar, the United Arab Emirates and the others which could hardly be called 'developing' at all, judged by some criteria. The OPEC group, however, was by no means composed wholly of wealthy states. Although after the succession of oil price rises in the 1970s the 320 million citizens in OPEC countries enjoyed a mean per capita income of $4,542 (at 1975 prices), OPEC still numbered among its populations millions of people who remained virtually untouched by the rising living standards elsewhere in their countries. These millions, who have been termed the 'village underclass', or the 'rural excluded', remained little better off after the decades of official development effort.

As was mentioned earlier, dissatisfaction with the First Development Decade was due largely to the increasingly frequent discovery by economists that high rates of economic growth, particularly in a country with a medium to large population, were in themselves no guarantee that personal living standards throughout the country were rising. Writing on the theme of growth and redistribution, Chenery emphasised that 'a decade of rapid growth in under-developed countries has been of little or no benefit to perhaps a third of their population. Although the average per capita income of the third world has increased by 50% since 1960, this growth has been very unequally distributed among countries, regions within countries, and socio-economic groups' (Chenery, 1974).

Thus it came to be widely recognised that 'growth' — which could be fairly easily measured by standard macroeconomic indicators — and 'development' — which by nature could easily be appraised — were two distinct concepts. Some writers maintained that while the two were conceptually different, growth was not a sufficient condition for development; others took the view that under certain circumstances the two could even by antithetical.

In some ldcs, differentiation between groups of residents has been growing more and more obvious at this internal level. In rural areas, the growing pressure on the land in certain parts of the developing world, coupled with large real earnings differentials between towns and rural areas, was a factor inducing a massive drift to towns in search of work. Those who found work and remitted part of their earnings to their families left behind would help create diverging standards of living in the rural area. Those who returned to the villages would contribute to the local stock of skills, and perhaps equipment, attitudes and prestige as well. In the case of areas in which the high yielding crops and other innovations introduced through the 'Green Revolution' had been a success, there was a further source of differentiation. On this point Griffin concluded his analysis of the green revolution as follows: 'The peasantry ceases to be a homogenous class (if it ever was) and the analysis has to be conducted in terms of a more sophisticated model . . . The minimum degree of elaboration is a division of the rural community into four classes' (Griffin, 1974, p. 252). Again, it was stressed by other writers (this time dealing with African peasants) that 'there can be among the peasants different peasantries, differentiated according to their structural position at a specified moment of time' (Saul and Woods, 1971, p. 104).

Similarly, in case studies of Asia, not only within the countryside were there 'unmistakeable signs of growing regional inequality', but 'there is evidence supporting the even stronger proposition that in many areas the absolute standard of living of a significant minority of the rural population has declined' (Griffin and Ghose, 1979). Central here has been access to irrigation and land redistribution. Some years earlier, in his study of urban/rural divergences, Lipton had similarly concluded that 'the worst-off one-third of mankind comprises the village underclass of the third world. This underclass has become less prone to malaria and illiteracy since 1945. It has thereby become more fit and better fitted to enjoy the good things of life. Yet these good things have not become available to it' (Lipton, 1977, p. 38).

Furthermore, it was increasingly thought by some economists that just as growth rates and per capita incomes had diverged between ldcs in the 1960s and early 1970s, so had they within ldcs, depending on their stage of growth. The most comprehensive statement of the hypothesis that the share of, say, the poorest 40% of an ldc's population in total income moves significantly between various national average per capita income figures is that of Adelman and Morris (1973). Although later time series analysis by Ahluwalia (1974) established that no consistent and predictable relationship exists between changes in an ldc's income distribution and its growth rate, cross-sectional analysis tends to support the Adelman—Morris view. There is indeed some evidence that income equality deteriorates as per capita GNP rises towards $400, stabilises for per capita incomes between $400 and $1,200, and thereafter improves.

In practice this means that personal income inequalities tend to be increasing until a per capita income level equivalent to that of (say) the Philippines or Zambia today is attained. Afterwards there is a perceptible if gradual trend towards greater equity, although of course the extent of this will again vary markedly across individual nations.

The internal dynamics of income distribution during phases of GNP growth have, as has just been noted, occupied the attention of many economists in the 1970s. So too have trends in other social and economic proxies for well-being, among them infant mortality rates, availability of health services, urbanisation, and so on. In addition, efforts have been made to create composite indices of development, combining changes across a wide range of indicators. One of the most ambitious of these was the United Nations' 73-variable index, later reduced to 42 variables because of multi-collinearity among some of the others (Baster, 1972). A more recent effort is the Physical Quality of Life Index (PQLI) which is an amalgam of three indicators – life expectancy, infant mortality and the literacy rate. An assessment of this index as regards OPEC countries has recently been made by the OPEC secretariat *(OPEC Review,* 1979). The OPEC authors suggest that the index shows most OPEC member states are too poor to do without their petroleum revenues and that 'the oil price adjustments do not create an economic case for compensations through aid' *(OPEC Review,* 1979, p. iii).

In a more restricted way, the efforts of Harbison and his colleagues to compose an index of 'human resource development' for a range of ldcs can similarly be seen as part of the search for broader-based development guides. Later work by Harbison (1974) refined some of his indicators to capture the distributional implications of ldcs' rising education budgets. In addition to those already discussed, many other proxies for development have been put forward. The frequencies of facilities such as telephones or private automobiles per head of population are cited, while more recently the level of energy consumption has become of interest.

Finally, mention might be made of one of the more nebulous aspects of development, namely, autonomy in tastes and consumption. The literature on technological choice in ldcs has long stressed the idea that plant managers, scientists or aid donors acting in ldcs have access to a relatively limited 'shelf' of technologies from which they can purchase machinery. Since virtually all machine innovation is carried out in dcs decision takers in ldcs are faced with choice only between technologies suited to factor endowments and current costs in dcs. In turn these technologies will tend to reflect the type of products being demanded in dcs.

Lying behind studies such as those mentioned above which try to relate the distributional structure of a developing economy to its level of income is the search for uniformity of experience. A recent overview of this kind, that of Chenery and Syrquin, undertook such an analysis so as to draw up 'an agenda for theoretical analysis of the interrelated phenomena of development' (1975, p. 136). Certain strong statistical relationships have been identified by work such as this. Notable is the finding that as a result of larger ldcs' tendency to industrialise early (since they are able to capture economies of scale in such basic industries as paper, chemicals, basic metals, and so on), in large ldcs, exports are biased systematically towards industrial goods, irrespective of the income level of the ldc (Chenery and Syrquin, 1975, ch. 4).

There is, however, no comparable set of relationships with which to assess the impact of the higher oil price on ldcs, or on groups of ldcs; nor is there any *modus operandi* to assess easily the trade-off between (say) the higher price of oil imports against the higher value of aid obtained from various OPEC institutions. For the evidence in the years since the major oil price increases in 1973 shows just how unpredictable has been the outcome. Even by 1975 some oil importing ldcs (Colombia, Ivory Coast, Liberia) were more or less in payments balance, and several others were by 1976.

Furthermore, within certain ldcs, immediate moves were made to seek out alternatives to oil imports, with India and Brazil taking the lead along with other countries such as South Africa, with kerosene burners, gobar gas and alcohol fuel research and development. The disparate response of ldcs therefore defies simple categorisation, just as it defied simple prediction in late 1973.

The following chapters in this book elaborate on these points. After a discussion of the genesis of OPEC as a successful cartel in Chapter 3, Chapter 4 deals with some of the consequences of the price rises for individual ldcs and for groups of ldcs. Later, Chapter 9 reviews the impact that these price rises had on the growth pattern of the developing world, and attempts to assess how far and in what respects growth rates and other macroeconomic variables were blown off course by the OPEC action. In this it is addressing above all the subject of inter-developing country conflict — the consequences for some of the world's poorest people of what Vallenilla has called 'the era of petroleum nationalism' (Vallenilla, 1975, p. 155).

Notes

1 This is non-oil exports: SITC 0 to 2 plus 4 and 68.
2 The net barter terms of trade is defined as the export price index divided by the import price index. Terms of trade indices can also be constructed to show the relationship between product groups, for instance primary product terms of trade would be an index of manufactures prices or oil prices (see Chapter 4).

2

The Changing World Economic Climate

Discussion of world economic conditions in the last ten years and the factors which brought them about is an integral part of the analysis of this book since these conditions have influenced the OPEC members' relationships with the rest of the world. At the simplest level, if OPEC is seen by policy makers as playing a dominant causative role in the world economic recession, the tone and possibly the substance of its relationships with any of its trade and aid partners will be different than if this is untrue.

Some early analyses of the world economy after the oil price 'shock' blamed stagflation (the combination of stagnation and inflation) almost entirely upon the OPEC cartel. Even as late as 1977 variants of this argument could still be found. The Bank for International Settlements (BIS) pointed out in its 48th Annual Report that the world economy operated 'under the converging influence of three depressive factors: the global oil imbalance, the external payments disequilibrium among the oil consuming countries and persisting inflationary disturbances inherited from the late 1960s and early 1970s' (BIS, 1977). Throughout its report the BIS stressed that the oil deficits played the major and perhaps a decisive role.

However, this view did not persist throughout the decade after 1974. For instance, those economists associated with the April 1979 issue of the *Cambridge Economic Policy Review* argued that 'while the OPEC surplus was a contributory factor, especially between 1974 and 1977, the main cause of continuing recession has been slow growth in the EEC (taken as a whole) and Japan, which were *not* balance of payments constrained . . . Continued recession since 1975 in Japan and the stronger EEC countries, with rapidly improving balance of payments positions, was due to anti-inflation policies which made their governments unwilling to accelerate growth in demand' (p. 10). Moreover, in the Cambridge view, not only was OPEC rather unimportant as a destabilising factor in the world economy in 1979, but 'a new round of *steep* OPEC price increases need not cause more than a minor disturbance to medium term prospects for world expansion, provided that the developed countries do not over-react' (p. 19).

In fact, as this chapter will attempt to show, many factors have contributed to depressed economic conditions in the developed countries and some developing countries since 1973. Inflation and unemployment have been much higher than in the 1960s, while economic growth rates have been much lower. Only the members of OPEC and a few other developing countries have avoided economic depression (see Chapter 9) although none of them has entirely avoided inflation either. Of course, the OPEC members' new wealth is derived from the substantial increase in oil prices that they engineered in October and December 1973 and maintained there-after. However, certain other major adverse events have also occurred and new trends developed in the world economy even before the oil price 'shock'. In the first place, the international monetary system that had operated successfully since 1945 was brought to a *de facto* end in August 1971 with America ending the gold-convertibility of the dollar. Moreover, even the new 'Smithsonian' pegged exchange rate arrangements of December 1971 soon fell apart. Without an efficient international monetary system, industrial countries were subsequently unable satisfactorily to adjust their balance of payments deficits. This meant that countries other than OPEC members, when they began to run large and persistent payments surpluses, also tended to exert a deflationary effect upon the world economy. Moreover, whereas the Bretton Woods monetary system had a tendency towards a stimulatory bias, which had encouraged high rates of economic activity, the new (non-) system possibly has something of a deflationary bias.

There is also a view emerging that in the early 1970s some developed economies were beginning to exhibit symptoms of structural imbalance of which chronic over-capacity in the shipbuilding, steel and textile industries were characteristic. The low rates of economic growth in much of the period after 1974 can be seen, at least if the Kondratieff cycle hypothesis is correct, as a cyclical reaction to the high rates of economic growth achieved in the previous twenty years. We will also discuss the view that trade protectionism has reappeared in developed countries, to the disadvantage of developing countries and the growth of the world economy as a whole. What needs to be shown then is that the oil price 'shock' of 1973 was not alone responsible for the stagflation which followed; other major factors were also at work.

Economic malaise

Economic conditions in the world economy are to a large extent governed by the performance of the industrial economies of North America, Western Europe and Japan. This is both because these economies form by far the largest part of the world economy itself and because changes in their economic circumstances influence economic conditions in other trading blocs including the NOPECs. Unfortunately, for most of the period since 1974 these major economies have experienced adverse economic conditions.

Inflation in the industrial countries was at historically high levels during most of the 1970s and after, really taking off in the late 1960s, as Figure 2.1 shows, even before the oil price rises of 1973. OPEC and NOPEC areas were similarly afflicted, although the take off of inflation was somewhat later in the latter's case. In the industrial countries this upturn of inflation rates was associated with an economic boom that was unusually widely spread and whose rate of acceleration from trough to peak was unusually fast (Cooper and Lawrence, 1975). By December 1973, the industrial countries' annual rate of inflation had reached 7.5%, but in Japan inflation was 19%, in the USA nearly 9% and, even in West Germany, inflation had risen to almost 8%. Twelve months later, in December 1974, inflation in the industrial countries had increased again (to 13%, Figure 2.1) and many more of these countries had double digit inflation.

A typical monetarist explanation links the 1972–3 economic boom and accelerating inflation to the very high rate of growth of international liquidity (the reserves that governments can use to purchase foreign goods, services and currencies) which was associated with large American expenditures to finance the Vietnam war. The international monetary system had become a 'perfect inflation machine' according to Karl Blessing.[1]

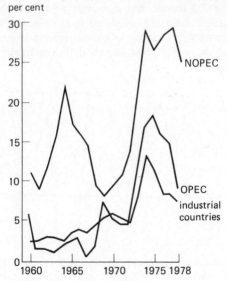

Figure 2.1 *Inflation Rates: NOPEC, OPEC, and Industrial Countries, 1960–78, percentages*

Source: IMF, *International Financial Statistics*

Since many countries (other than the USA) began to find that they had relatively strong balance of payments positions and increasing foreign exchange reserves, the external constraints on economic expansion were nearly everywhere lower than usual and, therefore, governments were able to adopt stimulatorary economic policies.

Once inflation had taken off most governments were unable to reduce it to the low levels recorded in the mid 1960s. Inflationary expectations, having adjusted to high inflation rates, subsequently did not adjust downwards sufficiently quickly. The strength of these inflationary expectations can be judged from the fact that even the 25% appreciation of the Deutschmark's effective exchange rate between 1976 and 1978 which, by itself, should have helped absolutely to reduce prices in West Germany as import costs fell, only helped to reduce inflation in that country to 3% in 1977. In Italy's case, it has been calculated that a 20% per annum inflation would arise if unemployment was reduced to 2.5% of the labour force (Modigliani and Tarantelli, 1977). In Britain also, where inflation peaked at over 25%, and despite the imposition of a series of income policies, inflation was only temporarily pushed into single figures. Just as soon as incomes policies were taken off, or thrown off (in 1978–9), inflation again rebounded upwards, well into double figures.

With inflation so difficult to control, it is hardly surprising that most industrial economies were and are being run with substantial excess capacity. As Figure 2.2 shows, real economic growth in the OECD area fell drastically in 1974 and 1975 compared to the two previous years and the subsequent recovery of economic growth rates was partial and temporary. By the end of 1977, industrial production in Western Europe was

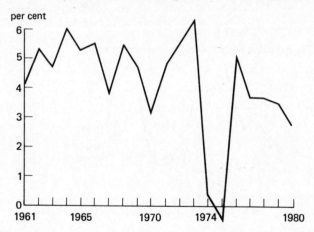

Figure 2.2   *OECD: growth of real gross domestic product, percent per annum.*

Source: OECD, *Economic Outlook*, No. 25, July 1979, pages 6 and 148.

20% below trend;[2] in Japan it was fully 70% below trend; while in the USA industrial production was only 11% below its trend level, largely thanks to high rates of economic activity in 1976 that were quite out of line with the rest of the industrial world.

Unemployment increased in association with the lower rates of economic activity. In the USA the average unemployment rate in 1966–73 was 5.9%, by December 1974 it had reached 7.2% of the labour force and it again increased to 8.3% in December 1975 (BIS, 1977). By the latter month the West German unemployment rate, at 4.8%, was well over double the 1966–73 average level. Even Britain, the country that probably struggled the most to prevent a rise in unemployment, had 5% of its labour force unemployed by the end of 1975 compared to only 2.8% one year earlier. Only Sweden and Italy of all the industrial countries actually managed to lower their unemployment in 1975 compared to their recent averages.

Some causes of the world economic malaise

As was pointed out in the opening paragraphs of this chapter the causes of the deteriorating world economic order from the early 1970s onwards are several, interdependent and disputed. This chapter will certainly not try and provide a definitive answer to the question of causality. Indeed, several monographs have already been, and no doubt are yet to be written, on that subject. Rather, the task here is far more limited, merely to point out that the quadrupling of oil prices in 1974 was by no means the only factor, indeed it may not even have been a major factor, in the economically depressed but high inflation economic environment that has existed in the world economy for much of the period since 1973.

OPEC's contribution to the world economic recession

The oil price increases of 1973 were extremely large and abrupt, as Figure 2.3 shows. Since the price elasticity of demand for oil is low at about −0.5 (see Chapter 3 for further details), expenditure on oil increased dramatically resulting in a sharp worsening of the OECD area's combined current account balance of payments deficit from $3 billion *surplus* in 1973 to $35 billion deficit in 1974. One response to this large deficit on the part of the industrial countries was to reduce economic activity by imposing restrictive fiscal and monetary policies. As a result, the industrial countries' aggregate current account deficit fell to $12 billion in 1975, with all of the improvement coming on the merchandise account as petroleum imports eventually were cut back. As growth in real GNP declined, coupled with higher unemployment rates, oil consumption fell. For example, in West Germany, Japan, the UK and France by the end of 1977 oil consumption in volume terms had fallen by between 10% and 16% of the 1973 level. In Italy oil consumption was 7% down. Only in the

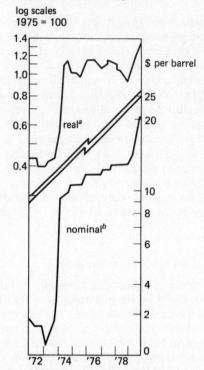

log scales
1975 = 100

^a The dollar price of crude oil divided by the dollar
price of world exports of manufactures.
^b Average contract price.

Figure 2.3　*Oil Prices*

Source: Bank of England, *Quarterly Bulletin*, Volume 19 No 3, September 1979, page 250.

USA did consumption of petroleum products actually increase over the 1973–7 period, and then by less than 2% (BIS, 1978).

The main case against OPEC as the major contributor to the world-wide economic depression is that, at a stroke, a substantial proportion of world income (perhaps 3% of the OECD's gross national production) was transferred to a group of countries who, it was believed, could not spend it quickly. The world's overall savings propensity had thus increased over-night. The concomitant reduction in world aggregate demand for goods and services would, it was argued (for example, by Park, 1976), lead to an increase in global unemployment and to slower economic growth.

OPEC members such as Saudi Arabia, Kuwait, the UAE, Libya and Qatar were thought to have low 'absorptive capacity', in that the relatively simple structure of their economies, together with the vast size of the revenues generated by the oil price increases of 1973, prevented them from finding a sufficiently large number of economic projects and activities to absorb all of these revenues usefully. The result was that the foreign assets of the Gulf members of OPEC (Iran, Iraq, Kuwait, Qatar, Saudi Arabia and the UAE) increased from $7 billion in 1972 to $117 billion in 1977 — representing 96% of all of OPEC's external holdings of reserves (*MEED*, 3 August, 1979). The largest part of these surpluses were invested in the USA (certainly until 1977), in European financial centres as well as in the 'off-shore' Eurocurrency markets (see Chapter 5). These savings constituted a withdrawal from world aggregate demand and only re-entered the 'circular flow' of world income when somebody else was prepared to borrow and invest them in real capital stock or to finance current consumption.

However, although some industrial countries were prepared in 1974 and 1975 to borrow external funds and to run larger current account balance of payments deficits, this alternative could not have been much more than a short-term palliative because continual borrowing on a very large scale would eventually have run the borrower up against a growing debt service problem. Moreover, the oil price shock has had secondary repercussions on the level of investment in the industrial countries. The continuing gloomy economic outlook, together with higher energy costs, has led to a reduction in investment intentions all around the OECD area. Furthermore, many governments resorted to the traditional deflationary means of bringing about an improvement in their balance of payments accounts, in turn tending to worsen the economic outlook and to lower investment intentions even further. Together these factors — depressed investment intentions, higher energy costs and balance of payments deficits — combined to bring about the world economic depression of 1974–5.

But these arguments really only apply to that two year period, 1974–5, because the oil-constraint on the world economy began to decline as the real price of oil fell (see Figure 2.3) and even the so-called 'low absorbers' began to spend their much increased incomes at rates that were (and still are) surprisingly high. Why was it then that economic conditions in the world economy continued to compare unfavourably to the experience of the 1960s?

Breakdown of the international monetary system

The breakdown of the international monetary system in the early 1970s was an event of major importance for the industrial countries' economic affairs. The monetary system agreed upon at Bretton Woods in America in 1944 had worked relatively smoothly for a generation during which world production and trade grew at unprecedentedly high rates for a period of time that was equally unprecedented in its duration.

The so-called Bretton Woods system (BWS) helped to create prosperity for the industrial countries, not only by providing a stable network of

foreign currency exchange rates, but also by providing a mechanism that
allowed governments to pursue economic policies that tended to encourage
fast economic growth. Both of these factors are important: stable exchange
rates encourage faster economic growth because they encourage world
trade. In each member economy of the system, businesses were encouraged
to specialise in the production of those goods and services which they
could sell on the world market because there was relatively little risk of
losses arising from unfavourable exchange rate movements. Exchange rate
stability has certainly not been a feature of the international monetary
system since 1971 with, for example, swings in the Deutschmark/dollar
exchange rate of up to 25%. Businessmen in the longer term are likely to
seek to reduce their foreign exchange risks simply by withdrawing at the
margin from world trade.

More important than even the stable exchange rate argument is the less
widely understood argument that the BWS encouraged governments to
run their economies with a high pressure of demand. This feature was
unfortunately also partly responsible for the accelerating rates of inflation
experienced in almost all industrial economies from the late 1960s which
spilled across the following decade and further.

A crucial feature of the BWS was that towards its end there was a surfeit
of international liquidity rather than a shortage. Most important here was
the large outflow of money from the 'key currency' countries – dollars
from the USA and sterling from an inflation-prone UK. In growing economies, governments are usually glad to add to their foreign exchange reserves
because it gives them greater scope to intervene in foreign exchange
markets should the need arise. Foreign exchange reserves can also be used
in emergencies to purchase, for example, food or petrol, or as a 'war
chest'. The advantage in this for the US and the UK was that they could
run larger payments deficits than if they had not provided the international monetary system's key currencies. Clearly, this was possible
because surplus dollars and pounds found their way into their trading
partners' foreign exchange reserves rather than being turned in for gold or
some other currency. Hence, to the extent that American and British
payments deficits were caused by high inflation in these countries, they
could 'export' their inflation to the rest of the world and suppress it at
home. With plenty of foreign exchange reserves around the world all, or
at least most, of the industrial countries ran their economies with a high
pressure of demand with relatively little fear of running into balance of
payments financing problems.

Moreover, outstanding reserves of dollars could always be adjusted
according to the demand for them. For countries wishing to obtain more
dollars could quite easily borrow them from internal US financial markets
or from the rapidly growing 'off-shore' Eurodollar market. Another
important feature here is the fact that in the 1960s the US usually financed
at least a part of its multinational companies' long-term investments in

Europe and elsewhere by borrowing foreign currencies short term. The counterpart accumulation of dollars by foreign central banks was, of course, an addition to their foreign exchange reserves. Thus, if anything, the BWS had a built-in bias towards high rates of economic growth as well as greater inflation.

When the industrial countries allowed the BWS to collapse in 1971, and moved over to floating rates in early 1973, the scope for a deflationary bias in the international financial system increased. Now countries with payments surpluses, like West Germany and Japan, have a certain amount of freedom to allow their currencies to rise on the foreign exchanges. In so doing they can avoid inflating their economies so quickly in the face of inflationary pressures from outside. Indeed, Otmar Emminger has said that is the most important reason why West Germany adopted floating exchange rates in 1973 (Emminger, 1979). Such countries have preferred to run their economies with a low pressure of demand and considerable excess capacity in an attempt to contain inflation. On the other hand, the balance of payments deficit countries like the US have found that they cannot stand by and watch their currencies constantly depreciating as their payments deficits have burgeoned. They also have been forced to apply deflationary policies much sooner than they would have liked. It is now all too apparent that, whereas once the US and, to a lesser extent, the UK could run their economies at near full employment and 'export' their currencies to the rest of the world, they must now adopt corrective deflationary economic packages or see the external value of their currencies collapse.

Uneven distribution of payments deficits

Another consequence of the failure to reconstruct an efficient international monetary system is that balance of payments deficits have been more unevenly spread between the major industrial countries and this also imparted a deflationary bias on to the world economy. Even in the 1973–5 period OPEC was not alone in having large payments surpluses, although it had the largest. The USA had a $12 billion current account surplus in 1975 and West Germany also had a large surplus, of almost $4 billion, despite the increased cost of imported oil. In the USA's case, imports fell by 17% in 1975, naturally reducing the size of the world market for manufacturers (American exports also fell, but by much less). The main factors contributing to the sizeable American payments surplus was the fall in American economic activity caused by a large reduction in investment, by more than in any other industrial country in fact. There was also only a relatively small rise in American public expenditure which might have mitigated these deflationary effects.

In some of the last years of the 1970s, West Germany and Japan both chose to adopt economic policies that resulted in large payments surpluses. Over the three years 1976–8, the combined West German and Japanese payments surplus totalled $48 billion. In 1978, West Germany and Japan

separately ran much larger surpluses than did OPEC. In fact, at $8 billion
the OPEC surplus was relatively small, but Japan's $16.6 billion and West
Germany's $9 billion surpluses were more difficult for the international
financial mechanism to cope with.

Further sharp increases in oil prices in 1979 again led to large OPEC
payments surpluses (about $60 billion). What will happen to these sur-
pluses over the next two to three years is impossible to forecast. The
1970s experience may repeat itself, with OPEC's current account surpluses
falling to manageable proportions. However, still higher oil prices could
lead to even larger surpluses despite continued rapid growth of expenditure
by OPEC members on imports.

Long-term cyclical factors
Monetary and oil price factors are by no means the only explanations of
economic depression in the OECD area since about 1973. N. D. Kondratieff,
a Russian economist, as long ago as 1926 noted that 'The idea that the
dynamics of economic life in the capitalistic social order is not of a simple
and linear but rather of a complex and cyclical character is nowadays
generally recognised' (1978, p. 41). Kondratieff's important finding that is
of relevance here, is that, as well as a seven to eleven year business cycle
(which he called an 'intermediate' cycle), there are also 'long waves' of
about fifty years' duration. Using the sometimes crude statistical data
available, Kondratieff identified these long waves in twenty-one time series
of up to 150 years' duration including commodity prices, interest rates,
wages, foreign trade and coal and iron production in the major capitalistic
economies of the UK, the USA and France. Both the cycle length and the
timing of the turning-points were found to be similar, with cyclical peaks
appearing in the 1914–20 period – that is, some fifty to sixty years ago.
Kondratieff did not advance an economic theory to explain his findings
and no satisfactory theory of 'long waves' has ever been advanced: indeed,
the economics profession has generally remained detached from the entire
subject. However, the findings are interesting because they indicate that
from the 1970s onwards and extending for upwards of twenty-five years,
capitalist economies will be in a downward phase of the Kondratieff cycle.

While Kondratieff did not put forward a theory to explain 'long waves',
he did argue that they were not caused by chance events such as wars,
revolutions, colonial expansion, technological revolutions or periodical
increases in gold production. Rather, the causality was reversed: the ebb
and flow of economic events producing socio-political tensions which led
to the observed non-economic events. Changes in the level of gold production and the application of new technologies were also explained as the
consequences not the causes of the 'long waves'. For example, gold production increased as the price level and gold production costs fell when the
Kondratieff cycle was in a downward phase. Thus, if any credit can be
given to the 'long wave' theory, the direction of causation between economic boom and depression on the one hand and high oil prices on the

other would run from the former to the latter. Oil prices were raised at an approximate peak of the Kondratieff cycle, and while this is of course reflective of the increased bargaining power of the oil exporting nations, it is also reflective of the acknowledged long-term scarcity of finite oil resources relative to greatly expanded demand.

One of the pioneers of trade cycle theory in Western economic circles, R. C. O. Matthews, has analysed economic conditions in Britain in the two decades after the end of the Second World War and his arguments certainly do not contradict the 'long wave' hypothesis. Matthews disagreed that government policy was responsible for the high level of full employment experienced in Britain during that period. Rather, higher levels of investment were the main causative factor and 'post-war investment has essentially the nature of a gigantic cyclical boom' (Matthews, 1968, p. 561). These high levels of investment were in turn a response to the low levels of investment in Britain that were typical of much of the first half of the twentieth century.

Of course, these notions of the 'long wave' and 'gigantic cyclical booms' are subjects which require much more research to establish their validity. However, the intention here is simply to point out that alternatives to the oil-shock-induced-depression hypothesis do exist even if a wholistic theory of the phenomenon has yet to be tested.

Structural factors

A further non-monetary factor which conditions the circumstances of the macroeconomy in most OECD countries is the emergence of structural problems. The ebb and flow of industrial strengths, Schumpeter's gale of creative destruction, has of course always been a feature of capitalist economies. The existence of stubborn pockets of structural resilience has, however, always embarrassed politicians and has frequently led them to alter national priorities or principles to accommodate them. In the UK, the north-east of England and west Scotland, with their traditional shipyard capacity, south Wales with its uneconomic coal mines and Lancashire with its textile mills have figured prominently. In France, Belgium and West Germany similar 'problem' industries and regions exist.

In many OECD countries certain steps were taken to mitigate these structural problems in the 1950s, and in retrospect it can be seen that these far-sighted measures were much to be preferred to the series of *ad hoc* initiatives taken in the next two decades whenever political expediency dictated. In the UK, the 1959 Cotton Industry Act was successful in slimming down the textiles labour force and should have opened the way for substantial liberalisation of trade in textiles and garments and a consequent improvement in the country's consumers' welfare. Similarly, in West Germany the footwear industry and in Belgium the coal industry were among those able to take advantage of prescient policies to reallocate resources away from low-productivity labour-intensive sectors which even then were coming into fierce competition from less developed country suppliers.

What made these policies (which have recently come to be termed 'adjustment' policies) economically desirable and politically practical at that time was the high overall level of employment in OECD countries. This meant that even disadvantaged groups in the labour force (the young, the old, the unskilled, and so on) were able to locate alternative jobs after tolerably brief spells of unemployment. And what made these same policies less practical in the eyes of OECD policy makers in the 1970s was precisely the reverse: the fact that unemployment was abnormally high, was resilient and was especially discouraging for the demographic groups likely to be involved. Given the lengthier spells of unemployment these people were now likely to confront, the pressure on politicians and policy makers to postpone structural adjustment exercises, which were no less economically desirable, became overwhelming.

The shipbuilding industry is perhaps the best-known instance of a 'structural' problem. By 1979 EEC official assistance for the industry was running at £500 million annually, and shipyards in the Community were operating at less than 30% capacity. The diagnosis is similar to that for many industries: expansion in the 1960s when national growth rates showed no sign of lapsing into the doldrums, and when confidence in governments' willingness and ability to smooth out temporary recessions was high, ranged against increasing competition from new sources of supply. In the case of shipbuilding, the new major source is of course Japan, which throughout the 1970s built around half the world's new tonnage. There are, however, strong less developed country challenges appearing too: South Korea, Taiwan, Brazil and Singapore are quickly establishing their own capacity.

Protectionism as a constraint on ldcs' exports

The burden of the arguments presented above is that the world economy has suffered from a number of adverse developments in the 1970s and after: high inflation, the breakdown and failure to reconstitute a new international monetary system, structural imbalances, and perhaps a downward turn in the long-term Kondratieff cycle. Oil prices are also a factor, but only one of this list. The non-oil exporting less developed countries have also suffered from the adverse influences of all of these elements as well as an additional factor investigated in this section: trade protectionism by developed countries.

It is not difficult to see that pressure from elected representatives and regional, industrial or craft-based interest groups to restrict allegedly harmful imports is less resistible in times of high unemployment. Given the deflationary impact of the OPEC price rises in 1973, and the compounding of this by deliberate government deflationary measures, the normal pockets of high unemployment, in certain regions of developed countries, and among certain demographic groups, were exacerbated. Because interest groups are concentrated and relatively coherent, while those individuals in an economy who stand on the other hand to lose from protectionism through higher prices and constrained choice are disparate and lack any lobby, the former are frequently able to swing government decisions in their favour. Throughout the early 1970s there were therefore many signs of a desire to curtail the trend towards the liberalisation of international trade that had characterised the 1950s and 1960s.

A wide range of policy instruments were brought into use by those who sought to constrain ldc suppliers' access to developed country markets. Frequent resort was made to Article XIX of GATT, the so-called 'safeguards' clause, which permits unilateral import quotas to be imposed by a country if it can show that a sector of its economy is suffering unduly from rapid import growth. In practice this relaxation of the multilateral most favoured nation principle of GATT allowed imports to be impeded without any guarantee needing to be given to the aggrieved suppliers about the resumption of unhampered trade. Moreover, the consumers in the country applying the safeguards clause receive no guarantee that the industries they are being required to support (through higher prices) will be forced into rationalisation. During the lifetime of the Tokyo Round of GATT negotiations voluntary export restraints (VERs) were imposed upon footwear, televisions and many other manufactures. Also, the Multi-fibre Arrangement was renegotiated, this time allowing still smaller growth of imports of textiles to the EEC in many sub-sectors.

Those product groups which attracted the greatest attention from protectionist lobbies in dcs in the 1970s were, naturally enough, those in which ldcs had made the greatest headway. By 1977 ldcs had come to represent over 10% of the total import value to dcs of six product groups — clothing (33.4% of total dc imports); processed food (20.8%); leather and footwear (20.3%); textiles (14.6%); wood products (11.8%) and miscellaneous light manufactures (11.3%) (UNCTAD, 1979b, p. 303). These shares of the import market were the result of very large annual increases in ldcs' trade effort: in the case of clothing, their exports to dcs rose by 31.2% annually over 1970–7. In volume terms, these market shares would be even greater, since a characteristic of ldcs' manufactured exports — at least in the initial years — is their typically low unit value.

Certain economists and politicians were not slow to condemn these moves. The IMF, in its 29th *Annual Report on Exchange Restrictions,* observed that protectionist measures were 'particularly harmful to those developing countries that have sought to sustain the growth of their economies through the expansion of non-traditional exports'. And the *Annual Report* of the World Bank in 1978 judged that 'developing countries are becoming increasingly concerned about the ability of policy-makers in the industrialized world to withstand pressure for imposition of new quantitative restrictions' (p. 16). The irony of these moves to constrain ldcs' manufactured and semi-processed exports to dcs in this period was that very few dc based industries were actually being put in peril at all by this source of competition. A multitude of studies confirmed that the net employment loss directly attributable to trade with ldcs in any given industry or sub-sector of industry was a tiny fraction of total labour turnover — typically less than one-tenth of one per cent.

Finally, the fact that dcs in aggregate were by 1976 running a surplus on trade in manufactures with all ldcs of the order of $100 billion annually indicates the magnitude of the net employment gain that must have been accruing to dc firms and their employees from their trade with ldcs. As an exhaustive review of empirical evidence on the subject from UNIDO concludes: 'trade with developing countries is not a cause of unemployment in dcs and counter-measures are no means of reducing unemployment' (UNIDO, 1979b, p. 58).

Conclusions

Some of the major aspects of the 1970s world economic malaise have been examined in this chapter. The oil price shocks of October and December 1973 have been found to be only one of several contributory factors, although an important one, especially in the 1974–5 period. Also of great importance has been the breakdown of the international monetary system that had served the world economy well up to the end of the 1960s. One result of this is that the virtually constant high pressure of demand in all industrial countries that had been encouraged by the Bretton Woods international monetary system was no longer present and may have been replaced by one with a bias towards a lower pressure of demand and slower economic growth. Moreover, nearly all industrial countries have reluctantly chosen to run their economies with substantial excess capacity from the mid 1970s onwards in an attempt to contain the high rates of inflation that were apparent before the oil price shock. Another consequence of both the high rates of inflation and the new international monetary (non-) system is that the industrial countries have not been able satisfactorily to share their payments deficits amongst themselves and this has also had a net deflationary effect. Certain structural imbalances have also been contributory factors to the economic malaise, and the non-oil developing countries have suffered from growing trade protectionism in the developed countries.

Notes

1 Quoted by Otmar Emminger (1979), p. 4.
2 The trend is the log-linear regression 1955–74 computed by the Bank for International Settlements, *Annual Report*, 1978, p. 13.

3

The Organisation of Petroleum Exporting Countries

The objective of this chapter is to show how and under what circumstances the oil exporting countries were able to take control of oil prices in the early 1970s. It is control over oil prices, especially the ability to raise prices and to keep them at high levels, that has enabled the oil exporting countries to differentiate themselves from the mass of Third World countries. Without high oil prices, the oil exporting countries would to a large extent be just another set of single-commodity exporters. None of them would head the World Bank's international league table of per capita incomes as some of them do. But the nature of the oil exporters' cartel, OPEC, is far more complex than is often supposed — a topic confronted later in the chapter.

The economic power of the oil exporting countries stems from a number of factors: these include the dominance of the world oil economy by OPEC in terms of these countries' high shares of world crude oil production, exports and proven reserves; the difficulty that the oil importing countries have in quickly substituting other energy reserves for oil; the new independently wielded control that the OPEC members have over their oil industries; as well as the lasting stability of the OPEC cartel. These issues are confronted separately in this chapter.

The chapter ends with a theoretical discussion of the effects of higher oil prices on the oil exporters' and importers' welfare levels. The impact that much higher oil prices have had on the terms of trade between oil and manufactured goods and primary commodities is, however, not quantified; this is left to Chapter 4.

OPEC's importance in the world oil economy

OPEC is composed of the thirteen member states shown in Table 3.1. Listed in order of their shares of OPEC crude oil production in 1978 they are: Saudi Arabia, Iran, Iraq, Venezuela, Kuwait, Libya, Nigeria, UAE, Indonesia, Algeria, Qatar, Gabon[1] and Ecuador. In each year between 1973 and 1978 the OPEC members produced over 58% of world crude oil

Table 3.1   *OPEC's crude oil output and exports*

	1973	1974	1975	1976	1977	1978
Total OPEC output billions of barrels per annum	11,299	11,200	9,935	11,241	11,469	10,907
	%	%	%	%	%	%
Share of OPEC producers in world output[a]	62.6	62.7	59.9	62.4	61.5	58.5
Share of Arab OPEC members in OPEC output	58.0	57.3	58.7	60.2	61.3	61.9
Algeria	3.5	3.3	3.5	3.5	3.5	4.1
Iraq	6.4	6.1	8.3	7.8	7.9	8.8
Kuwait	9.8	8.3	7.7	7.0	6.3	7.0
Libya	7.0	4.9	5.5	6.2	6.6	6.6
Qatar	1.8	1.7	1.6	1.6	1.4	1.6
UAE	4.9	5.4	6.1	6.2	6.3	6.1
Saudi Arabia	24.6	27.6	26.0	27.9	29.3	27.7
Saudi Arabia and Gulf states	41.1	43.0	41.1	42.7	43.3	42.4
Iran	19.0	19.7	19.8	19.3	18.1	17.5
Nigeria	6.6	7.3	6.6	6.7	6.7	6.6
Venezuela	10.9	9.7	8.6	7.4	7.1	7.2
The rest						
Ecuador	0.7	0.6	0.6	0.6	0.6	0.7
Gabon	0.5	0.7	0.8	0.7	0.7	0.7
Indonesia	4.3	4.5	4.8	4.9	5.4	5.5
OPEC's share of world[a] crude oil exports	92.5	92.0	90.8	92.5	91.5	

Notes
[a] World, excluding Sino-Soviet area.
Totals may not add to 100% due to rounding.

Sources: Petroleum Economist, September 1979, p. 391; US Department of Mines, *International Petroleum Annual,* various issues.

output (excluding the Sino-Soviet area), often over 62%. Even more impressively, these thirteen countries contributed over 90% to world crude petroleum exports during the same period. As will be shown in the next section, the dominance of OPEC in world crude oil production and foreign trade is an important factor enabling the thirteen countries to manipulate crude oil prices so successfully.

The largest producer is quite easily Saudi Arabia with nearly 28% of OPEC's crude oil production in 1978 — a share that actually *increased*

Table 3.2 *Proven reserves of crude oil and natural gas liquids, end 1978*

	billion tonnes	Percentage of world excluding Sino-Soviet area
World	88.9	
World excluding Sino-Soviet area	76.1	
OPEC	60.9	80.0
Abu Dhabi	4.1	5.4
Iran	8.1	10.6
Iraq	4.3	5.7
Kuwait	9.5	12.5
Libya	3.3	4.3
Saudi Arabia	23.1	30.4
USA	4.6	6.0
UK	2.2	2.9
Mexico	2.2	2.9

Source: Institute of Petroleum, London, 1979.

compared to 1973. Iran stands alone as the second largest producer with 17.5% of OPEC production in that year. There then follow nine countries each with between 4% and 9% of OPEC's total output. The OPEC membership is completed by Ecuador and Gabon with tiny shares of production. The seven Arab member states of OPEC together produce about 60% of OPEC output, but the Arabs' share is not always an important factor in policy formation because they often split between the radical states (usually identified as Iraq, Libya and Algeria) and the more conservative Saudi Arabians and Gulf states. Even so the latter group (four countries in all) produce over two-fifths of OPEC's crude oil.

The OPEC members also dominate in their share of the world's proven reserves of crude oil and natural gas (Table 3.2). At the end of 1978, proven reserves outside the Sino-Soviet area amounted to about 76 billion tonnes with OPEC accounting for 80% of this total. Saudi Arabia alone accounted for over 30% of these reserves. By contrast, the USA holds only about 6% and the UK 2.2% of world crude oil reserves.

The timing of the massive oil price rises in 1973 and the rise of OPEC itself have resulted from the complicated interplay of certain historical, political and economic forces. The OPEC members, of course, first had to gain independent control over their oil sectors before they were able to manipulate oil prices so effectively. The rise of OPEC is itself a fascinating subject — rooted as it is in the conditions which developed in the post-colonial era. However, as the history of OPEC is well documented elsewhere (Kubbah, 1974; al-Otaiba, 1975; Penrose, 1979; and Vallenilla, 1975) only brief attention will be paid to the subject here.

The rise of OPEC

OPEC was founded in 1960 between Iran, Iraq, Kuwait, Saudi Arabia and Venezuela as a response to the unilateral reduction in posted oil prices by the oil companies. But OPEC's roots go back further than this: exploratory meetings were held between the Venezuelans (the prime movers in the early days) and the Iranians even in 1947, and Venezuelan representatives toured the Middle East in 1949. In 1951 the Venezuelans advised the Middle East oil exporters of the advantages of the new profits tax system that they had recently negotiated with the oil companies. From the beginning the oil exporters recognised the need for a united front against the oil companies in order to avoid the companies playing one host country off against another — something that was relatively easy in a period of excess supplies of oil and emerging oil suppliers. The Arabs were also in touch with each other on sensitive oil industry policy issues through the Arab League and in 1953 a formal agreement to exchange information was signed between the Saudis and the Iraqis. Then in 1959 an important Arab Petroleum Congress was held in Cairo with Iran and Venezuela attending as observers. The following year OPEC was formed.

However, none of these early contacts was to have a significant impact upon the development of the international oil industry in the 1950s. Nor were the oil exporters, either individually or collectively through the OPEC, much more successful in the 1960s. But in the space of less than one decade relationships in the international oil industry changed. By the early 1970s the OPEC members could show a united front against the, by then disunited, international oil companies, reversing the situation of only a few years earlier. While Penrose finds it 'difficult to estimate the comparative importance of the several elements involved here' (1979, p. 18), Adelman is able quickly to unravel the complications. He points out that 'it is axiomatic that a good discovery of oil reserves means a dissatisfied landlord who wishes he had held out for more. He will look around for any possible way of getting more. Once this basic relation is understood a great deal of history can be compressed into a single page' (Adelman, 1972, p. 207). Initially lacking petroleum know-how, market outlets for their crude oil, skilled personnel and capital resources, the countries that were to become the large petroleum exporters invited foreign petroleum companies to prospect for oil and the governments agreed to generous terms relating to the division of revenues. Sometimes the countries were still colonies and some of them were subsequently to claim that they were not free agents when drawing up these agreements. Moreover, with time, the oil exporting countries improved their own technical competence in the oil industry, availability of capital was shortly to become only a minor problem, and technology could be obtained other than from the leading international oil companies, the so-called 'seven sisters'. Above all, the emergence of the independent oil companies, which were seeking new sources of crude oil, increased the range of policy alternatives open to the oil exporting countries.

Even so, during the 1960s the oil exporting countries were able to make only small gains: the formation of OPEC in 1960 is thought to have dissuaded the oil companies from making further unilateral cuts in posted prices, but OPEC was not successful in raising posted prices throughout the entire decade. Some headway was made on the question of royalty expensing. The companies were originally allowed to treat royalty payments as a credit against income tax paid to the host countries. The OPEC members wished to change this system so that royalties were treated as an operating cost (that is, not tax deductible). In 1964 the companies gave way on royalty expensing, but the gain for the host countries was small since they in turn agreed to grant the companies an allowance on posted prices. Another small gain for the oil exporting countries was that the companies eventually agreed to a reduction in the countries' contributions to marketing expenses.

However, during the 1960s there was a marked change in the tone of OPEC conference resolutions, from moderation to militancy. The first OPEC conference in 1960 only resolved to 'devise ways and means of ensuring the stabilization of prices in international oil markets'. To the limited extent that oil prices did not fall further after the formation of OPEC, the Organisation was successful here. The 1968 Declaratory Statement on Petroleum Policy was somewhat more ambitious, as it was resolved that the posted price 'shall move in such a manner as to prevent any deterioration in the relationship to the prices of manufactured goods traded internationally'. And two years later, at Caracas, the OPEC membership resolved 'to establish a uniform *general* increase in the posted prices'.[2] OPEC was, of course, to be successful in this resolve.

In 1971, with the companies under the threat of embargo, the Tehran Agreement began the trend of dramatically rising oil prices. Posted prices were immediately raised by 33 cents per barrel, and a schedule of price increases (tiny compared to those enforced in 1973) was also agreed. Agreements were shortly to be signed at Tripoli and Geneva and each time oil prices were raised. But none of these price increases were to compare in size to the rise in posted prices announced by the six Gulf states in October 1973 when at once prices were increased by 77% over the June level to $5.119 per barrel (Arabian light 34°). Then in December came the announcement that the price of oil would be raised again to $11.651 per barrel — quadrupling the June price. (Figure 2.3 shows posted oil prices.)

However, the success of the oil exporting countries in raising oil prices so dramatically stems from more than the newly acquired ability to organise themselves. Perhaps the single most important economic factor governing their success is the oil importing countries' dependence upon oil from OPEC sources, even long after prices have been very substantially increased. That is, the price elasticity of demand for OPEC's oil is low.

The elasticity of demand for OPEC's oil

The price elasticity of demand for a cartel's product in world trade depends upon three factors: first, the price elasticity of demand for the product in final consumption; secondly, the price elasticity of supply from non-cartel members; and thirdly, the share of world exports supplied by the cartel members. The more inelastic is final consumption demand, the lower is supply elasticity from the rest of the world, and the larger is the share of the cartel in total world exports, the better it is for the cartel members as demand for their production will be more inelastic.[3]

Econometric estimates show that the price elasticity of demand for oil in final consumption is indeed low. The US Federal Energy Office's estimate of the long-run price elasticity of demand for oil in consuming areas (the USA, Canada, Europe, Japan and NOPECs) is in the range between -0.2 and -0.6 (reported by Kalymon, 1975, p. 345). Burrows and Domenich's estimates (reported by Kalymon, 1975) correspond closely with this finding: in the USA the price elasticity of demand for oil is put at -0.5 (pp. 119–29). Short-run demand elasticities for oil must be even lower given that in 1974, immediately after the quadrupling of OPEC prices, consumption of refined petroleum in Western Europe, the USA and Japan (as a group) fell by only 4.3% compared to 1973.[4]

Additionally, the other two factors which influence the price elasticity of demand for OPEC's oil are also favourable (from OPEC's point of view). OPEC's share in world crude oil exports is high – about 92% (see Table 3.1) – and the price elasticity of supply of crude oil from the rest of the world is in the low range of 0.2 to 0.4 (Kalymon, 1975).

On the basis of these estimates, then, the long-run price elasticity of demand facing the OPEC cartel lies somewhere between -0.24 and -0.68, that is, is rather inelastic. Moreover, as it is still doubtful that there has been any significant change in these three parameters in recent years, the demand for OPEC's oil is still price inelastic despite the enormous price increase of the 1970s.

Forecasts of the demand–supply balance for OPEC oil in industrial countries confirm that these countries will remain dependent upon oil supplies from OPEC throughout the 1980s. A comprehensive Central Intelligence Agency analysis of energy demand and supply potentialities in the OECD area in 1982 points to an energy supply gap of 3 to 5 million barrels per day oil equivalent even if OECD countries were to grow at only 3.5% per annum and OPEC members were to produce oil at preferred levels (CIA, 1979). This energy gap must, of course, be closed in some way, either by even slower growth in the OECD area (less than 2% per annum) or by much improved energy conservation. Increased energy supplies from non-OPEC sources of oil, gas, nuclear power or 'non-traditional' energy forms are highly unlikely to relieve the energy constraint on economic growth. And as an authoritative oil industry journal has observed: 'most forecasters . . . do see a decade of chronic tight [energy] supply in spite of prospects for slowing demand growth' (*Oil and Gas Journal,* 12 November 1979, p. 163).

If newly acquired organisational freedoms and favourable market circumstances have been factors conditioning the rise of OPEC, it is apposite to ask what is the true nature of OPEC. Is it, for example, a tightly organised cartel or can it more nearly be described as a loose confederation of several oil exporting countries? And who is responsible for fixing oil prices: is it OPEC or do certain dominant oil exporters determine price policy to the exclusion of the rest of the membership?

The chimerical nature of OPEC

OPEC is usually seen as being a price fixing cartel. Indeed, a Minister of Petroleum and Mineral Resources from an OPEC member state has written in these terms: 'all are agreed that one of the objectives of OPEC is to stabilize the prices at which crude oil is sold and, of course, to raise them whenever possible' (al-Otaiba, 1975, p. 1). The subject of cartels is well researched in economics, with even first year economics textbooks showing that competitive firms can raise their profit levels by colluding on prices and rationing output between themselves. The exercise is so familiar that it will not be repeated here. The three essential elements of this standard treatment of cartel theory can be summarised thus: there is agreement among the cartel membership on the objective function to be maximised (profits in the standard case or sometimes total revenues); agreement on the price level needed to maximise the objective function; and agreement on the output prorationing required to make agreed prices stick. Sometimes it is observed that monopolists cannot fix both output and prices, so they have to experiment, either setting output and letting price find its own level, or setting price and letting demand determine total output. These problems arise only because the cartel does not have full information about demand and cost conditions. The comprehensive nature of the act of collusion remains unquestioned, however.

None of this standard theory holds any surprises. But what is surprising, given OPEC's spectacular success, is that it seems that little of it applies to the OPEC cartel. Precise objective functions have never been agreed upon; output prorationing has not been practiced; and most surprising of all, according to at least one leading oil industry expert, OPEC is not even responsible for setting oil prices. The most spectacular cartel in history is but a façade on this view. True power lies elsewhere, not with OPEC *per se* but with certain of its members, especially the largest oil producers.

Edith Penrose is of the view that OPEC 'is in fact extremely important but not as a restrictive cartel' and 'OPEC as such has little influence on the price or supply of oil' (Penrose, 1979, p. 24). A distinction is thus drawn between the power of OPEC — an organisation run by a secretariat — and the power of the individual countries that form the membership of OPEC. It is observed that OPEC's secretariat 'has been weak, and deliberately kept so' (Penrose, 1979). The membership, while recognising the need for close communications and policy discussions among themselves, have still sought individually to control at the local level oil prices and differentials, output, tax, royalty and participation policies. Major decisions on oil prices are not, for example, taken by majority vote in the OPEC. Indeed, a large number of historical changes in the oil industry have been forced by individual governments acting outside the aegis of OPEC. Examples are fiscal changes imposed by Libya on the oil companies in 1970 and new participation agreements between the latter and Saudi Arabia, Iraq and Kuwait later in the decade. Moreover, even the oil price rises of 1973 were not orchestrated by OPEC. Rather, the October price rise was enforced by the Ministerial Committee of the Gulf States and the much bigger price rise in the December of that year has been seen as the responsibility of the Shah of Iran. Thus, it appears that some large oil exporting countries do possess a great deal of leverage over oil prices and it is the governments of these countries which make oil price policy and run OPEC, not the other way around. Indeed, it has been observed that Saudi Arabia, the UAE, Libya and Iran are the 'dominant market power aristocracy' (Kuenne, 1979, p. 710) and Parker has referred to 'the medium term irrelevance of OPEC' (1978, p. 32).

However, these price leaders, if such a term can be used, do need to know that the other oil exporters will not undercut their oil prices. The OPEC forum is, at very bottom, a meeting place where such assurances can be given. It is a place where 'informal voluntary co-operation' can take place (Willet, 1979, p. 54). And its propaganda has fixed in mass psychology the idea of a world energy crisis which has made the oil importing countries almost receptive of higher oil and energy costs (Adelman, 1972).

Ability to control supply is the essential factor which has given OPEC, or some of its members, the power to raise oil prices. Adelman is convinced that the oil price rises of the early 1970s were not due to excess demand for oil, but to the power of the producers to control supply: 'monopoly means control of supply, hence the power to stop it' (Adelman, 1974, p. 59). Really, the importance of higher oil prices overrides that of the discussion of whether OPEC should be properly viewed as an effective monopolistic cartel, as a forum for the exchange of ideas and policy intents, or, even, almost an irrelevance on the world stage. In his 1972 *magnum opus* on the world oil industry, then unaware of the oil exporters' still untested ability to limit production, Adelman forecast that the new oil prices agreed under the 1971 Tehran Agreement could not be sustained.

He observed that already the price of oil was several times its cost of production. Easy profits from oil production would lead to higher output and to falling prices. (See also *The Economist,* 5 January 1974, 2 March 1974, 22 June 1974.) The forecast could not have been more wrong as it turned out. The oil exporters are able to control production, but not through formal prorationing. Saudi Arabia as the 'Mr. Big in the cartel' (Adelman, 1974, p. 61) is able, but not without some difficulty, to stabilise oil prices at the chosen level.

The fact that OPEC's strength derives from its being a cartel is a chimera can be seen in the many different economic models that have been developed to forecast its price and production behaviour. Willett is explicit that 'OPEC has been organized at least as much like an oligopoly with a dominant firm (Saudi Arabia) as like a genuine monopoly cartel' (1979, p. 54). One study of power relationships in OPEC adds to the confusion: a mathematical model of *oligopoly* power realtionships between eleven OPEC members is developed but in the paper OPEC continues to be described as a 'cartel' (Kuenne, 1979). Altogether Fisher, Gately and Kyle (1975) and Gately (1979) have reviewed twenty-two such formal models, emphasising their different economic and econometric structures. OPEC's objective function is variously defined in these models as, for example, the maximisation of the value of net foreign asset holdings at a specified future date plus the undiscounted value of oil still left in the ground at that date; or, more straightforwardly, as the maximisation of the total discounted value of oil reserves. And the list of objective functions that have been used could quite easily be extended. The problem for the modellers is that they have no real idea of OPEC's true objective function, nor can they even be sure that OPEC has an agreed and unchanging objective function.

Perhaps more interesting is the treatment given to OPEC's oil price and production policy in these formal economic models of the cartel. Many of the models recognise the fact that OPEC-wide production prorationing does not occur. Instead, the separate models assume that certain OPEC members will act as residual suppliers, reducing their production sufficiently to ensure that agreed minimum prices are not threatened by overproduction. Usually, Saudi Arabia, by far the largest producer, is taken to be the residual supplier, but others have also been taken as likely candidates — Kuwait, Abu Dhabi, Qatar, Iran, Libya and sometimes even Iraq. So universal is the belief that only a few oil producers act as residual suppliers, while the other members set output according to some other criterion (for example, maximising production in order to maximise foreign exchange earnings), that it is possible to speak of an OPEC *subcartel*. In essence, this sub-cartel notion recognises that only a few oil exporting countries, notably Saudi Arabia, are in a position to make oil prices agreed in OPEC stick. In the oil markets of the 1970s, Saudi Arabia, by moving its oil production down by two or three million barrels of oil per day from the average 8–9 million barrels per day, could have forced oil prices up to even higher levels. Or, if she could have been persuaded to raise output by the same amount, oil prices would almost certainly have fallen from the levels actually reached.

The sub-cartel idea is interesting for several reasons. First, it recognises that OPEC is not a monolithic cartel with all its members having an effective say in oil price and production policy. Secondly, the residual suppliers are identified as those countries with large oil production capacities but small populations and large balance of payments surpluses – the so-called 'low absorbers'. In technical terminology these residual suppliers have low rates of time preference and are supposed almost to welcome the chance to leave their oil in the ground for exploitation in the more distant future. And, thirdly, the very idea of an OPEC sub-cartel had to be invented by the economic modellers because agreed production prorationing is not a feature of the actual OPEC cartel.

However, it is not entirely clear that even the 'swing producer' sub-cartel notion in its strict form (a few OPEC members cutting output while the others maximise their production) is entirely accurate in OPEC's case. It is true that only four countries (Saudi Arabia, Kuwait, Iran and Iraq) together accounted for about 75% of OPEC's unused capacity in 1978 – see Table 3.3, columns 2 and 4. However, it is also apparent that leaving aside Indonesia and Gabon, all the other OPEC members have operated with 10% or substantially more unused capacity as columns 1 and 3 show. Moreover, the swing producer notion is likely to be even less relevant in the future as demand for OPEC output begins to outrun supply (see next section). Many of the largest OPEC producers have set oil production *ceilings* below current production capacities – Saudi Arabia, Kuwait, UAE, Iraq and Iran.[5] It is quite possible that OPEC members will eventually move over from a system of setting prices (with demand determining output and *ad hoc* rationing allocating this output among producers) to a system where the major producers fix output and let the market determine prices.

That production prorationing is not required in order to fix oil prices has been a source of great strength for OPEC. Squabbles over production levels have not occurred – at least not in public. Unfortunately for the more militant Libyans and Algerians, the main disadvantages of the absence of a formal OPEC machinery for controlling price, production and production quota levels is that there are no levers which can be pulled to make the more moderate members change tracks. But this is why Saudi Arabia and the Gulf states have distanced themselves somewhat from the OPEC forum and retained control over their own oil price and production policies.

One final note in this brief review of the modelling of OPEC must be reserved for the effect of the residual supplier/sub-cartel system on oil price levels. The Saudis are politically moderate in many respects: it is not

Table 3.3 *Estimated unused crude oil production capacity,[a] October 1977*

	PIW[b]		CIA[c]	
	Country's unused capacity %	% of total OPEC unused capacity	Country's unused capacity %	% of total OPEC unused capacity
	1	2	3	4
Algeria	21	3	12	2
Ecuador	20	0	20	0
Gabon	8	0	8	0
Indonesia	9	2	4	1
Iran	19	14	17	17
Iraq	29	10	27	12
Kuwait	44	16	44	21
Libya	16	4	9	3
Nigeria	19	5	15	5
Qatar	20	1	13	1
UAE	20	4	18	5
Saudi Arabia	27	35	18	27
Venezuela	14	4	10	4
		100		100
Estimated unused capacity (million b/d)	9.12		6.77	

[a] 90 days sustainable production.
[b] *Petroleum Intelligence Weekly*, overall design capacity of installed equipment.
[c] Central Intelligency Agency estimates based on technically feasible production.

Source: calculated from Salamon Brothers, *Biweekly Bulletin*, vol. III, no. 8, 25 January 1978, Table 2.

one of their objectives to bring down the system of Western capitalism. Moreover, the Saudis have an interest in the economic stability of the West, since Saudi Arabia has enormous financial investments in Western financial markets (some $70 billion) and these already yield her a sizeable income (up to $8 billion per year). Oil price policy must therefore take into account the value of these investments as well as current earnings from oil exports. If higher oil prices mean a weaker dollar, then at least until the bulk of the Saudi's financial assets have been diversified out of dollar-denominated paper, Saudi oil price policy will take account of the effect of oil prices on the dollar. And there are other arguments that suggest that Saudi Arabia has an interest in a moderate oil price policy. High oil prices, with Saudi Arabia as the main residual supplier, would require disproportionately large production cutbacks by that country and its revenues would be correspondingly lower. Moreover, so vast are Saudi Arabia's oil reserves that it would be sensible not to raise prices to the monopoly level because that would encourage more rapid substitution of alternative energy sources, so reducing the demand for Saudi oil in the longer term. Indeed, the OPEC model simulations run by Kalymon show that oil prices are lower under a residual supplier arrangement than under an output prorationing system.[6]

Is then OPEC a cartel? In the strict form described by the standard economic theory of cartels, it is not. However, we will continue to describe OPEC as a cartel, if for no other reason than everybody else calls it a cartel. Moreover, the sub-cartel idea described above also does not adequately describe the true nature of OPEC. Rather surprisingly some of the largest and low population producers, like Saudi Arabia, the United Arab Emirates and Libya, have not experienced reductions in their shares of OPEC's oil production since 1974. This is contrary to what would be predicted by the sub-cartel theory. And when OPEC has required to make relatively deep cuts in production, as in 1975 and 1978, most members have reduced their production levels − a fact that sits easily with the notion that OPEC is a cartel.

So it must now be asked: how stable is OPEC as a cartel-like organisation? Will it survive for the next five to ten years at least?

The stability of OPEC

The view that the large difference between oil prices at over $11 per barrel in 1974 and oil marginal production costs in the Middle East of about 15 cents to $1 per barrel would quickly lead to the breakup of OPEC turned out to be wrong. Certainly it was true that in the 1960s many OPEC members were desperate to increase oil exports so as to finance their development plans. But this was at the low price levels dictated by the oil companies, not the much higher prices that some OPEC members were able to impose on the world market in the subsequent decade. As the chairman of Gulf Oil observed in 1974: 'They'd have to be utterly mad to do anything so stupid as to go out and compete with each other to drive down the prices of oil' (quoted by Sampson, 1976, p. 296).

The standard economic models of cartel behaviour make clear the advantages to individual members of cheating. With prices well above production costs, profits can be increased by secretly giving discounts on the agreed cartel price. This increases total revenue to the cheater. But if everybody cheats, the cartel will soon collapse. However, as was demonstrated in the previous section, OPEC does not accord well with the standard cartel model − an objective function to be maximised has not been agreed upon by the membership, production prorationing does not occur, nor even does the membership exert collective control over oil price levels.

An important factor that gives the OPEC cartel resilience during periods of weak demand for oil is the willingness of most OPEC members to cut back production — an observation which does not square with the sub-cartel notions. For example, in 1975 when total OPEC production fell back by 11% all OPEC members other than tiny Gabon cut their output, while Libya and the UAE recorded only marginal increases in output. And again in 1978, with OPEC production down by 5%, all but four OPEC members cut output (they were a different four).

Another factor pointing to the continued stability of the OPEC cartel is that the demand for OPEC's oil has not fallen by very much — even in 1975, the worst year, demand was down only about one-eighth. Indeed, OPEC's share of world petroleum exports has held up well since 1973, as Table 3.1 shows. Moreover, there was agreement among the fifteen economic models of OPEC examined by Gately that real oil prices are unlikely to fall in the mid to late 1980s because by that time demand for OPEC oil would at least match supply. And the question of the likely behaviour of real oil prices during the first five years of the 1980s was quickly settled by the more than halving of Iranian production in the first half of 1979 compared to one year earlier and the related 40–60% increase in oil prices which took real oil prices above even their 1974 levels (see Figure 2.3). Even if real oil prices were to weaken over the next five years, it is unlikely that tensions within OPEC over price and production levels would be severe enough as to threaten the cohesion and stability of that organisation.

So OPEC is likely to survive for several more years at least. What then have been the effects of higher oil prices upon economic welfare in the oil importing and exporting countries? In the next section a theoretical economic model is developed to show these welfare effects and in Chapter 4 these terms of trade effects are quantified.

The welfare effects of cartelisation

The international welfare effects emitting from the cartelisation of the market of an internationally traded commodity can be put with some precision with geometric arguments. The geometric techniques used are familiar to students of international economics but other scholars might also find the analysis illuminating. However, those readers in a hurry can pass over this section without losing the thread of the arguments in the rest of the book.

Assumptions. We start out by making some simplifying assumptions about the 'world' in which international trade and the cartel operates.

First, the world is composed of only two countries, cartel members and petroleum importers. These, of course, are groups of countries rather than single countries; international cartels are after all formed between two or more countries. However, it can be assumed that *within* each group, countries are identical to each other with respect to factor endowment, demand patterns and technology. Thus, one country drawn from the cartel membership can be taken as representative of that group, and a country drawn from the petroleum importers can represent the rest of the world.

Secondly, it is assumed that only two commodities are produced in each country: petroleum and a composite commodity of all other goods.

Thirdly, the cartel member, being relatively well endowed with petroleum relative to the domestic demand for petroleum, exports this commodity in exchange for the composite all other goods. Thus, it is assumed that the cartel member has a comparative advantage in petroleum and the representative of the rest of the world, a comparative advantage in the composite commodity.

Assumptions 1 to 3 are needed to adapt the famous Heckscher—Ohlin theory of international trade to the analysis of the welfare effects that follow from the cartelisation of an international commodity market. However, several more assumptions are used to establish the Heckscher—Ohlin theory itself. As these assumptions are discussed in many standard international economics textbooks, the exercise will not be repeated here. The reader is referred to Paul Samuelson's classic paper on the subject (1948). An important assumption of the international trade model under discussion is that competitive conditions rule in all sectors of the 'world' economy. It is this assumption, and only this assumption, that is broken by the formation of a cartel in the following analysis. Of course, a cartel is specifically designed to replace competition between producer-exporters by collusive price fixing arrangements.

The *geometric technique* used here is that of the offer curve developed by James Meade and neatly explained by Charles Kindleberger (Meade, 1952; Kindleberger, 1973). Again, students of international economics will be familiar with offer curves, the international trade indifference curve maps from which the offer curves are derived and the terms of trade construction between the traded commodities.

In Figure 3.1, OC and OI are the cartel member's and the petroleum importer's international trade offer curves respectively constructed according to Meade's methodology from each country's trade indifference curve map. The offer curves show the quantities of exportables that each country will offer in exchange for imports. They are concave because a unit increase in exports will be offered only if a disproportionately greater increase in importables is obtained in exchange.[7] OI, the petroleum importer's offer curve, turns downwards at the point X, as to the right of X the demand for imported petroleum is price inelastic.[8]

Each country's level of welfare corresponding to this pattern of imports and exports can be judged from its trade indifference curve map. Two of the cartel member's trade indifference curves are shown in Figure 3.1, IC_{c1} and IC_{c2}; similarly IC_{i1} and IC_{i2} are two of the petroleum importer's

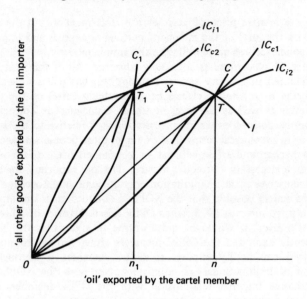

Figure 3.1   *Welfare effects of cartelisation*

trade indifference curves. Trade indifference curves are analogous to the concept of indifference curves familiar to economists. The cartel member prefers IC_{c2} to IC_{c1} because, as the former lies above the latter, more all other goods imports are obtained in exchange for the same quantity of petroleum exports. Similarly, the petroleum importer prefers IC_{i2} to IC_{i1}.

Under competitive conditions trade initially takes place on the inelastic part of the petroleum importer's offer curve at the point T. The terms of trade between petroleum and all other goods is OT; 'On' petroleum is exported in exchange for Tn all other goods: and the cartel member is on IC_{c1} while the petroleum importer is on IC_{i2}.

However, through colluding to fix export prices with other petroleum exporters, the cartel member can raise the price of petroleum to OT_1. The cartel member's offer curve is also seen to swing anti-clockwise from OC to OC_1 Petroleum exports fall from On to On_1 and the cartel member's imports of all other goods rise to $T_1 n_1$ from Tn. The welfare effects of cartelisation are also clear, the cartel member moves to a higher trade indifference curve IC_{c2} – representing a higher welfare level – while the petroleum importer moves to a lower welfare level compared to the pre-cartel situation.

OT_1 is the best terms of trade from the cartel member's point of view. It cannot reach a higher trade indifference curve as IC_{c2} is tangential to OI. It is doubtful, of course, that OPEC members have actually tried to optimise the relative price of petroleum in this manner, but the impact of OPEC on the level of the members' petroleum exports and imports of all other goods accords quite well with this simple model.

The non-oil exporting less developed countries. All of this analysis has been conducted under very special assumptions, but it has shown either the *damaging* or *corrective* effects of a petroleum cartel on the traders' welfare levels as well as the level of trade. 'Damaging' or 'corrective' of course can be defined either in objective terms — relative to the starting-point — or in ideological terms. For example, those people who see OPEC against a background of imperialist or neo-imperialist exploitation will view it as a necessary corrective device. The oil exporters are able to protect themselves against exploitation only by combining together.

It is of course possible that the NOPECs obtained their oil imports at too low a price prior to 1973, when OPEC raised the price of oil so dramatically. However, it would be quite untrue to argue that the NOPECs have recently exploited the OPEC members either through monopolistically priced commodity exports to OPEC members or through their ownership of multinational oil companies. Nor have the NOPECs had an exploitative imperial relationship with the OPEC members (unless certain Arab countries are motivated by the memory of the Ottoman Empire).

It would seem, therefore, that the NOPECs are innocent bystanders in the conflict between the industrial countries and the OPEC members over the appropriate price of oil. However, the NOPECS have had to bear a severe deterioration in the price of their exports *vis-à-vis* petroleum imports as well as an associated dramatic worsening of their trade accounts with the OPEC members. While the theoretical analysis laid out above is simple it can hardly be disputed that the NOPECs' welfare was reduced by the steep increases in the price of oil in 1973 and again in 1979.

In the next chapter the extent of the adverse terms of trade and balance of trade effects on the NOPECs caused by the rise in oil prices will be discussed. And Chapter 5 will discuss the worsening debt position faced by these countries.

However, the OPEC members are not insensitive to the way higher oil prices have been received by the NOPECs. They can point to the moral and diplomatic support given to NOPECs in the Paris Conference of 1975, in UNCTAD and in other fora (see Chapter 10). The OPEC members can also point to their enlarged expenditures on imports from the NOPEC area (see Chapter 7); to large remittances of wages to NOPECs from the OPEC area (Chapter 8); and to much enlarged flows of OPEC aid (Chapter 6). Some oil exporting countries have also tried to win the support of the NOPECs by identifying themselves only as the economic leaders of the Third World in the post-colonial era — OPEC was to be only the first of many commodity cartels.

Notes

1 Gabon is an associate member.
2 Italics added.
3 The relationship between these three variables has been precisely defined (Takeuchi):

$$Dec = \frac{1}{m} \cdot Dew - \frac{1}{m}(1 - m)\,Ser$$

where *Dec* is the price elasticity of demand for the cartel's product; *Dew* is the price elasticity of demand for the production in final consumption; *Ser* the price elasticity of supply from non-cartel members; and *m* is the share of the cartel in world trade. If the demand for the cartel's product is price inelastic, a cut in total sales by the cartel membership will lead to both an increase in market price and total receipts received by the cartel membership. It is elementary that the more inelastic is the demand curve facing the cartel, the greater will be the rise in total revenue caused by a given cut in sales by the cartel. Moreover, if it can be presumed that the cut in production also leads to a reduction in production costs, total profits must necessarily increase and they are likely to increase so long as the marginal cost curve is not too steeply rising (for *lower* output).

4 Statistics from *International Petroleum Annual*, 1975 and 1976. It would be incorrect to simply conclude on the basis of these figures that the price elasticity of demand for oil in 1974 was -0.014. It is, of course, necessary to take into account income changes which will have also influenced the demand for oil. However, that the short-run price elasticity of demand for oil is very low is not in dispute.

5 Saudi Arabia is thought to have imposed a production ceiling of 8.5 million barrels per day since 1974; Kuwait a ceiling of 2 million barrels per day; UAE a ceiling of 80% of capacity; Iraq 2.4 million barrels per day; and Iran 3.5–4.0 million barrels per day (CIA, 1979).

6 The US Federal Energy Authority source quoted by Fisher, Gately and Kyle (1975) estimated that by 1985 excess oil production capacity in the OPEC area would be 7% if the price of oil was $6 per barrel (1974 prices) and 46% if $9 per barrel. For a sub-cartel of Saudi Arabia, the Gulf states and Libya, 12% and 51% production cutbacks (in these countries only) at these prices respectively would be required.

7 J. S. Mill explained the concavity of the traders' offer curves in terms of the diminishing marginal utility of imports relative to the increasing marginal utility of exportables as the former become more abundant at home and the latter less abundant.

8 Since fewer all other goods are offered for export to the right of X in Figure 3.1, domestic expenditure on them in the non-cartel member must have increased as the price of petroleum declined. This country's expenditure on imported petroleum must, therefore, have declined. Thus, *lower* expenditure on petroleum imports will have occurred as petroleum prices fell, and this condition is consistent with inelastic demand for petroleum imports.

4

Energy and the NOPECs' Terms of Trade

Between 1970 and 1979 the prices received by the non-oil exporting ldcs (or NOPECs) for their commodity exports increased by 383%.[1] The price that they paid for oil over the same nine years (to July) increased from $1.80 per barrel to $18 per barrel — an increase of exactly 1,000%.[2] The industrial countries' export price index[3] increased by 260% and consumer prices in the industrial countries increased by 195%.[4] Price movements of these magnitudes have naturally had a pervasive effect on world economic performance as was pointed out in Chapter 2. International economic relationships between the NOPEC and OPEC groups, as measured by the behaviour of the terms of trade between primary commodities and oil and the trade balances between the two groups, have also undergone a marked change since 1973.

This chapter opens by pointing out the large and relatively inflexible extent of the NOPECs' dependence upon oil imported from OPEC. A consequence of the rise of oil prices is that NOPECs now run much larger trade deficits with the OPEC members than was the case prior to the oil price rise. All the NOPECs have suffered in this respect; conversely with the OPEC members. Indeed, such is the force of the impact of higher oil prices and the OPEC members' continuing ability to control oil prices that it is argued later in this chapter that there has now been added to the old dependency relationship that many of the NOPECs have had with the industrial countries, a new dependency relationship with the oil exporting countries that has almost inadvertently been created by the fact that the oil exporting countries have been able to create a hugely successful cartel and the NOPECs have not.

Energy import dependence

As Table 4.1 shows, there are substantial differences in the degree of energy import dependence between ldcs. The table is arranged to show up, first, those ldcs which import less than 25%, 25–75%, and over 75% of

Table 4.1 *NOPECs' energy import dependence and per capita energy consumption, 1975 (number of countries)*

| | | Per capita commercial energy consumption, kilos of coal equivalent | | |
		Less than 200	200–1,000	More than 1,000	Total
Net imports of energy as % of commercial energy consumption	Less than 25	1	2	3	6
	25–75	4	4	2	10
	More than 75	32	21	8	61
Total		37	27	13	

Source: Abstracted from UNCTAD (1978b), p. 18.

their net commercial energy consumption; and second, how much commercial energy is consumed per capita in each of those countries. Note that this table presents energy data from only one year, 1975, and refers exclusively to commercial energy. Since commercially sold energy will play a diminishing part in total energy use the poorer a country, this tends to overstate the degree of the poorer ldcs' import dependence. The poorer countries are aligned in the left-hand boxes of Table 4.1, low per capita energy consumption being associated with low per capita income. It should be noted also that energy imports refer almost exclusively to oil imports: ldcs are 97% self sufficient in coal and other conventional fuels (Lambertini, 1976, p. 10). Examination of Table 4.1 indicates that those non-oil exporting ldcs with less than 25% energy trade dependence number only six, but as India is included in this category, 709 million people (in 1978) live in these countries. A further ten ldcs, with 313 million inhabitants, are import dependent to between 25% and 75% of consumption, while the most dependent countries number sixty-one and contain 485 million people. The most countries (thirty-two) appear in the lower left-hand box, which accounts for 318 million people.

The NOPECs' dependence upon imported energy, even several years after the oil price increases of the early 1970s, stems from several factors. The barriers to initiating and efficiently carrying out a series of policy initiatives to diminish reliance upon imported energy can be divided into physical, financial and administrative and they are reviewed briefly here. Regarding the physical constraints, the choice of energy sources other than oil is restricted in many ldcs. Ldcs' coal reserves, for instance, are chiefly located in one country, India, leaving others almost devoid of coal resources at economic prices. Other ldcs have relatively little access to hydroelectric power. Nor have commercially competitive alternatives to the 'traditional' energy forms yet been developed in the NOPECs.

Financial factors clearly prevent ldc governments from carrying out all the energy-saving and/or energy-source diversification plans they would like. Friedman has gone so far as to suggest that 'in the short and medium-term, the so-called "energy crisis" is not one of resources or technology but mainly a financial crisis' (1976, p. 38). The latest IBRD projections show that the NOPECs will have to invest annually an enormous \$5,625 million and \$1,225 million in oil and gas projects respectively over the years 1976—85 inclusive.

Moreover, crude oil production costs are predicted to rise particularly quickly. In 1979 an average 'low cost' well cost \$2,000 per barrel per day of output to explore and set up. For 'medium cost' wells such as those in the North Sea the cost was nearer \$8,000/b/d. But by the end of the century it has been predicted that at current prices the cost will have risen to \$33,000/b/d. This will push up the total capital needed by the industry for reinvestment from \$20 billion in 1970 to \$70 billion by 2000 (*Oil and Gas Journal*, 17 September 1979, p. 55).

In ldcs the cost of drilling normally exceeds typical US levels, due to poorer infrastructure and normally harder terrain, by a factor of 3 or more. Offshore exploration is particularly costly, entailing outlays of \$20—50 million for a three to ten year effort. Rig prices have risen quickly in the 1970s, and by mid 1979 drilling to a depth of 10,000 feet in the US cost approximately \$3.4 million in rig equipment. Drilling to 25,000 feet cost \$5.2 million (*Oil and Gas Journal*, 24 September 1979, p. 99). Spot rig rates vary widely by season and location, but in the southern USA a 10,000 feet drilling rig would cost \$5,500 per day. An anchored drill ship in the Gulf of Mexico would, by contrast, cost \$16—19,000 per day.

Administrative problems also beset ldc policy initiatives, although probably no more so in energy than in any other area. Particular difficulties in this regard may arise because of reluctance to use prices fully to reflect real scarcities; political commitment to projects which will be continued or initiated irrespective of the energy inputs needed and the consequent cost inefficiency; and a tendency for the planning outlook to be affected by 'urban bias' and view energy needs and means in an urban rather than rural, non-commercial perspective (Lipton, 1977). However, energy conservation efforts have been quickly started in some ldcs.

Table 4.2 *Non-oil exporting developing countries' trade balances, 1971–7 ($ billion f.o.b.)*

	1971	1972	1973	1974	1975	1976	1977	1978	1979
NOPECs' exports to the world, fob	37.8	45.5	66.5	96.5	93.7	114.2	136.0	156.1	n.a.
NOPECs' imports from the world, fob	51.0	57.3	80.6	128.9	133.5	144.5	165.7	197.6	n.a.
NOPECs' trade balance with the world	− 13.2	− 11.8	− 14.2	− 32.4	− 39.8	− 30.3	− 29.7	− 41.6	− 47.0[a]
NOPECs' trade balance with OPEC	− 2.5	− 2.6	− 4.5	− 16.9	− 15.3	− 20.7	− 20.4	− 19.0	− 34.2[a]
NOPECs' trade balance with OPEC as % of their total deficit	18.9	22.0	31.7	52.2	38.4	68.3	68.7	45.7	72.8

[a]Estimated.
Source: IMF, *Direction of Trade*, various issues.

Premier Michael Manley of Jamaica, for example, initiated a National Energy Plan for the 1978–82 period, which includes the conventional higher tax on petrol, more hydroelectric investment by the government, faster removal of peat from deposits and enhanced use of sugar for bagasse fuel. Brazil and some other ldcs have followed a similar course of action (*Petroleum Review*, April 1979, p. 23).

The NOPECs' trade accounts

The enormous rise in the price of oil, together with the NOPECs' inability to reduce their dependence upon it, led to a worsening of their trade accounts, as shown in Table 4.2. The NOPECs' trade deficit was only $14 billion in 1973, the year of the oil price shock (which was delivered late in the year), before jumping upwards in 1974 to $32 billion. High oil prices were the main reason for these larger trade deficits: as a proportion of their worldwide trade deficit that with the OPEC members increased from about one-fifth prior to 1973 to over one-half after that year. The year 1975 is seen to be rather anomalous in that OPEC's 'share' of the NOPECs' trade deficit fell quite substantially. This was due to the collapse of the NOPECs' export markets in the industrial countries. In fact, while the value of the NOPECs' export earnings in 1974 was a record $20 billion above the 1967–78 growth trend, earnings collapsed to the trend level in 1975. In real terms (measured against the industrial countries' export price index) the collapse was even more dramatic. For real export earnings fell from a record above-trend to a record below-trend deviation to the extent of $23 billion (at 1975 values). Clearly, the NOPECs' foreign trade experience cannot be understood only in terms of the price of oil. But higher oil prices are an important component, as is indicated by the much larger NOPEC trade deficits with OPEC and the larger share of these deficits in the NOPECs' worldwide trade deficit (see Table 4.2).

The data in Table 4.2 are drawn from one source only, the IMF's *Direction of Trade*. However, due to data collection problems the detailed measurements of trade flows tend to vary somewhat according to the source used. In an attempt to deal with this problem similar calculations to those shown in Table 4.2 have been performed with data from the IMF's *International Financial Statistics* and the United Nations *Yearbook of International Trade Statistics*. When the NOPECs' trade balance with OPEC measured as a percentage of the former's total trade deficit is averaged for these three sources together the result is to raise somewhat the estimated share of the payments deficit with OPEC. The averaged data is as follows: 1972, 25%; 1973, 42%; 1974, 59%; 1975, 40%; 1976, 74%; 1977, 76%; 1978, 45%; and 1979, 73%. These results confirm the finding that the share of the NOPECs' foreign payments deficit with OPEC members has increased very markedly since 1973.

Table 4.3 NOPECs' trade balances with OPEC members, 1971–7 ($ million fob)

	1971	1972	1973	1974	1975	1976	1977
Algeria	− 12	− 21	+ 101	+ 136	+ 99	+ 176	+ 249
Indonesia	− 96	− 14	− 70	− 659	− 972	− 879	− 1,264
Iran	− 437	− 435	− 540	− 2,210	− 1,640	− 2,640	− 2,793
Iraq	− 86	− 44	− 260	− 910	− 1,307	− 1,774	− 1,988
Kuwait	− 311	− 384	− 660	− 2,399	− 2,297	− 2,504	− 1,530
Libya	− 135	− 109	− 117	− 553	− 307	− 418	− 828
Nigeria	− 21	− 45	− 325	− 1,073	− 848	− 2,133	− 2,897
Qatar	+ 2	− 49	− 147	− 318	− 381	− 440	− 329
Saudi Arabia	− 499	− 647	− 1,381	− 6,183	− 5,389	− 7,444	− 5,469
UAE	+ 23	+ 43	+ 61	+ 158	+ 33	− 256	− 637
Venezuela	− 878	− 811	− 1,196	− 2,845	− 2,191	− 2,291	− 2,827
Ecuador	+ 15	− 27	− 165	− 301	− 153	− 235	− 172
Gabon	− 39	− 10	− 21	− 112	− 31	− 119	− 414
Total	− 2,474	− 2,553	− 4,720	− 17,269	− 15,384	− 20,957	− 20,899

Source: IMF, Direction of Trade, various issues.

Table 4.4 *Selected ldcs' Petroleum Imports ($ million current, and as shares of each country's total imports)*

	1972	1973	1974	1975	1976	1977	1978
Latin America							
Argentina[a]	32	83	328	223	289	337	
% of imports[b]	2	4	9	6	10	8	
Brazil[c]	537	986	3,233	3,300	4,083	4,201	4,600
%	12	14	23	24	29	31	30
Paraguay[a]	5	6	35	25	29	28	
%	6	5	18	12	13	9	
Uruguay[a]	31	45	141	164	160	186	
%	15	16	29	30	27	26	
Central America and Caribbean							
Bahamas[a]	231	442	1,662	2,110	2,429	2,452	
%	45	58	79	85	84	86	
Costa Rica[c]	11	17	36	24	24	31	40
%	3	4	5	4	3	3	5
El Salvador[a]	10	19	48	46	48	85	
%	4	5	9	8	7	9	
Guatamala[a]	21	27	80	70			
%	6	6	11	10			
Honduras[a]	15	21	55	61	50	45	
%	8	8	14	15	10	8	
Jamaica[c]	48	70	192	184	200	241	
%	8	11	21	16	22	28	
Nicaragua[a]	12	17	51	63	57	78	
%	6	5	9	12	11	11	
Africa							
Burundi[c]	2	2	3	3	4	6	6
%	5	5	6	5	7	8	6
Ethiopia[c]	16	20	49	68	54	65	
%	8	9	17	22	15	19	
Gambia	4	5	9	13	22	32	45
%	4	5	7	7	6	8	11
Ivory Coast[a]	25	26	129	146	149	170	
%	6	4	13	13	12	10	
Kenya[a]	41	47	191	259	249	286	
%	8	8	19	28	26	22	
Madagascar[a]	12	15	45	68	89		
%	6	8	16	19	18		
Malawi[c]	9	9	15	18	22	24	27
%	7	6	8	7	11	10	

Table 4.4 Cont.

	1972	1973	1974	1975	1976	1977	1978
Africa Cont.							
Mauritius[c]	9	12	28	32	31	41	
%	8	7	11	10	9	9	
Morocco[a]	37	55	227	221	238	276	239
%	5	5	12	9	9	9	9
Niger[c]	6	7	13	13	15		
%	9	8	14	13	12		
Senegal[a]	15	21	58	60	71		
%	5	6	12	10	11		
Sudan[c]	25	86	96	89			
%	6	13	10	9			
Tanzania[c]	34	48	141	80	94	102	
%	9	10	18	10	15	14	
Togo[c]	4	5	11	13	12	20	
%	5	5	9	8	7	7	
Upper Volta[c]	5	n.a.	9	13	11	18	
%	9		7	9	8	9	
Zambia[a]	10	13	37	39	61	62	
%	3	5	9	8	14	13	
Asia							
Bangladesh[c]	n.a.	n.a.	92	97	122	172	156
%		8	7	13	14	13	
Cyprus[c]	21	24	50	46	62	83	78
%	7	5	12	15	14	13	11
India[a]	189	308	1,165	1,152	1,060		
%	9	10	23	18	19		
South Korea[a]	206	277	966	1,271	1,611	1,926	2,152
%	8	7	14	18	18	18	16
Malaysia[a]	63	72	204	232	283	354	393
%	4	3	5	7	7	8	3
Pakistan[a]	33	55	137	254	255	251	253
%	5	6	8	12	12	10	15
Philippines[a]	140	166	570	710	801	859	880
%	98	9	16	19	20	20	17
Singapore[c]	477	661	2,007	1,995	2,484	2,673	2,290
%	14	13	24	25	27	26	24
Thailand[a]	116	173	507	592	679	806	836
%	8	9	16	18	19	18	16
Turkey[c]	155	207	763	812	1,125	1,470	1,281
%	10	11	20	17	22	25	32

Table 4.4 Cont.

	1972	1973	1974	1975	1976	1977	1978
Oceana							
Fiji^c	16	20	43	47			
%	10	9	16	17			

Notes
^{a} crude petroleum
^{b} oil imports as percentage of cif imports
^{c} petroleum products
In certain cases refined oil imports are also quite large and would increase the figures shown here. In the cases of Argentina, Paraguay, Guatamala, Honduras, Malaysia, and Pakistan refined products imports were, by volume, about one-third those of crude oil in 1975. In Thailand the share was 25% and in India 20%.

Source: IMF, *International Financial Statistics*. Note: import values and percentages have been rounded to leave no decimal places.

The oil accounts

This deterioration in the NOPECs' trade deficit with OPEC is reflected both in the size of the individual OPEC members' payments surpluses with the NOPECs and in the individual NOPECs' expenditures on imported oil. (Chapter 7 discusses the converse, the NOPECs' exports to OPEC members.)

In 1972 the NOPECs taken as a group had a trade deficit of over $0.5 billion with only two OPEC members – Venezuela ($0.8 billion) and Saudi Arabia ($0.6 billion) (see Table 4.3). However, by 1974 the NOPECs had deficits of over $0.5 billion with eight of the thirteen OPEC members – Indonesia, Iran, Iraq, Kuwait, Libya, Nigeria, Saudi Arabia and Venezuala. In 1977 the UAE was added to this list. Only with Algeria did the NOPECs retain a trade surplus and even this was small – smaller, in fact, than their deficit with the tiny OPEC member Ecuador.

Over the four year period 1974–7 the NOPECs ran large trade deficits both with OPEC members ($75.5 billion in all) and with the industrial countries as a group ($63.5 billion in all). While two of the three largest NOPEC trade deficits in this period were with developed countries – Japan ($30 billion) and France ($14 billion) – six of their largest collective deficits were with OPEC countries. The ten in order of size were: Japan, Saudi Arabia, France, Venezuela, Iran, Kuwait, West Germany, Nigeria, the USA and Iraq.

Table 4.5   *Oil imports: changes in value and volume, 1972–4*

	Value %	Volume %
Argentina	936	98
Brazil	502	41
India	516	14
Ivory Coast	412	n.a
Jamaica	419	23
Kenya	367	13
South Korea	368	13
Pakistan	320	−11
Singapore	320	17
Thailand	339	13
Turkey	391	33
Uruguay	350	13

Sources: Value figures taken from IMF, *International Financial Statistics* and volume figures from *International Petroleum Annual*.

Considering the obverse of these relationships, immediately after the 1973 price rise, in 1974, twenty-one NOPECs allocated more than 10% of their total merchandise import expenditures to oil[5] (see Table 4.4). The largest ten according to the share of oil in imports were: Brazil, (23%), India (23%), Jamaica (21%), Turkey (20%), Kenya (19%), Philippines (16%), Thailand (16%), South Korea (14%), Honduras (14%) and Ivory Coast (13%).[6] By comparison, in 1972 only one of the countries included in Table 4.4 showed its share of oil in total import value exceeding 10%, and that was Brazil.[7] Even by 1977, when there had been time to adjust expenditure on oil imports, there had been no withdrawals from the group allocating over 10% of its imports to oil imports. Of all the NOPECs, Brazil spent the most on oil imports in 1978, $4.6 billion. The next five biggest spenders on oil imports were South Korea ($2.2 billion), Turkey ($1.3 billion), India ($1.1 billion in 1976), Philippines ($0.9 billion) and Thailand ($0.8 billion).

The fact that it was the oil price rises rather than import volume increases that largely accounted for the deterioration in the major NOPEC trade balances with OPEC is shown in Table 4.5. This shows that the percentage increases in expenditure on oil between 1972 and 1974 were in all the cases listed more than 320% while import volumes increased by less than 25% except in the three cases of Argentina, Brazil and Turkey.

Fluctuations in the terms of trade

It follows from the foregoing that an important aspect of the NOPECs'

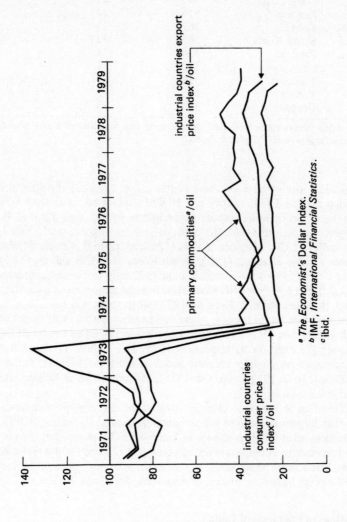

Figure 4.1 Terms of trade indices with oil (Arabian 34°) 1970 = 100

^a The Economist's Dollar Index.
^b IMF, International Financial Statistics.
^c ibid.

Table 4.6   *Terms of trade: Selected developing country groups* vis-à-vis *petroleum exporters (1970 = 100)*

	1971	1972	1973	1974	1975	1976
Non-oil developing countries	85	86	83	36	33	32
of which:						
(a) Fast-growing manf. expts.	105	89	80	30	30	30
(b) All other ldcs	86	89	86	36	35	35
of which:						
GNP over $800	89	95	89	40	36	36
$300 – $800	84	84	85	36	36	36
under $300	87	90	80	32	30	31
of which:						
(i) 29 lldcs	89	93	83	33	31	34
(ii) other Africa	78	74	77	32	25	28
(iii) other Asia	91	96	82	32	32	31

Source: UNCTAD, Handbook of International Trade and Development Statistics, Supplement 1977, Table 2.3. Based on unit value indices of exports.

balance of payments experience in the 1970s is the behaviour of the prices of the commodities that they exported relative to the prices of the goods they imported — especially oil and industrial country exports. It is to this issue that attention is now turned.

Figures 4.1 and 4.2 show terms of trade indices between primary commodities, oil, industrial countries' export prices and consumer prices. As these indices are crucial to the analysis that follows a technical comment on them is in order. Since oil dominates the oil exporting countries' export patterns and primary commodities other than oil the NOPECs' exports, price indices for oil and non-oil primary commodities have been taken to represent the export price indices for the oil exporters and the NOPECs respectively. Saudi Arabian light 34° marker crude has been used to represent 'the' price of oil because this is the price most usually referred to by the oil industry. However, the correspondence between primary commodity prices and the prices received by developing countries is less exact than that between oil prices and revenues received by the oil exporting countries. This difference arises because about 40% of the NOPECs' non-oil merchandise exports are of manufactured goods (1977 figure). However, comparing the terms of trade between primary commodities and oil (as shown in Figure 4.1) with the terms of trade between certain groups of NOPECs and the oil exporting countries (as shown in Table 4.6) shows that no violence is done to the economic facts. Table 4.6 shows that the terms of trade of the NOPECs against oil measured by either method showed the same degree of deterioration between 1970 and 1976. The primary producers' terms of trade as measured by *The Economist*'s dollar index of primary commodity prices and oil prices fell to 35.9 in 1976 (see Figure 4.1), while the NOPECs' terms of trade calculated by the other method fell to 32 for the group as a whole and to 35 if the fast growing manufactures exporters are excluded from the NOPEC group (see Table 4.6).

Between 1971 and 1973, before the increases in oil prices, the price of primary commodities against oil actually increased, as Figure 4.1 shows. In 1971 the terms of trade of primary commodities *vis-à-vis* oil stood at only 79.7 (1970 = 100) but in 1972 it had improved to 88.4 and actually reached the decade's annual average peak in 1973 at 114.9. However, this improvement was quickly wiped out. The October 1973 oil price rise to $5.12 per barrel reduced the relative price of primary commodities from 135.6 in the third quarter of 1973 (1973III) to 82.7 in 1973IV – an 'overnight' fall of 39%. Looked at another way, the same volume of primary commodity exports could purchase 39% less petroleum.

The oil price rise announced for the end of 1973 had an even more dramatic effect upon the primary producers' terms of trade against oil. In 1974I the index tumbled to 37.1 – a sudden 55% fall, and down 73% in just three months. It should be noted that this deterioration was wholly due to the higher oil prices since *The Economist*'s non-oil primary commodities dollar price index was actually higher in 1974I than in the second half of 1973. That is to say, primary commodity prices increased as did oil prices, but by much less.

Commodity cartels

As far as the NOPECs are concerned they have less control over their export prices, much less their terms of trade, than do the members of OPEC or developed country exporters. The oil exporters took over control of oil export prices by colluding to some extent within OPEC itself, but developing country based cartels exist in no other commodity markets. Many primary commodities are priced on free international markets which are from time to time subjected to fluctuations in demand from both speculative and final user sources. Moreover, since it is difficult to alter the supply of most primary commodities very quickly, fluctuations in demand rather than supply are more frequently the cause of price changes (Brook and Grilli, 1977). Sometimes primary commodity export prices are agreed on long-term contracts with multinational corporations and the basis of bargaining power between the two sides therein can shift about. For example, in 1979 the Jamaican government had to renegotiate the 7½% export tax levied on the five American companies that run the Jamaican bauxite industry. The tax was first levied in 1975 when the government was in a strong position, but the companies complained from the beginning that the tax was too high and responded by cutting back on investment and even closed one plant. This, together with the collapse of a proposed arrangement with the Mexican government, brought the Jamaican government back to the negotiating table, only to accept less favourable terms (*FT*, 25 July 1979).

As was pointed out in Chapter 3, the success of OPEC stems from a number of factors: first, there are the purely technical factors such as the fact that the demand for oil in the importing countries is unresponsive in the short term even to very large price increases; there is also the lack of significantly large and quickly recoverable new oil supplies from non-OPEC sources and there is the inability of the oil importing countries quickly to substitute other types of energy for oil. Few, if any, of these economic and political factors are present in other commodity markets however. A study of fourteen non-renewable mineral markets by Hallwood (1979) showed that in only three cases are the NOPECs able to exert even a small degree of market power. The International Bauxite Association (IBA), established in 1974 by ten bauxite exporting countries (including Australia), has had some influence on bauxite export prices and taxes levied upon the multinational corporations operating the mining concerns. If the IBA members had been able to agree on a cartel pricing formula they could have raised their income by about $2 billion in present value terms over the 1974–85 period (Charles River Associates, 1976). Morocco has also had some limited success in raising phosphate rock export prices and Zaire may even have been pricing cobalt near its monopoly price level.

However, in another five cases (zinc, uranium, palladium, platinum and diamonds) developed country interest groups have manipulated prices. And in five more cases prices are either influenced by an international commodity agreement (tin) or NOPECs are not dominant suppliers (iron ore, chromite, nickel and manganese). The remaining case, copper, has often been quoted as a possible NOPEC cartel but nothing has materialised so far. An international commodity agreement with suppliers is the more likely outcome.

Prospects for NOPEC cartels in reproducible raw materials are also limited. Most tropical products have temperate area substitutes and, in the important cereals category, the NOPECs are importers, with the USA, Canada, Australia, the EEC and Argentina being the dominant suppliers. Rubber has come into an international commodity agreement with consumers rather than being cartelised by the major south-east Asian producers. As a final example, in coffee, Brazil's aggressive export tax measures of the mid 1970s had to be largely withdrawn in 1978 and 1979 as coffee prices tumbled. Moreover, the Bogota Fund, set up by Latin American coffee producers in 1978 to intervene on the international coffee market, has been used only to cushion falling prices.

Centre-periphery relationships

Notwithstanding the persistent claims by OPEC spokesmen that their countries are 'full members of the "Group of 77"', it would be an error to

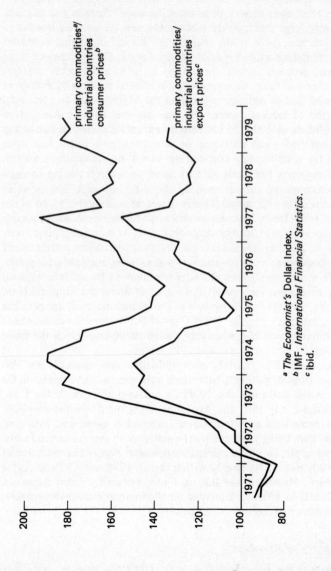

Figure 4.2 Terms of trade indices with industrial countries' prices 1970 = 100

a The Economist's Dollar Index.
b IMF, International Financial Statistics.
c ibid.

view the NOPECs and the oil exporting countries as part of a homogenous bloc. For the success of OPEC in controlling oil production and prices has not only been a shock for the industrial countries; it has also created new relationships with the developing world. To use the terminology of Raul Prebisch, this could loosely be called a centre–periphery relationship. The OPEC members control the prices of their oil exports and have stead-fastly refused to give NOPECs price discounts;[8] they also draw in labour and commodity imports from these countries. Moreover, as Chapter 8 shows, over a million NOPEC citizens now work in OPEC countries, and the oil exporting countries have become some of the NOPECs' fastest growing export markets – as Chapter 7 demonstrates.

If the events of 1973 and 1974 showed that OPEC members had increased their economic power *vis-à-vis* the industrial countries the events of 1975 showed that the NOPECs were still experiencing periphery relationships with the industrial centre. The industrial countries' response to the oil price shock was severely to deflate their economies, as Chapter 2 showed. They would probably have deflated anyway because inflation was already out of control in several countries even before OPEC delivered its blow, but the deflation would in all probability have been less severe. In any event, in 1975 the industrial countries' GNP actually fell after decades of growth. Allied to this was the rising prices of consumer goods and goods exported by industrial countries. In the year up to 1975IV consumer goods prices in the latter group of countries increased by 9%. The two factors combined caused the terms of trade between primary commodity prices and industrial countries consumer good prices to fall by 22% in the year up to 1975IV and by 30% in the eighteen months up to that date (see Figure 4.2).

The NOPECs' terms of trade deterioration measured against industrial countries' export prices was marginally less severe – declining by 15% in the year up to 1975IV, and by 30% in the twenty-one months up to that date. These differences between the two indices arose because, first, the rise of the dollar in 1975 tended to lower export prices from countries other than America (the IMF's export price index is calculated in dollars); and secondly, because declining export markets probably led to greater price competition between exporters.

The year 1975 is only one example showing the dependence of the NOPECs' terms of trade on economic events in the industrial countries. Hallwood (1979) has pointed to the cyclical behaviour of the ldcs' terms of trade – a cycle that is predominantly generated by changes in economic activity in the industrial countries. In the interwar period the relationship between the cycle of industrial production and the primary producers' terms of trade *vis-à-vis* industrial goods prices is highly correlated. More-over, no trend is discernible. While the deteriorating terms of trade argu-ment has been important in political circles, for instance it has been used by the UNCTAD as a justification for more official development assistance, and was given economic content by Prebisch (1967), it has not been evident as a sustained long-run phenomenon.

However, this does not mean that the dependence of developing countries upon the industrial centre is any weaker. Because of the typically long supply-response lags for many primary commodities — several years in the case of copper and many other minerals, coffee, cocoa and rubber — primary product prices tend to rise sharply in industrial booms. However, when a trade cycle eventually turns downwards, primary product suppliers find it difficult to reduce planned output quickly — partly because of financial considerations and partly because the investments in new capacity made during the boom years will be in the process of being added to productive capacity. The resultant glut then leads on to falling commodity prices. By contrast, industrial goods' prices are more stable over the trade cycle. This is partly because of the oligopolistic structure of many markets, enabling manufacturers to control prices, and partly because in manufacturing industry output is more responsive to changes in demand. The resulting greater instability (on average) of primary commodity prices relative to manufacturers leads to improved terms of trade for the primary producer during industrial booms and to worsening terms of trade during the slump phase.

For various reasons, some of which are still not entirely clear, this cyclical behaviour was absent during the 1950s and 1960s. Probably the fact that growth in industrial countries' GDP in this period was more stable than at any other time was a central factor.

However, the cyclical terms of trade pattern reasserted itself in the 1970s, as is shown by Figures 4.1 and 4.2. Against industrial countries' exports, the primary producers' terms of trade peaked in 1974I, 1977II and 1979II which were also peaks in growth of industrial activity. Conversely, troughs in the terms of trade in 1975 and 1978I correspond with troughs of industrial activity.

Conclusions

Looked at through the prism of prices received in foreign trade and the degree of independent control over these prices, it seems that the economic relationships between the NOPECs and the oil exporting countries as a bloc changed fundamentally in 1973. It is indeed true that all the terms of trade indices shown in Figures 4.1 and 4.2 had, as a result of the June 1979 OPEC decision to raise oil prices, returned to almost precisely the same level as in January 1974, immediately after the oil price shock. Clearly, OPEC member countries share many economic characteristics with the NOPECs, especially their dependence upon Western technology, skilled labour and, in certain respects, multinational corporations. However, it can reasonably be claimed, after looking at the evidence in this chapter, that OPEC members have gained a new authority in their economic relationships with the NOPECs that did not previously exist. It is also clear that the NOPECs' old dependency with the established industrial centre continues. This chapter has however discussed only some aspects of this new authority gained by the OPEC members. Other aspects are discussed in the chapters which follow: the debt situation and OPEC aid in Chapters 5 and 6 respectively; labour flows to OPEC from NOPECs and related matters are discussed in Chapter 8; and OPEC as a market for NOPECs' products is discussed in Chapter 7.

Notes

1 *The Economist*'s commodity dollar price index. It was chosen here both because the dollar is the major international currency and because oil prices are fixed in dollars.
2 Saudi Arabian 34° marker crude – usually quoted by commentators as 'the price' of oil.
3 Export unit value index of industrial countries calculated by the IMF in *International Financial Statistics*. Taken to represent average import prices paid by NOPEC and OPEC members for imports from the industrial countries.
4 Calculated by the IMF in *International Financial Statistics*. Used here for comparisons with export unit value data.
5 In fact the number is twenty-five but Bahamas, Singapore, Tanzania and Uruguay are left out because of their substantial re-export trade in petroleum products.
6 Omitting Fiji and Madagascar as small importers and Bahamas, Singapore, Tanzania and Uruguay because of their re-export trade in petroleum products.
7 Again, not including those countries excluded by note 5.
8 There was a suggestion from one OPEC member – Venezuela – in 1975 that it would charge only $6 per barrel to certain Caribbean oil importers, but this scheme was never properly implemented. See Chapter 10.

5
OPEC and Debt in the Developing World

The fall in the NOPECs' terms of trade with the oil exporting countries and their balance of payments deficits caused by the oil price increases of 1973 were serious – an argument set out in the preceding chapter. In this chapter answers are sought to questions about the NOPECs' external debt situation. It would be difficult to deny that the NOPECs' debt problems have worsened in the 1970s compared to earlier years and institutions such as the IMF, the World Bank, the OECD and the Bank of England have expressed their concern. But by how much have the NOPECs' debts grown in the 1970s? Indeed, did the oil shock make a fundamental difference to the level or growth rate of the NOPECs' foreign debts, and are these countries now moving towards a debt crisis either as a bloc or individually?

These are the big issues, but there are several other developments in the field of the NOPECs' international debt that are also of great interest: what changes have occurred in the 1970s in the sources of foreign capital flow and what factors were responsible for these trends? Have these changes, in particular the move to a much larger share of private capital in the flow of external capital to the developing countries, any important implications for the NOPECs' debt position and their ability to service debt outstanding? What is the relationship between the Eurocurrency banking system, the NOPECs and the members of OPEC and can the system continue to recycle 'petrodollars' as it has since 1973?

The most important conclusion that is brought out in this chapter is that the NOPECs' debt positions have worsened since 1973, partly because the level of debt outstanding has increased and partly because of higher interest rates and the shortening of repayment periods. Another notable feature is that while the Eurocurrency banking system has been of great importance as a mechanism for recycling 'petrodollars' to the NOPECs, only a few countries have been really significant borrowers from this source. It is also observed here that criticism of the role of the Euro-currency banks in this recycling process has been misplaced because no other mechanism was in place to take over the task.

The rest of this chapter is organised into six sections. First, the debt position before the oil shock is discussed in order to set the background to the subsequent developments. The second section discusses the balance of payments effects of the oil price rise, viewing the developments as an aspect of the international transfer problem. The worsening debt position after 1973 is discussed next, and is followed by a discussion of the NOPECs' relationships with the Eurocurrency markets. Since OPEC has been an important source of funds for the Eurocurrency banks, the relationship between the two is briefly discussed in the penultimate section. In the final section of the chapter the nature and extent of the NOPECs' debt problems are assessed and generally pessimistic conclusions are drawn.

The debt position before 1974

In the decade before the oil price shock in 1973, the debts of the NOPECs were already increasing at an explosive rate, whether measured either in nominal or real terms. The developing countries first became significant borrowers of foreign capital in the middle of the 1950s when their external debt outstanding (total borrowing less repayments) stood at about $8 billion.[1] Debt was to increase at an accelerating rate in each of the quinquenniums beginning in 1955 and 1960 and in the six year period beginning in 1967, as Table 5.1 shows. In the first of these periods debt outstanding grew at an average annual rate of 14.8%, increasing to 16.5% in the second period and accelerating again to 16.8% in the third period. By 1967 the NOPECs' debt outstanding stood at over $31 billion and by 1972 their foreign debts were nearly to double again to over $60 billion (IBRD, *World Debt Tables*, 1975).

These high growth rates were a constant worry even before the oil shock led to another acceleration in the rate of growth of debt and several NOPECs had to renegotiate the terms and conditions of their debt service obligations with their creditors. For example, in the one-and-a-half decades

Table 5.1 *The growth of medium- and long-term debt of developing countries, 1955–76[a] (average annual percentage growth rates)*

	Current prices	Deflated by developing countries' export price index
1955–60	14.8	14.7
1960–5	16.5	16.3
1967–72	16.8	12.6
1973–6	21.0	9.1

[a] Including developing oil exporting countries

Source: Abstracted from Hughes (1977).

before 1973 Indonesia had to draw up no fewer than four rescheduling agreements; India, Ghana and Argentina three each; and another eight countries also found it necessary to enter into such arrangements on at least one occasion.

The Pearson Commission on international development pointed out the extent of the crisis for the developing countries in 1969: 'Debts already contracted by many developing countries cast a pall over the short- and long-term management of their economies' (Pearson Commission, 1969, p.74). Even if capital flows to the developing countries were to rise at 8% per annum, by 1977 debt service would absorb up to nine-tenths of new lending, the Commission pointed out. Debt relief, lower interest rates and a long-term structure of debt were recommended. However, debt relief other than in the form of postponements of repayments was delayed for nearly a decade after the Pearson Commission's report and even then only a few developing countries benefited.[2] Moreover, changes in the structure of capital flows to the developing countries in the 1970s have tended to raise interest rates on loans and to shorten term structures. Reference here of course is to the growth of borrowing on commercial terms from the Eurocurrency banks. Although borrowing from these banks really took off in 1971, discussion of the importance of this trend is postponed until the section which deals with post-1973 developments when the Euro-banking system grew to dominating importance as a financial recycling mechanism.

Measuring the debt burden

Various measures have been devised to gauge the extent of the burden of debt and debt service on the NOPECs. The World Bank uses the ratio of a country's debt service on public and publicly guaranteed debt to annual export earnings (which is referred to here as *the* debt service ratio). The total debt service ratio (inclusive of unguaranteed private debt service); the adjusted debt service ratio (which incorporates a projection of debt service payments over the next fifteen years); and the ratio of external debt outstanding to gross national product are alternative measures and several more could be listed (Sofia, 1979).

High debt service ratios may of course leave a country vulnerable to adverse changes in its foreign trade sector. A fall in export earnings or rise in expenditure on 'necessary' imports (caused by a crop failure or higher import prices, for example) may leave the country with few substitution possibilities because of the large fixed obligation to service foreign loans. Default on debt service payments may result and in turn this might preju-dice potential creditors against future loans. Moreover, the need to cut back on capital goods and intermediate product imports is likely to cause the rate of economic growth to falter.

The near doubling of debt outstanding between 1967 and 1972 was

Table 5.2 *Debt burden indicators: NOPECs, 1967–8 and 1971–2[a]*
(public and publicly guaranteed)

	Debt service as % exports	Debt service as % GNP	Debt outstanding as % GNP
Higher income countries			
1967–8	11.6	1.6	10.2
1971–2	10.0	1.5	10.8
Middle income countries			
1967–8	7.4	1.5	15.2
1971–2	10.6	2.0	16.4
Lower income countries			
1967–8	12.1	1.1	15.5
1971–2	13.6	1.1	17.3

Notes
a annual averages
Countries are classified for 1972 per capita as published in the *World Bank Atlas*, 1974, viz.:
Higher income countries, per capita income over $375
Middle income countries, per capita income $200–$375
Lower income countries, per capita income below $200.

Source: IBRD, *World Debt Tables*, 1975, p. xxvii.

accompanied by an increase in the NOPECs' debt burden as measured by these coefficients, but by a smaller proportion (see Table 5.2). This was mainly because the developing countries' economic growth and export performances were generally quite good after 1967. Even so debt outstanding as a percentage of GNP increased in all categories of the NOPEC group, higher-, middle- and lower-income. But the increase in the debt burden seems to have been relatively less for the higher income countries, for, as Table 5.2 shows, their debt service as a percentage of exports and GNP actually fell. Countries in the other categories were, on average, less fortunate however.

These relatively small increases in the simple measures of the debt burden during 1967–73 were accompanied by other favourable factors: the world economy was still buoyant, the IMF had just liberalised its compensatory finance facility (in 1966), negotiations were going on within UNCTAD that were to lead to the establishment of the Generalised System of Preferences and trade-protectionists were generally in eclipse. The Pearson Commission was right in 1969 to point to deteriorating trends in the debt position of the developing countries, but for a few more years, conditions did not deteriorate too rapidly.

The diverse experience of individual members of the NOPEC group should however be recognised. By 1973, while the NOPECs' average debt service ratio was 10.3% (lower than the average in the six previous years

Table 5.3 NOPECs' external financial deficits ($ billion)

	1972	1973	1974	1975	1976	1977	1978	1979	1980
(1) Current account deficit [a]	6.0	6.0	23.5	37.5	25.5	23.0	35.0	45.0	60.0 [b]
(2) Deficit with OPEC [c]	2.8	5.0	17.7	16.0	21.1	21.3	19.0	34.2 [d]	34.2 [d]
(3) Non-oil current account deficit (1−2)	3.2	1.0	5.8	21.5	4.4	1.7	16.0	10.8	25.8
(4) NOPECs' export price index [e]	73.5	100.0	136.0	132.1	140.3	164.3	168.9	182.4 [f]	n.a.
(5) Real non-oil current account deficit (3 ÷ 4)	4.4	1.0	4.3	16.3	3.1	1.0	9.5	5.9	n.a.

n.a. not available

a OECD, *Economic Outlook*, no.23 (July 1978) and no.25 (July 1979).
b OECD estimate made before the December 1979 oil price increases.
c IMF, *Direction of Trade*, various years.
d Estimated, 1979 and 1980 deficit increased in proportion to the increase in the price of Arabian light crude during 1979, i.e. 80%.
e IMF, *International Financial Statistics*, various years.
f Estimated on the basis of the first five months of 1979.

because of a remarkable boom in primary commodity prices and export earnings), twelve NOPECs had debt service ratios more than 1.5 times this average. In some countries (Egypt, India, Israel, Mexico, Peru, Uruguay and Zambia – a list that was to lengthen after 1973) debt service absorbed more than 20% of export earnings.

The oil shock and the transfer problem

The oil shock to the NOPECs' balance of payments was substantial: their oil import bill increased by 450% between 1972 and 1974 to reach $21.5 billion and while only in one case (Brazil's) did oil imports account for more than 10% of total expenditure on imports in 1972, the number increased to 21 in 1974. Moreover, the NOPECs' terms of trade *vis-à-vis* the oil exporting countries deteriorated sharply (see Chapter 4). The effect of these adverse developments is shown by the dramatic deterioration in the NOPECs' payments deficits – see Table 5.3. The current account deficit reached $24 billion in 1974 and $38 billion in 1975, when it had stood at only $6 billion two years earlier.

At a theoretical level, the impact of higher oil prices on the NOPECs' debt position can be analysed within the context of the so-called 'transfer problem' model. J. M. Keynes and B. Ohlin discussed the transfer problem with reference to Germany's post-1918 war reparations. They debated how a *financial* transfer of war reparations levied on Germany would result in a *real* transfer of resources to the recipient countries. For the purpose of economic analysis, the balance of payments effects of the steep rise in oil prices in 1973 can be viewed similarly. The sudden rise in oil prices acted like a tax upon the oil importing countries payable to the members of the OPEC. However, the financial transfer to OPEC would result in a real resource transfer in the same direction only if the OPEC members were to run a larger non-oil current account deficit (or a smaller surplus) and the oil importing countries a larger non-oil current account surplus (or a smaller deficit).[3] Under these circumstances a real transfer will occur because the OPEC members, when running a larger non-oil current account deficit, would be *ceteris paribus* absorbing more non-oil resources than previously.[4] Similarly, the oil importing countries, by running a larger non-oil current account surplus (or smaller deficit), would be left with fewer non-oil resources for domestic absorption. As far as the NOPECs are concerned, it seems that they did not make a real transfer of resources to the oil exporters in 1974 or 1975 but they did so in 1976 and 1977. Moreover, such was the extent of the reduction in the NOPECs' current account deficit that the real transfer was made as early as 1977 or even 1976. The argument unfolds as follows.

Immediately after the oil price rise in 1973, the NOPECs' non-oil current account deficit (as opposed to their aggregate deficit) increased to $6 billion in 1974 and to over $20 billion in 1975 – see Table 5.3, line 3.

Table 5.4   *OPEC current account surpluses, 1973–9 ($ billion)*

1973	1974	1975	1976	1977	1978	1979[a]
6	68	35	40	32	6	63

a IMF staff projections

Source: IMF, *Annual Report*, 1979.

In terms of the model set out above, while the oil shock led to a financial transfer from the NOPEC to OPEC members, a real transfer did not occur at this time. Rather, OPEC as an entity chose to accumulate financial claims, allowing their current account surpluses to increase sharply, as shown in Table 5.4. Through various channels and by different means, the NOPECs as a group were able to finance their payments deficits by borrowing international capital in 1974 and 1975. In other words, the concomitant of OPEC's large current account surplus was a large current account deficit for the rest of the world, with the NOPECs taking their share. But in avoiding an immediate real transfer of resources to OPEC to pay for the higher priced oil, the NOPECs accumulated foreign debts in 1974 and 1975 even more quickly than in earlier years.

However, there was to be a sharp reduction in the NOPECs' payments deficits in 1976 and 1977, especially when measured in real terms. Indeed, in 1977 the real non-oil deficit was the same as in 1973 and much lower than in 1972, the last full year before the oil shock (see Table 5.3, line 5). This reduction in the non-oil current account deficit itself shows that the NOPECs, by increasing export earnings faster than expenditure on non-oil imports, were beginning to make a real transfer to finance higher priced oil imports. Since OPEC's current account surplus was also falling, they were receiving at least a part of this real transfer.

These developments helped to alleviate somewhat the NOPECs' growing debt problem that so many observers were warning of. Simply, the NOPECs were *earning* foreign exchange rather than needing to *borrow* it in 1976 and 1977. Moreover, it was the really big debtors — Brazil and Mexico — that did most to reduce their current account deficits. These two countries did not stop borrowing however. Rather, they used borrowed funds to increase their foreign exchange reserves which in turn encouraged the Eurocurrency banks to make further loans to them and generally to improve the stability of that recycling mechanism.

However, the rise in the NOPECs' current account and real non-oil current account deficits in 1979 and 1980 is a warning that the higher oil prices set during the course of 1979 would again cause the NOPECs to increase their foreign net indebtedness. Whether they will be able to effect for a second time the subsequent real resource transfers that they earlier made is still problematical at this time. But if the NOPECs do not, then their foreign net indebtedness is almost bound to grow at least as quickly as after the 1973 oil shock.

Foreign exchange reserves. Another factor that enabled the NOPECs to reduce the extent of their new borrowing after 1973 was that they were able to draw upon their accumulated foreign exchange reserves in 1974 and 1975. Indeed, the NOPECs were better prepared for the oil shock when it came in 1973 than at any time during the 1960s. Throughout that decade and the early 1970s, the NOPECs built up the real value of their foreign exchange reserves from SDR15 billion in 1960 to SDR33 billion in 1973 — see Figure 5.1. Their foreign exchange reserves as a proportion of annual imports increased from 34.5% to 44% over the same period peaking at 46% in 1972 — see Figure 5.2. When the oil shock came, together with the subsequent decline of export markets in the industrial countries and rising prices of imported manufactured goods, the NOPECs drew upon these enlarged foreign exchange reserves so as to maintain import levels without too dramatically increasing their gross foreign indebtedness. As a result, the real value of their foreign exchange reserves was drawn down by almost one-quarter in the two years after 1973, and reserves, which had covered more than five months' imports in 1973, could purchase less than four months' imports in 1975.

It would be incorrect, however, to blame higher oil prices entirely for the deterioration in the NOPECs' payments accounts after 1973 as other factors from time to time made a contribution but none has had a systematic effect. First, there is the behaviour of the NOPECs' export prices

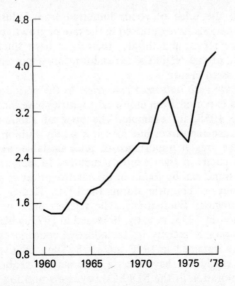

Figure 5.1 *NOPECs' real value of foreign exchange reserves* (SDRs billions deflated by industrial countries' export price index, 1975 = 100)

Source: IMF, *International Financial Statistics,* various years

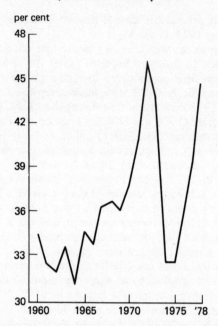

Figure 5.2   *NOPECs' foreign exchange reserves as percentage of annual imports*

compared with the price of goods imported from industrial countries; secondly, fluctuations have occurred in the rate of growth of the NOPECs' exports in value terms; and thirdly, there have been fluctuations in the rate of growth of the NOPECs' expenditure on imported goods. These factors are discussed in turn.

Terms of trade with industrial countries. In the period since 1973 the prices of goods exported from industrial countries have increased steadily, by 63% up to 1978, for example. The price of goods exported from NOPECs have also increased, but in a less steady fashion, as one would expect given the greater importance of price unstable raw materials and semi-processed goods in their export structures. In fact, as was shown in Chapter 4, no trend can be found in the relative prices of goods exported by the two groups of countries during the 1970s. Rather, the experience was one of irregular fluctuations. The relative price of the NOPECs' exports increased in 1973, in early 1974 and in 1977, which were periods of sustained economic activity in the industrial countries, while relatively low prices were obtained in 1975 and 1978. Thus, relatively high manufactures prices could not have been a systematic contributory factor to the sharp deterioration in the NOPECs' payments position. Only in 1975 was this the case, and this was due more to the collapse of primary commodity export prices in that year than to much higher manufactures prices.

This price collapse was itself associated with economic depression in developed countries which was in turn partly a reaction to higher oil prices.

NOPEC exports. Fluctuations in the real value of exports from the NOPEC area contributed to the NOPECs' increased payments deficits only in 1975 (real values were calculated here as nominal export values deflated by industrial countries export prices). For in that year, NOPEC exports, by real value, fell to nearly 14% below their 1961–78 trend, whereas they had been 2% above that trend only one year earlier. Moreover, the real value of NOPEC exports returned to their trend level in 1976 and rose above the trend in 1977 and 1978. However, NOPEC exports in volume terms (that is, NOPEC export nominal values deflated by NOPEC export unit values) performed much less well in the second half of the 1970s than during the first five years of the decade: deviations from the 1966–78 growth trend were negative rather than positive. One very likely cause of this is the poor performance of the NOPECs' main export markets, the industrial countries, during the middle and late 1970s. If this is the case, then it is arguable that the NOPECs have again suffered from the effects of another external factor (oil prices being the other) over which they have little or no control.

NOPEC imports. The NOPECs' worsening payments position since 1973 cannot be blamed upon excessive growth of imports measured in real terms. The NOPECs have not experienced an internally induced boom and they cannot collectively be accused of economic mismanagement in this respect. For when the nominal value of the NOPECs' imports is deflated by the index of imports unit values, to yield a measure of the NOPECs' real import growth, it is found that they cut down import growth to below the 1961–78 trend in both 1975 (when their export markets virtually collapsed) and 1976 (when these markets and the real value of NOPEC exports recovered), and in 1977 and 1978 imports calculated in this way were only slightly above trend.

Thus most of the deterioration in the NOPECs' payments balances after 1973 can be explained by developments in their foreign trade with the oil exporting countries. In fact, as a proportion of the NOPECs' aggregate merchandise account deficit, the deficit with the oil exporting countries increased from about one-quarter in 1972 to three-quarters in three of the last four years of the 1970s.

The debt position after 1973

As a result of the deteriorating international economic environment after 1973, the growth of the NOPECs' debt accelerated despite the use of foreign exchange reserves. The main reason for this was, as pointed out above, that the NOPECs were not able to reduce their international

Table 5.5 *External debt[a] of eighty-seven NOPECs ($ billion)*

	1974	%	1975	%	1976	%	1977	%
Public debt	90.7	75.6	110.0	75.8	134.7	76.6	164.5	77.9
Official sources[b]	55.6	46.3	65.0	44.8	75.6	43.0	89.0	42.1
Private sources[c]	35.1	29.3	44.9	30.9	59.1	33.6	75.5	35.7
Private debt[d]	29.3	24.4	35.2	24.2	41.2	23.4	46.8	22.1
Total	120.0	100	145.2	100	175.9	100	211.3	100
Per cent growth p.a.			21.0		21.1		20.1	

a Defined by the World Bank as 'debt outstanding' (disbursed only). Amounts outstanding represent principal only (that is, excluding interest except in cases where interest is reported as part of the principal) and are net of past repayments.
b Governments and multilateral agencies.
c Financial markets, suppliers credits and others.
d '40 countries in which private non-guaranteed debt is believed to be significant' (p. 3). Mainly medium- and long-term Eurocurrency loans.

Source: IBRD, *World Debt Tables*, 1978.

payments deficits to any great extent until 1976. In 1974 their outstanding public debt amounted to $91 billion and it grew to $165 billion in 1977 (see Table 5.5). To these totals should be added private non-guaranteed debts; accordingly, total debt outstanding was $120 billion in 1974, increasing to over $210 billion in 1977. Debt outstanding as a proportion of exports increased from 72% in 1974 to 90% in 1975, reversing a downward trend that had lasted for some years (Figure 5.3).

Future chapters will allude to the relatively concentrated impact of OPEC upon the NOPECs in respect of their aid, export penetration and labour remittances. In the matter of debts, however, there was no clear concentration of the impact of the OPEC price rises. The external public debt of the NOPECs is in any event rather highly concentrated in a few countries. In fact, the World Bank lists eighty-three NOPECs according to their public and publicly guaranteed debt outstanding and only ten countries (Mexico, Brazil, India, Israel, Korea, Pakistan, Egypt, Argentina, Turkey and Chile in order of size) accounted for over 64% of these debts in 1976. The other seventy-three countries accounted for only 36% of these debts. While there has been a slow but steady erosion of the share of the public debt owed by the biggest ten debtors (the share had been 68% in 1970), the decline is probably due to the limited coverage of the World Bank's data base rather than an actual downward trend in concentration. For as Table 5.5 shows, private non-guaranteed debt formed over one-fifth of the NOPECs' debts in the mid 1970s. Nor was the level of debt and its

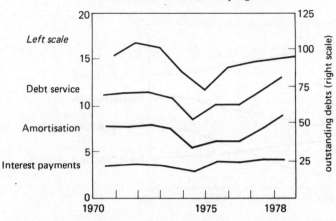

^a The debt and debt service ratios plotted in this chart relate only to medium-term and long-term external public, or publicly guaranteed, debt.

Figure 5.3   *Non-Oil developing countries:public and publicly guaranteed debt and debt service, 1970–78*[1] *(as a percentage of exports of goods and services)*

Source: IMF, *Annual Report, 1978* page 27.

increasing rate of acceleration the only problem. The source of international debt was also changing in an unsatisfactory way according to some observers. The share of public and publicly guaranteed debt owed to official creditors fell steadily, while that of private creditors increased — the Eurocurrency banks were the dominant factor here (Figure 5.4). One of the main problems was that as the terms of commercial loans were harder than on official loans, future debt service problems were more likely to arise. And these worries were not unfounded. Reference to Figure 5.3 shows that interest payments and amortisation as a proportion of export earnings increased rapidly from 1976 onwards even though the ratio of debt outstanding to exports remained fairly stable — a feature that is to be expected given the hardening of terms and conditions.

Since borrowing from the Eurocurrency banks has been a dominant feature of debt patterns in the post-1973 period it is worthwhile giving the subject deeper consideration.

Borrowing from the Eurocurrency banks by the developing countries first took off in 1971 and this embryonic trend was reinforced by developments after 1973. Of course, one of the main reasons for this was the need to finance burgeoning payments deficits and another was the fall in interest rates on Eurocurrency loans which made them more attractive to borrowers. The banks had plenty of funds to lend as deposits by OPEC members grew very rapidly. The three months interbank dollar deposit rate, for example, fell from 14% in 1974 to only 5.5% in early

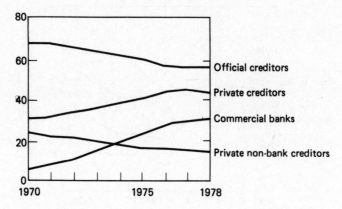

Figure 5.4   *Non-oil developing countries: share of external debt owed to various groups of creditors, end 1970 to end 1978* (as a percentage of total debt outstanding)

Source: as Figure 5.4.

1976 and interest rates on other currency deposits also fell sharply — fortunate developments for the NOPECs.

Another reason why some NOPECs turned to the Eurocurrency banks for credit after 1973 was the continued slow growth of official development assistance from the industrial countries. The oil price rise had weakened the dcs' international payments positions, and foreign aid was one of the first avoidable expenses to be cut in real terms. Moreover, there was another factor at work to constrain the growth of official development assistance since the early 1960s — the declining importance of official aid as an instrument of foreign policy. Nor did the rapid growth of foreign aid from OPEC members make good the decline in aid from the more traditional sources. As the next chapter will show, OPEC's aid was initially far too concentrated geographically to have given much relief to most of the countries in the NOPEC group.

Foreign aid. The low levels of official development assistance from the developed countries have been a constant focus of criticism. Not only were aid flows too small to make an impact upon debt but aid was project tied and procurement tied; and, as a result of the monopoly position conferred upon suppliers in the 'protected' donor countries, purchases by the recipients of aid were often over-priced (UNCTAD, 1968). These criticisms were hardly, if at all, to change in the post-1973 years and some aspects might even have worsened. For example, the differences between aid flows and aid targets widened, and (as is shown in Chapter 6) even though OPEC aid has grown rapidly, its geographic distribution has been determined by the political needs of the donor countries, rather than the economic and social development needs of the NOPECs. And yet it was recognised that once loans had been made to a developing country, further

Table 5.6   *Outstanding borrowing from Eurocurrency banks, end 1978 ($ billion)*

Brazil	31.9
Mexico	23.4
South Korea	7.0
Argentina	6.0
Philippines	4.0
Taiwan	4.0
Israel	3.9
Peru	3.4
Chile	2.8
Thailand	2.6
Total	123.4
% of all[a] NOPECS	72.1

a Offshore Eurocurrency banking centres excluded.

Source: BIS, *Annual Report,* 1979, pp. 112–13.

loans (or grants) would be needed on an increasing scale in order to keep net flows from becoming negative, that is, flow in the reverse direction (Strange, 1967).

As one would expect from the uneven distribution of their overall debts, NOPECs' debts to the Eurocurrency banks are not evenly distributed. In 1978 only ten countries accounted for 72% of the NOPECs' borrowing from foreign banks (see Table 5.6). Brazil, with 26% of these debts, is the largest borrower and Mexico is another very large debtor. Other major borrowers are South Korea, Argentina, Philippines, Taiwan, Israel, Peru, Chile and Thailand. Nearly all the other NOPECs have been small borrowers, if they have used this source at all. Amongst the black African NOPECs only the Ivory Coast's and Zaire's net borrowing from the Eurocurrency banks is greater than $1 billion, while most have borrowed less than $100 million.

After a surge of new borrowing by the NOPECs from the Eurocurrency banks between 1974 and 1976 when their *net* debts (that is, borrowing minus lending) to these banks increased to $31.1 billion, 1977 saw a break in the rapid upward trend. In fact, in that year the NOPECs deposited *more* than they borrowed from the Eurocurrency banks to the extent of over $1 billion. As the Bank for International Settlements observed, this was 'a turnaround that must have surprised even the most optimistic observers of the international financial scene' (BIS, 1978). This development was mainly caused by the improvement in the NOPECs' payments deficits that was discussed above. Even in 1976, the NOPECs were borrowing large sums from the Eurocurrency banking system and redepositing

Table 5.7   *External positions^a of Eurocurrency banks^b with NOPECs^c (year end, $ billion)*

	1975	1976	1977	1978
Bank lending *to*:				
OPEC	14.3	24.1	35.4	57.2
All NOPECs	63.0	80.9	92.0	123.4
Latin America^d	43.5	57.4	63.8	80.8
Middle East	3.3	4.4	4.6	6.6
Asia	12.9	14.7	18.1	24.8
Africa	3.3	4.4	5.5	11.2
Bank borrowing *from*:				
OPEC	51.8	64.2	77.6	83.8
All NOPECs	37.0	49.8	62.0	78.0
Latin America^d	16.3	22.3	25.3	33.9
Middle East	6.0	7.3	10.0	13.8
Asia	10.6	14.9	20.0	22.9
Africa	4.1	5.3	6.7	7.4

a   With bank and non-bank sector in the reporting area.
b   Eurocurrency banks are those banks holding positions in domestic and foreign currencies outside their home country. These banks are those of the Group of Ten countries and Switzerland and the foreign branches of US banks in the Caribbean and Far East.
c   The bank for International Settlements excludes those countries which are 'offshore' Eurocurrency banking centres from the group of NOPECs because the large inflows and outflows of funds would distort the data. These excluded countries are: Bahamas, Barbados, Bermuda, Cayman Islands, Hong Kong, Lebanon, Liberia, Netherlands Antilles, New Hebrides, Panama, Singapore and other British West Indies.
d   Including those countries in the Caribbean area which cannot be considered as offshore banking centres.

Source: BIS, *Annual Report*, various issues.

a large proportion, and in so doing built up their foreign exchange reserves which had been depleted.

Unfortunately, on a longer term view, it will probably turn out that the years 1976 and 1977 were only a temporary respite in the growth of the NOPECs' net foreign borrowing. In 1978 net borrowing from foreign banks increased very substantially (by over $15 billion), gross outstanding debts to these creditors reached $123 billion and net indebtedness grew to $45.4 billion (Table 5.7). Moreover, in 1979 the new rounds of oil price increases caused payments deficits to increase yet further. The debt service ratio continued to increase as grace periods on hastily raised and expensive Eurocurrency loans ran out (Figure 5.3 again).

Given the scale of borrowing from the Eurocurrency banking system by the NOPECs, the ever-increasing price of oil and the continued failure of official development assistance to increase quickly, it is difficult to see how these countries can reduce their net indebtedness to these creditors in the short to medium term. A withdrawal of credits by foreign banks would almost certainly cause a spate of sovereign defaults and impose severe economic restraint upon the debtor countries. The NOPECs will remain locked in with the international banks for several more years at least.

OPEC and the Eurocurrency banks

The oil price rise, leading as it did to a dramatic rise in the OPEC members' current account surpluses, was of course the main reason for the rapid net flow of funds from this source to the Eurocurrency banks. By 1975, OPEC members' net deposits with these banks had reached $35.7 billion with gross deposits standing at $52 billion (see Table 5.7). But as the difference between these gross and net figures indicates, some OPEC members were already becoming large borrowers from the Eurocurrency banks. In fact, a clear division soon appeared between those OPEC members which were net creditors and those that were net borrowers. The so-called 'low absorbers', Kuwait, Qatar, Saudi Arabia and the UAE, continued to be large net depositors to the extent of about $30 billion per annum between 1976 and 1978. On the other hand the rest, the 'high absorbers', became less important as net depositors until, by the end of 1978, they had actually become net borrowers. Venezuela, for example, borrowed about $5 billion from foreign banks in 1978 alone, Algeria and Iran about $2.5 billion each and Nigeria $1.2 billion.

What is the extent of the NOPECs' debt problem?

The sharp rise in the NOPECs' debt service ratio since 1974 – shown in Figure 5.1 – was paralleled by an increase in debt and debt net of foreign exchange reserves as percentages of the combined GDP of the twenty largest NOPECs (see Table 5.8). By 1978, external debt outstanding

Table 5.8   *External debt indicators: twenty largest NOPECs, 1973–8*[a]

	1973	1974	1975	1976	1977	1978
External debt as % of GDP	18.9	18.3	21.1	22.6	24.2	25.1
External debt net of reserves as % of GDP	12.7	13.2	16.9	17.2	18.2	17.9

a In terms of the value of their external trade: Argentina, Brazil, Chile, Colombia, Egypt, India, Ivory Coast, Kenya, Korea, Malaysia, Mexico, Morocco, Pakistan, Peru, Philippines, Singapore, Taiwan, Thailand, Tunisia and Turkey.

Source: Morgan Guaranty Trust (May 1979, p. 8).

amounted to 25% of these twenty countries' GDP when it had been only 19% in 1973. Debt net of reserves is not as high, but the proportionate increase during this six year period (inclusive) was even greater.

However, the problem with these proxy measures for the debt burden is that they are too simplistic to reflect the whole complex of factors which determine a country's ability to service its outstanding debts. In fact, there are so many factors bearing upon a country's ability to service its foreign debts that it is instructive to discuss them in a little detail.

The ability to increase export earnings is clearly a major factor that determines whether an external debt service obligation becomes a burden. A country may be unable to earn sufficient foreign exchange because of structural factors such as inelastic foreign demand for the country's exports, or immobile domestic resources which prevent a rapid expansion of the export sector. Nor need the inability to earn sufficient foreign exchange only have structural causes. Indeed, Sargen has gone as far as to suggest that debt problems are 'monetary phenomena' caused by governments' maintaining overvalued foreign exchange rates (Sargen, 1977), a policy which leads to worsening balance of payments difficulties, a growing need to borrow foreign capital and, ultimately, to debt servicing problems.

A high degree of unforeseen fluctuation in export earnings makes external debt management difficult, especially when foreign exchange reserves — owned or borrowable — are small. Again, structural factors such as price inelastic foreign demand and domestic supply are important here, as are fluctuations in the level of foreign demand associated with business cycles. Debtor countries have little control over any of these variables — even the lagged response of supply to export price changes is often governed by technological factors (for example, the time it takes coffee, cocoa or rubber trees to reach maturity or to increase mining capacity). Moreover, attempts to stabilise market prices by the use of quotas or buffer stocks operated under international commodity agreements have so far been very largely unsuccessful. Nor have compensatory finance arrangements such as the IMF's Compensatory Finance Facility or the EEC's Stabex done anything like enough to compensate developing countries during periods of shortfall in export earnings.

The willingness of existing or potential lenders to roll-over outstanding debts is also relevant to a country's ability to service outstanding debts and to raise its debt service ratio. Oil-rich Mexico, with high potential foreign exchange earnings, has little difficulty in rolling-over debts, while countries with bleak export potential suffer great difficulty in servicing relatively small debts because new loans cannot be raised on a sufficiently large scale.

The term structure of debt repayments can also impinge upon the debt burden question. For example, when repayments are bunched in time, so that a large proportion of debt outstanding is paid back in a single year, a change in economic conditions such as a temporary decline in export earnings could set off a debt crisis if banks are discouraged by the current difficulty to repay these debt obligations. A more dispersed term structure of debt repayments would in general be preferred to bunched patterns (IBRD, *World Debt Tables*, 1979).

Countries with more sophisticated economic structures can produce domestically a wider range of products and are better able to practise import substitution should the need arise. Countries with a narrow economic base may find that a large fixed obligation to service foreign loans means that under certain circumstances, necessary imports must be cut back, with adverse effects on welfare standards and economic growth.

To illustrate the point that the various types of debt service ratio do not encompass all of the factors related to a country's ability to service foreign debts, consider the case of Brazil. Brazil has the largest foreign debt of all developing countries – $49 billion at the end of 1979 including public, publicly guaranteed and private non-guaranteed (IBRD, *World Debt Tables*, 1978, p. 7). Debt service is also unusually high and the ratio of debt service to export earnings has been over 40% in most years during the 1970s. Yet Brazil did not seem to have a debt service problem: its credit rating remained good amongst the Eurocurrency banks. This success was mainly due to Brazil's ability to raise its debt service capacity along with its debt service obligations: export growth rates and economic growth remained high during the 1970s relative to the performance to most other developing countries.

In contrast with this Brazilian position, other NOPECs performed much less well during the 1970s. Indeed, since 1973, eight NOPECs had to reschedule debt repayments, in India's case no fewer than five times. The Indian example is interesting because in addition to its debt outstanding being lower than Brazil's, less of it is owed to Eurocurrency banks, implying that India is able to borrow on softer loan terms. Moreover, in some years Brazil's public debt service ratio alone was higher than that of India.

Returning to the subject of the NOPECs' overall debt position, the IMF was seriously worried by the rapid deterioration in their current accounts in the year or two after the oil price rise in 1973. In its 1977 *Annual Report* the IMF observed: 'It is clear that the upsurge of current imbalances among the NOPECs from 1973–75 *overshot the mark*. In meeting the emerging pressures of that period, when a strongly adverse cyclical swing was compounded by the increased costs of energy and foods, many of these countries relied on external borrowing *at rates and costs that were not sustainable*, either from their own standpoint or from that of their creditors' (p. 20, italics added). Moreover, despite the respite in the growth of new debt in 1976–7, debt service ratios continued to rise (Figure 5.3).

However, there is no substance to the view of the Development Assistance Committee of the OECD that much increased borrowing from the Eurocurrency banks adds 'uncertainty concerning the adequacy of future [foreign] capital availability to meet investment needs' (DAC, 1978, p. 23). There is really no reason to suppose that private capital flows are 'less certain' than public capital flows. After all, the latter have failed to grow quickly in the 1970s; their level and distribution is governed in large measure by political expediency; aid targets are virtually never achieved; and the practices of project and procurement tying reduce their real value and slow the rate of disbursement to the recipient countries. In fact, such is the extent of disarray in industrial countries that it is difficult to see how else funds would have been recycled to the NOPECs other than through the Eurocurrency markets.

Moreover, the prospect of bank failures caused by NOPEC debt service default does not seem to be a serious problem. Even when the growth of NOPEC borrowing from international banks was at its height, the banks' exposure was limited. For example, in 1975 unguaranteed dollar term loans to NOPECs were equivalent to only 2.5% of the total assets of the major twenty-one American banks involved in lending to developing countries, and no single NOPEC accounted for more than 2.5% of these banks loans to the NOPECs (Cleveland and Bruce Brittain, 1977).

It was thought that as the Eurocurrency banking system does not have an obvious 'lender of last resort', the system could collapse should one or more important banks find themselves in a liquidity crisis. However, it is notable that the few bank failures of the 1970s were not caused by losses sustained in the Euro-loans sector. Moreover, as Eurodollar deposits are ultimately the liabilities of American banks, the Federal Reserve Board is perforce closely associated with the Eurodollar market (the largest sector of the Eurocurrency market) and conceivably would act as a lender of last resort should the need arise. So would the other central banks for the Euro-Deutschmark and Euro-Swiss Franc markets, and so on. Nor does it seem likely that fund switching by the large OPEC depositors could bring the system down. Presumably, the switched funds would have to be redeposited somewhere else in the world banking system and could, therefore, be re-borrowed by the banks from which the funds were originally withdrawn (Mendelson, 1979).

Sniping at the Eurocurrency banking system's relations with the NOPECs is somewhat irrelevant because these relationships are in the nature of technical machinery rather than a fundamental cause of the NOPECs' worsening debt situation. These fundamentals are found in the sluggish rates of world economic growth, high world inflation rates and are exacerbated by increasing energy costs. Since these fundamentals will not improve in the next few years (indeed, they will worsen), the prospect for an improvement in the NOPECs' debt situation is bleak.

Moreover, while the previous discussion has suggested that the debt 'problem' is to be measured in terms of the inability, or the future inability, of debtors to service outstanding debts, such a restrictive criterion need not be used. As Gamani Corea has observed a debt problem can be deemed to have arisen when a country's debt service repayments impinge upon the ability 'to meet its minimum economic and social *objectives*' (Corea, 1976, p. 60, italics added). And on this view many more NOPECs already have a debt problem than with 'the ability to service' criterion.

Notes

1 Including private debts guaranteed by the public sector but excluding unguaranteed private debts with maturities of less than one year.
2 The UK announced in August 1978 that it was writing off debts with $900 million owed by seventeen of the world's poorest countries. West Germany and the Netherlands announced smaller write offs at about the same time ($196 million and $130 million respectively.) *The Times* and *International Herald Tribune*, 1 August 1978.
3 There is an added complication because of the existence of other trading blocs, but broadly the argument is correct. However, a possible situation could have been that the NOPECs managed to reduce their non-oil deficit, while OPEC did not reduce its collective current account surplus. Should this situation have occurred, the financial transfer would have been from the NOPECs to OPEC while the real transfer was from the former group of countries to some other trading bloc. For a more detailed consideration of these matters refer to J. Tumlir (1974)
4 The 'absorption approach' to the balance of payments was first developed by S. S. Alexander (1951). Using the national income identities it can be shown that:

$$I + X = S + M$$
$$\text{therefore}$$
$$X - M = S - I$$

where I is investment; X is exports; S is saving; and M is imports. If $X < M$ (a balance of payments deficit), it follows that $S < I$ which implies that insufficient domestic resources have been released from domestic consumption to support the level of investment. The extra resources come from the surplus of imports over exports. The current account deficit must be financed by a 'below the line' surplus or by a running down of foreign exchange reserves.

6

OPEC Aid

The dimensions of foreign aid from OPEC, mainly the Arab member countries, only became large after the 1973 oil price increases and the resulting vast increases in their foreign exchange earnings. The phenomenon of OPEC aid, its scale and the factors that have motivated the donor countries to give it, are discussed in this chapter. So is the balance between increased outlays on imported oil and receipts of OPEC aid by Third World countries.

The marked geographic concentration of OPEC aid, together with policy statements by members of the donor governments, suggest that political motivation has been the major factor behind most of the Arab countries' aid programmes. All the Arab foreign aid donors – Saudi Arabia, Kuwait, Qatar, the UAE, Iraq and Libya – have used their financial resources to aid the so-called 'front line' states against Israel – Egypt, until she withdrew in 1978, Jordan, Syria and the Palestine Liberation Organization. Other Arab states have benefited from acts of Arab solidarity, a financial Pan-Arabism without the rhetoric. But here again, Arab aid signifies a shift of political power within the Arab orbit towards the oil exporting countries.

Regional security is another important motivating factor behind Arab aid. For example, Saudi Arabia has given aid to Somalia and Oman to counter Soviet influences that might threaten her oil-trade routes. The former country overlooks the Red Sea route to the Suez Canal and Oman overlooks the Strait of Hormuz at the exit from the Persian Gulf. Similarly, Saudi Arabia has turned North Yemen, the largest country by population on the Arabian Peninsula, into a client state in an attempt to secure political stability which is threatened by neighbouring Marxist-leaning South Yemen.

Saudi Arabia and some other Arab aid donors have also used aid in support of ideological and religious causes, especially the strengthening of Islam, both in Arab countries and in fringe Muslim countries. The main ideological issue here is the use of aid to combat the spread of communism: the cases of Somalia and Oman can again be cited and, in addition, distant

Mauritania, which until August 1979 was fighting the Marxist-leaning Polisario Front guerrillas in the former Spanish Sahara, has received aid from Kuwait and Saudi Arabia.

Aid from the other conservative Arab states such as Kuwait, Qatar and the UAE is motivated by similar impulses to that of the largest aid donor, Saudi Arabia: the Arab conflict with Israel, regional security and other ideological and religious factors. Moreover, 'revolutionary' Iraq gives about 80% of its aid to Arab causes. Libyan aid mainly goes to the same end, although President Gadaffi prefers to channel aid bilaterally, with Uganda until lately being a favoured partner. Iran's aid, until 1978, was motivated by regional security factors. Its contributions to Pakistan were in support of the Central Treaty Organisation arrangement that existed between the two countries. Afghanistan has also received Iranian aid. Both programmes could be seen as efforts to out-do Soviet aid in the area.

The rest of the Third World has received relatively little OPEC aid, certainly not enough to compensate for the higher outlays on imported oil. Latin America, Central America and the Caribbean received almost nothing until quite recently. Non-Muslim black African countries have even complained about the unsatisfactory amounts of OPEC aid that have been disbursed to them. Even OPEC aid disbursements to India, which averaged about $290 million per annum between 1974 and 1977, were not large in relation to India's extra outlays on imported oil as is shown below. Nor have the non-Muslim countries of East Asia, such as Hong Kong, Singapore and Taiwan, received much in the way of Arab aid to compensate them for the higher oil prices.

As was suggested in the Introduction, however, OPEC members do not concede that higher oil prices in themselves constitute a case for concessional aid. Moreover, a Nigerian suggestion to sell crude oil to African states at reduced prices was rejected in February 1975 as being contrary to OPEC rules (Baker, 1977). Rather, the OPEC members, preferring to shift the ground of debate, lend moral support to Third World countries in their pursuit of higher primary commodity export prices. They have also pledged $100 million to the UNCTAD's Common Fund for commodity price stabilisation and related matters. OPEC members have not, however, given financial assistance to support other primary commodity cartels.

OPEC members, however, are not unconcerned about their aid policy towards the rest of the Third World. Indeed, in the last two or three years there has been some diversification of their aid towards these countries. Again political factors are important, especially in winning diplomatic support for the Arab case against Israel and in promoting Third World solidarity. The latter really means minimising Third World criticisms of high oil prices as well as lining up on issues such as technology transfer, tariffs, the control of multinational corporations and the law of the sea negotiations. A spur to greater diversification of Arab aid came at

UNCTAD V held in 1979 when the Latin Americans tried unsuccessfully to get oil prices on the agenda.

The way OPEC members have used foreign aid for political ends, indeed the very fact that they have an aid programme at all, is yet another factor that distinguishes them from the rest of the Third World. OPEC members, especially the Arabs, have a newly acquired degree of economic and political power to which other Third World countries cannot aspire. OPEC controls oil export prices to these countries while the non-oil exporting countries have minimal control over their own export prices to OPEC members (see Chapter 4); OPEC aid disbursements do not compensate for higher oil prices – see below; while OPEC markets are becoming important for the NOPECs the reverse is not happening (Chapter 7); also several Arab OPEC members absorb migratory labour and remittances from these countries are important to several NOPECs (Chapter 8).

We proceed now to discuss in some detail the dimensions of OPEC aid and then consider its motivations in greater depth. The cost of aid to the donor countries is also given consideration. The final sections point out the balance between OPEC aid and the Third World countries' extra expenditure on imports caused by higher oil prices.

OPEC aid: the dimensions

OPEC aid disbursements have grown very quickly since 1973.[1] In that year OPEC aid was already above $1.3 billion. It increased to about $3.4 billion in 1974 and then to over $5.5 billion in each of the years 1975, 1976 and 1977 – see Table 6.1.

Most of OPEC's aid has originated from those member countries with large balance of payments surpluses – especially Saudi Arabia, Kuwait and the United Arab Emirates. Two other countries, Qatar and Iran, have run much smaller aid programmes as have Iraq and Libya. The other six OPEC members aid programmes have been much less important or even non-existent.

The OPEC aid effort measured as a proportion of OPEC GNP is far more impressive than that of the industrial country members of the OECD's Development Assistance Committee (DAC). While in 1977 the DAC members gave only 0.31% of GNP in official development assistance, the OPEC members gave 2.65%, well above the United Nations' 0.7% target agreed upon at the 1970 UN Special Session. Moreover, the aid efforts of some OPEC members is even more impressive: since 1973 Qatar and the UAE have each given more than 10% of their GNP in foreign aid, Saudi Arabia disbursed 5% of its GNP and Kuwait 6.5%.

Bilateral aid from OPEC members is much greater than their multilateral aid. Between 1973 and 1977 total OPEC aid (bilateral and disbursements to multilateral agencies mainly financed by OPEC as well as

Table 6.1   OPEC net aid disbursements to developing countries and multilateral agencies[a] ($ million)

	1970	%	1973	%	1974	%	1975	%	1976	%	1977	%
Algeria	1.0	(0)	25.4	(0.02)	46.9	(1.4)	40.7	(1.0)	53.6	(1.0)	46.1	(1.0)
Iran	3.6	(1)	1.9	(0)	403.8	(11.8)	593.1	(10.8)	752.5	(13.5)	202.1	(3.5)
Iraq	2.0	(1.0)	11.1	(0.01)	422.9	(12.3)	218.4	(4)	231.7	(4.1)	53.4	(1.0)
Kuwait	130.0	(36.4)	345.2	(26.4)	621.5	(18.0)	975.3	(17.7)	614.3	(11.0)	1,441.8	(25.1)
Libya	63.0	(17.6)	214.6	(16.4)	147.0	(4.3)	261.1	(4.7)	93.6	(1.7)	109.4	(1.9)
Nigeria	0	(0)	4.7	(0)	15.3	(0)	13.9	(0)	82.9	(1.5)	63.6	(1.1)
Qatar	0	(0)	93.7	(7.2)	185.2	(5.4)	338.9	(6.1)	195.0	(3.5)	117.6	(2.0)
Saudi Arabia	155.0	(43.4)	304.9	(23.3)	1,029.1	(29.9)	1,997.4	(36.2)	2,407.1	(43.1)	2,373.0	(41.3)
UAE	0	(0)	288.6	(22.1)	510.6	(14.8)	1,046.1	(19.1)	1,060.2	(19.0)	1,261.8	(22.0)
Venezuela	2.5	(1.0)	17.7	(1.4)	58.8	(2.0)	31.0	(1.0)	95.9	(1.7)	71.5	(1.2)
Total	357.1		1,307.8		3,445.6		5,515.9		5,586.8		5,740.9	

a Contributions both to multilateral institutions largely financed by OPEC members and contributions to other multilateral institutions such as IDA, IBRD, United Nations and regional development banks.
Source: UNCTAD (1979b), Table 5.11.

to other multilateral agencies such as the World Bank, IDA and the United Nations) was $21.6 billion (Table 6.1) while OPEC bilateral aid amounted to $17.4 billion or 81% of the total. It is argued below that the predominance of bilateral over multilateral aid in the case of OPEC members, as in the case of DAC members, is related to the desire to use aid for political leverage, and bilateral aid affords the donor greater manipulative control. Another factor here is that the rapid growth of OPEC aid has been so recent that it has outrun the development of new institutional machinery. As this new machinery — the plethora of mainly Arab multilateral aid institutions — has been established (see below) there has been some diversification away from bilateral aid.[2]

Geographical distribution of OPEC aid

On a continental basis, Africa has received most of OPEC's aid disbursements in the 1973—7 period — 48.5% in fact (see Table 6.2). Africa's predominance is almost entirely accounted for by Egypt's presence as easily the single largest OPEC aid recipient. There are also several other Muslim countries in Africa that have received relatively large aid disbursements, in particular Sudan, Mauritania, Somalia and Morocco. West Asia, which constitutes the Arab Middle East, Pakistan and Afghanistan (both Muslim countries), is the second largest recipient of OPEC aid — 27.6% in the five year period under review. Aid disbursements by OPEC members to South and South-East Asia have been relatively small — only 17.2% of the total, mainly to India. Latin and Central America and the Caribbean have received very little OPEC aid.

Multilateral Arab aid (or aid from 'Regional Institutions' in Table 6.3 which lists the major Arab aid institutions) tends to be as heavily geographically concentrated on Arab bilateral aid from 'National Institutions'. The Arab Bank for Economic Development in Africa (BADEA by its French initials) alone specialises in Arab aid to non-Arab African countries. The BADEA was established in 1974 after the Cairo Arab-African summit with a total commitment of $1.4 billion, 81% of which had been distributed by the end of 1977 (BADEA, *Annual Report*: 1978). However, the other Arab multilateral aid agencies specialise in aid to Arab countries or to Muslim countries — the Arab Fund for Social and Economic Development (established in 1973), the Islamic Development Bank (1973), the Arab Investment Company (1974) and the Arab Monetary Fund (1976). In addition, Arab countries have contributed more than half of the capital of the OPEC Special Fund (1976).

The heavy geographic concentration of OPEC aid is clearly illustrated when it is analysed on a country basis. Of the twenty largest recipients of OPEC bilateral aid in the 1973—7 period, all except India and Thailand are regarded as Muslim countries (Muslim Council of Europe definitions)

Table 6.2   OPEC aid^a to developing countries, 1973–7 ($ million)

	1973	1974	1975	1976	1977	% share 1973–7 inclusive
Bilateral	1,208.8	3,014.7	4,905.7	4,526.7	3,763.8	
Multilateral	–	116.7	159.9	422.4	1,489.0	
Total	1,208.2	3,131.4	5,065.6	4,949.1	5,252.8	100
America						
Bilateral	0.1	20.0	0.7	9.6	0	
Multilateral	0	0	0	0	7.6	
Total	0.1	20.0	0.7	9.6	7.6	insignificant
Africa						
Bilateral	699.0	1,142.0	2,698.1	1,535.7	1,451.8	
Multilateral	0	90.0	146.4	383.1	1,366.9	
Total	699.0	1,232.9	2,844.5	1,918.8	2,818.7	48.5
of which						
Egypt	652.1	839.2	2,072.7	1,278.8	2,121.6	
Sudan	3.3	42.6	174.1	224.7	103.7	
West Asia						
Bilateral	399.3	1,119.4	1,240.0	1,352.3	1,187.8	
Multilateral	0	25.8	12.5	31.5	34.5	
Total	399.3	1,145.2	1,252.5	1,383.8	1,222.3	27.6
South & South-East Asia						
Bilateral	18.2	626.9	732.3	1,458.7	460.7	
Multilateral	0	0	0	0	67.1	
Total	18.2	626.9	732.3	1,458.7	527.8	17.2
Oceania						
Multilateral	0	0	0	0.8	1.6	insignificant
Unspecified world						
Bilateral	91.5	106.4	234.7	170.4	663.5	
Multilateral	0	0	1.1	7.1	11.4	
Total	91.5	106.4	235.8	177.5	674.9	6.6

a Excluding aid to multinational agencies *not* mainly financed by OPEC members.
Source: UNCTAD (1979b), Tables 5.7 and 5.8B.

(see Table 6.4). The twenty largest recipients of disbursed OPEC bilateral aid received 87% of the total in the 1973–7 period. The eighteen Muslim countries amongst these twenty accounted for 81%; and the eleven Arab countries amongst them received 65% of OPEC's bilateral aid. In fact, the single largest recipient, Egypt, received $5.5 billion or 31.5% of all OPEC disbursed bilateral aid; the second largest recipient was Syria, also an Arab

Table 6.3 *Arab institutions for development assistance: loans by country group through 1977*

	Arab Countries	Non-Arab African Countries	Non-Arab Asian Countries	Other
	%	%	%	%
National Institutions				
Abu Dhabi Fund	79.9	4.1	16.0	0
Kuwait Fund	69.1	10.2	20.6	0
Saudi Fund	53.2	9.7	33.6	3.5
Regional Institutions				
BADEA	0	100	0	0
Arab Fund	100	0	0	0
Islamic Bank	63.7	26.4	9.9	0

Source: IMF, *IMF Survey*, 5 February 1979.

'front line' state, which received $2.4 billion of bilateral aid or 13.7% of the total; the third largest recipient was Pakistan, a large poor Muslim country that was also viewed by the Shah of Iran as of strategic importance within the Central Treaty Organisation; and the fourth largest OPEC bilateral aid recipient was Jordan (6.6% of the total) — another 'front line' state. However, OPEC's bilateral aid to nineteen African countries other than Egypt, Sudan, Mauritania, Morocco and Somalia was not niggardly: it amounted to $239 million in 1974; $398 million in 1975; $437 million in 1976; and it increased sharply in 1977 to $1.47 billion.

The much smaller bilateral aid handouts to these other African countries only reflects their lack of political or military importance to the major Arab aid donors in the latter's confrontation with Israel on the one hand, and with communist incursion into the Arab region on the other. Non-Muslim black African countries have fared even less well than the Muslim black African countries. For example, Kenya and Tanzania have been only minor recipients of OPEC aid. Even so, some OPEC aid has made its way to some of the poorest countries in the world (of the twenty largest recipients, ten had per capita incomes below $300), but this arose mainly because several Muslim countries happen to be very poor rather than because of a primary policy objective to aid the poorest countries.

Terms and conditions

Most OPEC aid is given on very favourable terms and conditions from the recipient's point of view. A large proportion of this aid is given on a grant

Table 6.4   *OPEC bilateral aid: The twenty largest recipients: 1973–7*

		$m	%	cumulative %	GNP per capita 1976 $
1	Egypt	5,488.2	31.5	31.5	280
2	Syria	2,391.0	13.7	45.2	780
3	Pakistan	1,648.2	9.5	54.7	170
4	Jordan	1,148.4	6.6	61.3	610
5	India	1,052.1	6.0	67.3	150
6	Yemen, Arab Republic	593.0	3.4	70.7	250
7	Sudan	548.7	3.1	73.8	290
8	Oman	440.6	2.5	76.3	2,680
9	Mauritania	299.7	1.7	78.0	340
10	Bangladesh	271.8	1.6	79.6	110
11	Somalia	262.8	1.5	81.1	110
12	Morocco	250.7	1.4	82.5	540
13	Yemen, Dem.	247.6	1.4	83.9	280
14	Lebanon	132.0	0.8	84.7	n.a.
15	Tunisia	112.1	0.6	85.3	840
16	Afghanistan	86.4	0.5	85.8	160
17	Thailand	75.9	0.4	86.2	380
18	Algeria	61.9	0.4	86.6	990
19	Senegal	50.7	0.3	86.9	390
20	Mali	50.2	0.3	87.2	100

Sources: UNCTAD (1979b); IBRD (1977a).

basis, otherwise loan terms are with low interest rates and long grace and amortisation periods.

The OPEC donors tend to favour project aid over non-project aid or aid for balance of payments support. Much of this project aid is provided under co-financing arrangements with institutions such as the World Bank, and the separate aid agencies mainly financed by OPEC members often work together in order to share their expertise. However, owing to the slow rate of disbursement of project aid (due to the difficulty of finding projects and slowness of implementation), non-project aid disbursements are relatively larger. In fact, this observation points to a more general problem.

While it is true that many recipient countries require the expertise that comes as part of a project aid package, most of them also require capital inflows for general balance of payments support – especially in view of the serious worsening of their foreign accounts since 1973. Moreover, there is also the general criticism of project aid that if the recipients would have undertaken the project without aid financing, then the aid funds can be readily switched to some other use (for example, the purchase of oil) – the so-called fungibility problem. In this case there seems to be little point in project-tying the aid at all. Alternatively, if the recipients would not have undertaken a given project in the absence of foreign aid, then the aid has simply promoted a low-priority project. In addition, under such circumstances, project aid donors have sometimes been accused of unwarranted interference in the domestic affairs of the recipient country.

The cost of OPEC aid to the donors

Just why is the OPEC aid effort so large when compared to the DAC countries' aid effort and why is it so heavily concentrated geographically? Most OPEC aid originates from those few OPEC members that have large balance of payments surpluses – Saudi Arabia, Kuwait, Qatar and the UAE. This aid is mainly distributed from funds that would otherwise accumulate in Western financial centres and, owing to inflation, earn negative rates of interest. Arab aid is concentrated geographically because the political and military benefits that the donors obtain from their aid are also regionally concentrated. The first of these aspects of the cost-benefit calculus, cost, is discussed in this section, and the mainly political benefits in the next section.

The Director General of the OPEC Special Fund has pointed out that 'The aid burden is heavier on an OPEC donor than is apparent at first . . . [because] aid is given from oil revenues which are in fact part income and part capital, as they represent, *to a large extent*, the monetary realization of a [real] asset' (Shihata and Mabro, 1979, p. 161). On a theoretical level the argument may be correct but the question arises: to what extent does the argument fit the circumstances? That is: is it really true that OPEC aid represents 'the monetarisation of a real asset'?

Just suppose that an OPEC aid donor actually had to produce and sell more oil in order to earn foreign exchange to increase its foreign aid programme to the NOPECs. What factors should be taken into account in the appraisal of the cost of this aid? In fact, since an oil reservoir is a finite depletable resource, the cost of an extra barrel of output today is composed of two parts: first, the current cost of production – labour costs and the cost of using capital equipment; and secondly, user cost. User cost is the discounted value of the future revenue that must be forgone because a unit of a depletable resource has been extracted and sold today rather than in the future.

The optimal rate of extraction of any depletable resource, according to strictly economic criteria, would occur at the point where the rate of interest on additional accumulations of financial assets is equal to the expected proportionate rate of price increase of the natural resource (Solow, 1974). For instance, if the expected proportionate rate of price increase was higher than the rate of interest on financial assets, the owner of the resource could increase its wealth faster by leaving the natural resource in the ground rather than transforming it into a financial asset. Conversely, if the rate of interest is higher than the expected proportionate rate of price increase, the rate of production should be increased so that more wealth is held in the form of financial assets and correspondingly less in the ground.

However, this strictly economic set of criteria of the optimal rate of extraction of a natural resource is rather simplistic because other factors are also relevant. For example, Saudi Arabia usually produces over 8 million barrels per day even though it has claimed that its domestic needs for oil and foreign exchange can be satisfied with about 5 million barrels per day. A few other OPEC countries are in a similar position. The reasons for these high rates of extraction lie in political factors not revealed by the purely economic criteria. The economic-political stability of the industrial oil importing countries is an important consideration for several of the OPEC countries, not least Saudi Arabia which has substantial financial assets placed in these countries and would not want to put them at risk by cutting back on oil production to a much greater extent and so destabilising their economies. Thus, to some degree, oil production in the OPEC is still influenced by demand factors in the industrial countries and OPEC has not had to squeeze very hard on supply to produce the over 1,000% rise in oil prices between 1970 and 1979.

The question now arises: have the major OPEC aid donors actually increased their oil output in order to give financial aid to the NOPECs? The facts of the case seem to point to the conclusion that they have not. Rather, these countries have determined their oil output according to the economic and political criteria mentioned above and one result, of course, has been a massive increase in their surplus financial assets.

The implication is that much of OPEC's foreign aid is given from financial assets that have already been accumulated and that oil-output policy has not been modified by the aid-to-NOPECs policy. Thus, the cost of OPEC aid is not really related 'to a large extent to the monetarisation of a real asset' as the Director General of OPEC Special Fund has claimed. The cost of aid given from existing financial assets (which have not been specifically acquired so as to give aid, but because of a much wider oil output and price policy together with the donors low absorptive capacity) should instead be measured against the forgone return on those financial assets which have been turned over to the aid programme.

It has been estimated by Chase Manhattan Bank that, after taking account of inflation and exchange rate depreciation of the dollar in which three-quarters of OPEC investments are denominated, the real rate of return on OPEC financial assets is between *minus* 2% and *minus* 4% annually, even though the nominal rate of return is about 7.9% (*MEED*, 3 August 1979, p. 6). Thus, the cost to the donors of mainly Arab OPEC aid is not all that great. Moreover, the perceived benefits are high in a region of the world where political instability is high — the Middle East.

The politics of OPEC aid

The political context of Arab OPEC aid has been put by Choucri (1976):
'The predominance of petroleum in the economy of the [Middle East and
North Africa] made the disbursement of oil revenues [i.e. foreign aid],
not trade regulations, the major issue of economic policy. Surplus revenues
gave the rich states a privilege. They sought to obtain a position of dominance in Arab politics' (p. 117). We are not going to embark upon an
analysis of inter-Arab politics here: that would be far too large a task.
Rather, we shall confine the discussion to showing how OPEC aid has been
used in particular cases.

Aid from the Arab oil exporting countries to Egypt is, perhaps, the
most obvious example of Arab aid being used for political purposes, with
the aid tap having been turned on or off according to circumstances.
Following the June 1967 war with Israel, Egypt received about $200
million per annum in aid from Saudi Arabia under the Khartoum Agreement, an arrangement that lasted for several years. Despite the defeat
by Israel in the October 1973 war, Egypt has remained the major military
counter-weight against Zionism. It is this factor, together with the huge
rise in oil revenues after 1973, that has encouraged Saudi Arabia and
other Arab oil exporting countries to raise their financial support to
Egypt. Accordingly, between October 1973 and the end of 1977, the Arab
oil exporting countries committed about $4 billion per annum to Egypt
in aid and debt service relief.

Actual disbursements were lower, but still substantial: nearly $1 billion
in 1974; over $2 billion in 1975; $1.3 billion in 1976; and over $2 billion
in 1977. Almost $2 billion of this aid came from the Gulf Organisation for
Development (GODE).[3] Saudi Arabia, the UAE and Qatar have also
financed the $1 billion Arab Organisation for Industrialisation (AOI),
based in Egypt for the purpose of improving the Egyptian and Arab arms
manufacturing capability. Six OPEC-financed multilateral aid agencies
have channelled large amounts of aid to Egypt − about $600 million up
to the end of 1978; the six funds are: the Kuwait Fund for Arab Economic
Development, the Kuwait Fund for Economic and Social Development,
Saudi Fund for Development, the ADFAED, IDB and the AMF. A lot
more aid came directly from bilateral Arab aid sources, especially from
Kuwait (about $350 million annually) and from Saudi Arabia (about
$650 million annually). These two countries have also placed large deposits
in Egypt's central bank − over $1 billion in Kuwait's case.

The change in Egypt's position *vis-à-vis* Israel, from one of confrontation
to one of tentative compromise, has, of course, led to a dramatic change
in the Arab oil exporting countries' aid relationships with Egypt. As
Egypt's policy towards Israel no longer conforms to that desired by the
Arab aid donors, the Arab aid donors, with more or less willingness, have
withdrawn their support to Egypt. Saudi Arabia at first tried to resist this

policy at the Baghdad summit in the spring of 1979, but ultimately she, too, supported the policy proposed by the more radical states of Syria and Iraq. Saudi ambivalence, as will be discussed in Chapter 10, in large measure stems from her perception of contemporary Egypt in her post-Moscow days as a valuable agent of regional stability (Dawisha, 1979). Following President Sadat's visit to Jerusalem in November 1977 Arab aid to Egypt was reduced to only $166 million in 1978. Relationships between Egypt and the Arab aid donors worsened considerably in 1979 following the signing in March of the peace treaty with Israel. At the March Baghdad summit nineteen of the twenty-one Arab League members voted to sever diplomatic relationships with Egypt. All capital transfers (except workers' remittances) and all technical and material aid were to be withdrawn. Prince Sultan Bin Abdel-Aziz, the Saudi Arabian defence minister, speaking about the closure of AOI is reported to have said: 'Egypt's unilateral steps in granting Israel legal and political recognition was, in the view of the leaders of the three participant countries [in AOI] in conflict with the reasons and objectives of setting up the Arab arms industries organization' (*MEED*, 18 May, 1979).

The closure of AOI was accompanied by other sanctions: new Arab aid commitments were immediately stopped; Kuwait gave notice in May that it wished to withdraw its bank deposits in Egypt; Arab trade relationships with Egypt — which are in any case limited — were severed; the headquarters of the Arab League was moved from Cairo; and at the July 1979 Organisation of African Unity summit (held in Liberia) Algeria and Libya, both Arab members of OPEC, tried to have Egypt expelled from the Organisation but they were unsuccessful. Opposition to Israel still persists of course and the Arab response has been to switch their aid to the remaining front line states, Jordan and Syria, by an extraordinary $35 billion.

Saudi Arabia has also used aid to influence political developments in its region in the Arabian Peninsula and the Horn of Africa. Hence, $400 million was committed to Somalia to be drawn once the Russians had left. Two other conservative Arab states — Abu Dhabi (a member of the UAE) and Kuwait — as well as the Arab Fund for Economic and Social Development — have also contributed to Somalia. South Yemen received small amounts of Saudi aid in the mid 1970s as the Saudis tried to weaken the country's links with the communist bloc — alternatively, Chinese and Soviet — but the attempt failed. Along with abortive initiatives with Syria and Algeria, the South Yemen débâcle well illustrates the point made in the Introduction that aid is not a sufficient condition for successful foreign policy. Saudi Arabia and Kuwait have financially supported Mauritania against the Marxist-leaning Polisario Front. But when it seemed that Mauritania was about to make peace with the guerrillas, Kuwait stalled on its aid contributions. It has been pointed out that by channelling its disbursements through selected channels, Saudi Arabia tries to maximise political leverage over its aid in other ways as well. Aid to multilateral institutions such as the World Bank, ABEDA and the Arab Investment Company is dwarfed by Saudi bilateral aid, over which the Saudis exercise independent control. Moreover, Saudi aid is usually given on a one-off basis, rather than, for example, for regular balance of payments support. Thus, Saudi Arabia is in a position regularly to review terms and conditions and even whether to repeat the aid donation whenever recipients make renewed aid requests.

Kuwait has since the early 1960s given large amounts of foreign aid, rising from $130 million in 1970, to $620 million in 1974, to $1.44 billion in 1977. The main political motivation driving this aid is Kuwait's need for international recognition; thus: 'Kuwait can justify her survival as a political entity in this age of regional interventionism only by serving effectively and importantly as a distributor of economic aid to her neighbours. Herein lies Kuwait's raison d'etre' (Shehab, 1964, p. 474).

The motivating factors behind the United Arab Emirates' aid programme are not dissimilar to those behind Kuwait's in that the UAE is also a small state only formed in 1971. Twenty per cent of oil revenues are regularly given as aid, mainly on grant or very soft loan terms. The aid disbursements pattern has been closely aligned with that of Saudi Arabia: the main recipients of the UAE's aid are the front line states against Israel, Egypt again suffering a moritorium after the Baghdad summit; other Arab countries, in particular, neighbouring Oman, North Yemen and Bahrain; and Muslim countries such as Bangladesh, Sudan, Afghanistan and Mauritania.

In Africa outside Egypt the link between Arab oil and the black African countries' position on the Israeli-Palestinian question is of paramount importance. As Chapter 10 explains, most black African countries severed diplomatic relationships with Israel during 1972 and 1973 and have since been induced to support the Arab position — although by no means all of the countries involved in this diplomatic volte-face were convinced of the policy's intrinsic merits. Malawi has not received aid from the Arab Bank for African Economic Development because it has maintained diplomatic relationships with Israel. After the March 1977 Afro-Asian summit (held in Cairo) the Arab aid donors committed an additional $1.5 billion to black African countries following African protests about the low level of Arab aid despite their support of the Arab cause against Israel, and Saudi Arabia is reported to have extended aid to an astonishing range of recipients.

Third World solidarity

The oil exporting countries share with the rest of the Third World a heritage of colonial relationships. Indeed, an irony not lost on African statesmen is the fact that in the Arabs' first incursions into Africa they played the role of slave traders and pillagers. But in the last decade more substantive solidarity with the rest of the Third World has been seen as a way of helping OPEC members in re-forming these relationships. President Boumedienne argued that 'If the Arabs can unify their points of view and capabilities at the lowest common level, and can build with speed and strength an Arab-African bridge, they will be able to change – both politically and economically – their relations with a large number of countries in their favour in record time and in the most fruitful way' (Choucri, 1976, p. 134). Or again, Ali Mohammed Jaidah, former Secretary General of OPEC: 'What is important is OPEC's solidarity with other developing countries towards bringing about the new international economic order' (*Worldview*, 1979, p. 44). As was pointed out above, OPEC members do not like to admit that their aid is a form of compensation for high oil prices. Rather, OPEC members prefer to argue that all Third World countries are deserving of higher export prices and that they support NOPECs to this end.

However, OPEC members are well aware of the danger that high oil prices, without adequate compensations in the form of aid or oil price discounts, might lead the NOPECs to join the developed oil importing countries in open and hostile criticism of OPEC's oil price policy. As early as November 1973, at the OAU extraordinary meeting convened to discuss the oil price rises, the Ghanaian delegation requested cut-price oil for black Africa. At meetings throughout the following years similar pleas were made, with a Tanzanian Minister of State in September 1975 going so far as to suggest that OPEC had 'turned their back on the developing countries'. This question of the balance between OPEC aid disbursements and higher expenditures on oil imports by the NOPECs is examined in statistical terms in the next section.

OPEC aid and the NOPECs' balance of payments deficits

OPEC aid and the current account deficit. If we begin by looking at the financing of the NOPECs' current account balance of payments deficits by capital inflows from the OPEC members it is apparent that the latter countries were aware of the problems faced by the former and made some partly compensatory capital donations. Taking concessional and non-concessional capital flows from OPEC members to the NOPECs as a proportion of the latter's overall current account deficit, OPEC's financing increased from 11.1% in 1973 to 11.5% in 1974 and further increased to 14.9% in 1975, 21.8% in 1976 and 22.5% in 1977. By contrast, official capital flows from DAC countries financed a declining proportion of the NOPECs' current account deficit, from an average of 50% in 1970–2 declining to an average of 36% in 1975–7 (UNCTAD, 1979b).

Table 6.5   *OPEC aid and NOPECs' balance of trade deficits ($ million)*

	1973	1974	1975	1976	1977
NOPECs' trade deficit with OPEC	4,554	16,892	15,319	20,654	20,352
OPEC aid to NOPECs	1,308	3,446	5,516	5,587	5,741
OPEC aid as a percentage of NOPECs' trade deficit with OPEC	28.7	20.4	36.0	27.1	28.2

Source: Table 6.1 and Chapter 5. OPEC aid disbursements include bilateral aid, aid distributed through institutions mainly financed by OPEC countries and aid through multilateral aid institutions such as the World Bank, the IDA and the United Nations.

However, this measure of OPEC's aid performance in relation to the NOPECs' balance of payments problems is too aggregative, for the NOPECs' current account deficit includes their deficits with the industrial countries as well as their large deficits on services account. It would be better, therefore, to compare OPEC aid specifically with the NOPECs' trade deficits with the OPEC members alone. Even so, neither of these aggregative views take into account the uneven geographic distribution of OPEC aid: as has been shown, some NOPECs have fared much better with respect to OPEC aid disbursements than others. Moreover, neither the current account nor the trade account deficits with OPEC show the true financial balance between higher oil prices and OPEC aid. The balance of payments accounts, of course, take into account increased exports to OPEC from the NOPECs and these have helped to pay for the higher cost of imported oil. In order to deal with this problem, OPEC aid should therefore be compared with the additional expenditure on oil imports caused by higher oil prices.

OPEC aid and the trade deficit. Table 6.5 compares OPEC aid with the NOPECs' balance of trade deficit with OPEC during the 1973–7 period inclusive. In fact, OPEC aid disbursements to these countries financed just over one-quarter (27.8%) of the NOPECs' trade deficit with OPEC over this period. In 1973 the difference between the NOPECs' trade deficit with OPEC and OPEC aid disbursements was only $3.2 billion. In 1974 the 'unfinanced' portion increased to $13.5 billion, and although falling to under $10 billion in 1975, it increased to over $15 billion in each of the following two years. This unfinanced part of the trade deficit with OPEC was financed from other sources: official development assistance from OECD countries, private foreign investment inflows, export credits, borrowing from the Eurocurrency markets and non-concessional capital flows from OPEC members.

Table 6.6 NOPECs' domestic consumption of refined oil products not supplied from domestic crude oil production (thousand barrels)

	1972	1973	1974	1975	1976	1977
Africa[a]	96,717	105,549	104,048	101,064	111,053	110,444
Asia[b]	473,247	482,654	443,355	452,168	565,486	534,859
South America[c]	224,607	301,156	346,034	355,607	407,518	425,916
Central America & Caribbean[d]	196,297	228,170	181,664	185,411	193,333	208,432

a Excluding bunkers and Angola, Egypt, Tunisia, Former Equatorial Africa (and Zaire from 1976) as net exporters.
b Excluding bunkers and Brunei, Indonesia and Malaysia (and Burma from 1976).
c Excluding bunkers and Bolivia, Colombia and Trinidad.
d Excluding bunkers.

Source: US Department of Mines, various issues.

OPEC aid and the higher price of oil

NOPECs' oil imports. The NOPECs' domestic consumption of petroleum products *not* supplied from domestic crude oil production is shown in Table 6.6. In other words, Table 6.6 shows the annual volume in barrels of petroleum products consumption that was supplied by net imports of oil either in crude or refined forms.[4] Petroleum products destined for sale to bunkers are excluded – data permitting – on the assumption that a large proportion of these sales would have been to carriers owned by developed country interests.[5]

Table 6.6 covers sixty-seven NOPECs: twenty-six in Africa, seventeen in Asia, ten in South America and fourteen in the Central American and Caribbean areas. In the 1974–7 period inclusive, Africa's net imports of petroleum products amounted to 426.6 million barrels; Asia imported almost 2 billion barrels over the same period; South America 1.54 billion barrels; and Central America and the Caribbean 769 million barrels. Together these sixty-seven NOPECs imported 4.73 billion barrels of petroleum products in the four years 1974–7.

The question arises: how much extra did these oil imports cost because of oil price rises in the 1970s?

Crude oil reference prices. If crude oil prices were 'index linked' to an index of world inflation they should have increased during the 1960s in any event as they had been pegged at $1.80 per barrel between 1960 and 1970.[6] Thus, a proportion of the oil price rises in the 1970s can be considered as correcting for the long period of fixed crude oil prices when industrial country and NOPEC export prices increased.

Additionally there is the question of the base price. In February 1959, the oil companies had deliberately cut crude oil posted prices by $0.18 per barrel and did so again in August 1960 when they took an extra $0.09 per barrel off posted prices, reducing Arabian marker crude to $1.80 per barrel. Naturally, these price reductions caused a great deal of displeasure in the oil exporting countries. As Abdulamir Kubbah commented in 1974: 'In 1970 [Kuwait, Iran, Iraq and Saudi Arabia] were losing, as a result of these price cuts about $1.62 million per day in tax proceeds on a combined production of about 12 million barrels per day' (Kubbah, 1974).

Accordingly, let us take an end-1960 posted price of $1.80 plus $0.27 (equals $2.07) and increase it according to the increase in the index of industrial countries' export prices. Thus, by 1973 the crude oil posted price should have been about 62% higher. The industrial countries' consumer price index also increased by the same amount.[7] Thus, by January 1974 the 'index linked' marker crude oil price would have been $3.36 per barrel. The price of primary commodities other than oil increased by 77% between 1960 and 1973,[8] and had the price of marker crude oil been 'index linked' against this price index, it would have stood at $3.66 per

Table 6.7　*Oil price terms of trade stabilised against industrial countries' export prices and primary product prices*

	1974	1975	1976	1977	1978
Section A					
Percentage rise p.a. in:					
1 Industrial countries export price index	24.7	12.0	0.7	7.9	13.3
2 Industrial countries consumer price index	13.2	10.7	7.9	7.9	6.8
3 The *Economist's* dollar price commodity index	22.6	-13.1	17.6	22.85	-1.95

Section B
Imputed oil price (to stabilise OPEC terms of trade 1960–78) dollars per barrel

	Imputed base price end 1973				
A Industrial country export price index	$3.36	4.19	4.69	4.73	5.1	5.78
B Industrial country consumer price index	$3.36	3.80	4.21	4.54	4.90	5.23
C Primary commodities other than oil	$3.66	4.49	3.90	4.59	5.63	5.52
Actual oil prices (average)	$11.65	11.53	12.38	13.09	12.70

Section C
Actual oil price minus imputed prices (dollars)

		1974	1975	1976	1977	1978
A Index		7.46	6.84	7.65	7.99	6.92
B Index		7.85	7.32	7.84	8.19	7.47
C Index		7.16	7.63	7.79	7.46	7.18

barrel at the end of 1973. In fact, Arabian light marker crude cost $11.65 per barrel in January 1974 – $8.29 higher than if oil prices had kept pace with prices in the industrial countries and $7.99 higher than if they had kept pace with the rise in non-oil primary commodity prices. On this basis, therefore, it could be argued that OPEC's price policy had added about $8 per barrel on to an 'index linked' reference price.

Table 6.7 shows these imputed 'index linked' marker crude oil prices for the 1974–8 period. Imputed prices for three separate price indices are shown in section A. On all three indices the 'index linked' price would have increased to about $5.50 per barrel by 1978 as shown in section B. Finally, section C shows the differences between imputed oil prices and

Table 6.8   *Estimated foreign exchange cost of higher oil prices to NOPECs ($ billion)*

	1974	1975	1976	1977	1974-7
NOPECS					
$4 per barrel extra	4.3	4.4	5.1	5.2	18.9
$6 per barrel extra	6.5	6.6	7.7	7.7	28.4
$8 per barrel extra	8.6	8.8	10.2	10.2	37.8
Africa					
$4 per barrel extra	0.4	0.4	0.4	0.4	1.7
$6 per barrel extra	0.6	0.6	0.7	0.7	2.6
$8 per barrel extra	0.8	0.8	0.9	0.9	3.4
Asia					
$4 per barrel extra	1.8	1.8	2.3	2.1	8.0
$6 per barrel extra	2.7	2.7	3.4	3.2	12.0
$8 per barrel extra	3.5	3.6	4.5	4.3	16.0
South America					
$4 per barrel extra	1.4	1.4	1.6	1.7	6.1
$6 per barrel extra	2.1	2.1	2.4	2.6	9.2
$8 per barrel extra	2.8	2.8	3.3	3.4	12.3
Central America and Caribbean					
$4 per barrel extra	0.7	0.7	0.8	0.8	3.1
$6 per barrel extra	1.0	1.1	1.2	1.3	4.6
$8 per barrel extra	1.5	1.5	1.5	1.7	6.1

Note: Totals may not add due to rounding.

Source: Table 6.6.

actual oil prices. On all three indices actual oil prices were between $7 and $8 higher than the 'index linked' price from 1973 onward.

However, it has been argued that 'the price of 1974 was not totally unjust' (Al-Janabi, 1979). Of course, in economics there is no such thing as 'the fair price'. Even so, OPEC has engineered several oil price increases during the 1970s and these price increases have substantially increased the NOPECs' oil import bills. Accordingly, the incremental cost of NOPECs' net imports of petroleum products has been calculated in Tables 6.8 and 6.9 for 'extra' oil prices of $8, $6 and $4 per barrel.

Additional oil import bills. Taking the NOPECs as a single group, over the four year period 1974-7 they spent an additional $38 billion on imported oil if the extra cost is taken to be $8 per barrel – see Table 6.8. Similarly, at $6 per barrel extra, the additional outlay is $28 billion; and at $4 per barrel $19 billion. Asia suffered the most from the oil price

Table 6.9 *NOPECs: oil imports by volume, additional outlays on oil, and compensatory OPEC aid (thousand barrels and $ million)*

	1973	1974	1975	1976	1977
Asia					
Afghanistan[a] oil imports	3,069	2,990	2,775	2,137	1,808
at $8/barrel extra cost		23.9	22.2	17.1	14.5
$6/barrel extra cost		18.0	16.7	12.8	10.8
$4/barrel extra cost		12.0	11.1	8.5	7.2
OPEC aid	0	28.6	21.6	14.7	88.6
Bangladesh[a] oil imports	5,033	5,414	8,864	9,469	11,237
at $8/barrel extra cost		43.3	70.9	75.8	89.9
$6/barrel extra cost		32.5	53.2	56.8	67.4
$4/barrel extra cost		21.7	35.3	37.9	44.9
OPEC aid	0	34.8	61.1	10.9	168.8
Burma[a] oil imports	9,938	205	580	n.a.	n.a.
at $8/barrel extra cost		1.6	4.6		
$6/barrel extra cost		1.2	3.5		
$4/barrel extra cost		0.8	2.3		
OPEC aid	0	0	0	0	2.2
Fiji oil imports	1,761[b]	1,500	1,648	1,726[b]	1,795
at $8/barrel extra cost		12.0	13.2	13.8	14.4
$6/barrel extra cost		9.0	9.9	10.4	10.8
$4/barrel extra cost		6.0	6.6	6.9	7.2
OPEC aid	0	0	0	0	0

Table 6.9 contd.

	1973	1974	1975	1976	1977
Hong Kong oil imports	26,084[b]	26,801[b]	24,479[b]	29,701[b]	32,427[b]
at $8/barrel extra cost		214.4	195.8	237.6	259.4
$6/barrel extra cost		160.8	146.9	178.2	194.6
$4/barrel extra cost		107.2	97.9	118.8	129.7
OPEC aid	0	0	0	0	0
India oil imports	107,807	110,086[b]	117,769	121,390[b]	124,807
at $8/barrel extra cost		880.7	942.2	971.1	998.5
$6/barrel extra cost		660.5	706.6	728.3	748.8
$4/barrel extra cost		440.3	471.1	485.6	499.2
OPEC aid	0	235.0	203.7	499.6	135.6
South Korea oil imports	99,538[b]	101,653[b]	110,036[b]	126,548[b]	153,716
at $8/barrel extra cost		813.2	880.3	1,012.4	1,229.7
$6/barrel extra cost		609.9	660.2	759.3	922.3
$4/barrel extra cost		406.6	440.1	506.2	614.9
OPEC aid	0	0	0	0	20.8
Malaysia[a] oil imports	1,608	6,372	533	n.a.	n.a.
at $8/barrel extra cost		51.0	4.3		
$6/barrel extra cost		38.2	3.2		
$4/barrel extra cost		25.5	2.1		
OPEC aid	0	0	1.1	1.5	7.5
New Caledonia[a] oil imports	3,649	5,836	5,246	4,492	4,134
at $8/barrel extra cost		46.7	42.0	35.9	33.1
$6/barrel extra cost		35.0	31.5	27.0	24.8
$4/barrel extra cost		23.3	21.0	18.0	16.5
OPEC aid	0	0	0	0	0

Pakistan oil imports	18,553	26,777	22,472	29,947	24,611
at $8/barrel extra cost		214.2	179.8	239.6	196.9
$6/barrel extra cost		160.7	134.8	179.7	147.7
$4/barrel extra cost		107.1	89.9	119.8	98.4
OPEC aid	18.2	328.4	421.2	821.3	69.8
Philippines oil imports	61,245	62,804[b]	68,362	72,609	78,809[b]
at $8/barrel extra cost		502.4	546.9	580.9	630.5
$6/barrel extra cost		376.8	410.2	435.7	472.9
$4/barrel extra cost		251.2	273.4	290.4	315.2
OPEC aid	0	0	0	0	0
Sri Lanka oil imports	5,928[b]	9,790	7,307	7,146	8,319[b]
at $8/barrel extra cost		78.3	58.5	57.2	66.6
$6/barrel extra cost		58.7	43.8	42.9	49.9
$4/barrel extra cost		39.2	29.2	28.6	33.3
OPEC aid	0	0	0	0	0
Taiwan oil imports	64,078	70,521[b]	68,445	92,066[b]	99,172
at $8/barrel extra cost		564.2	547.2	736.5	793.4
$6/barrel extra cost		423.1	410.7	552.4	595.0
$4/barrel extra cost		282.1	273.8	368.3	396.7
OPEC aid	0	0	0	0	0

Table 6.9 contd.

	1973	1974	1975	1976	1977
Thailand[c] oil imports	61,546	64,705	64,331	64,185	67,426
at $8/barrel extra cost		517.6	514.6	513.5	539.4
$6/barrel extra cost		388.2	386.0	385.1	404.6
$4/barrel extra cost		258.8	257.3	256.7	269.7
OPEC aid	0	0	0	75.6	0.3
Latin America					
Argentina oil imports	25,280	23,952	20,668	18,658	10,296
at $8/barrel extra cost		191.6	165.3	149.3	82.4
$6/barrel extra cost		143.7	124.0	111.9	61.8
$4/barrel extra cost		95.8	82.7	74.9	41.2
OPEC aid	0	0	0	0	0
Barbados oil imports	2,006	2,375[b]	1,789	3,325	1,744
at $8/barrel extra cost		19.0	14.3	26.5	14.0
$6/barrel extra cost		14.3	10.7	20.0	10.5
$4/barrel extra cost		9.5	7.2	13.3	7.0
OPEC aid	0	0	0.3	0	0

Brazil oil imports	216,323[b]	234,651[b]	248,440	289,084	306,062
at $8/barrel extra cost		1,877.2	1,987.5	2,312.7	2,448.5
$6/barrel extra cost		1,407.9	1,490.6	1,734.5	1,836.4
$4/barrel extra cost		938.6	993.8	1,156.3	1,224.2
OPEC aid	0	0	0	0	0
Chile[a] oil imports	28,163	25,593	24,408	23,757	24,329
at $8/barrel extra cost		204.7	195.3	190.1	194.6
$6/barrel extra cost		153.6	146.4	142.5	146.0
$4/barrel extra cost		102.4	97.6	95.0	97.3
OPEC aid	0	0	0	0	0
Guyana[a] oil imports	3,506	3,662	4,251	4,027	3,583
at $8/barrel extra cost		29.3	34.0	32.2	28.7
$6/barrel extra cost		22.0	25.5	24.2	21.5
$4/barrel extra cost		14.6	17.0	16.1	14.3
OPEC aid	0	15.0	0	5.0	0
Paraguay[a] oil imports	2,279	2,275	2,178	2,583	3,740
at $8/barrel extra cost		18.2	17.4	20.8	22.4
$6/barrel extra cost		13.7	13.1	15.5	22.4
$4/barrel extra cost		9.1	8.7	10.3	15.0
OPEC aid	0	0	0	0	0

Table 6.9 contd.

	1973	1974	1975	1976	1977
Surinam[d] oil imports	4,581	3,498	4,473	3,776	4,011
at $8/barrel extra cost		28.0	35.8	30.2	32.1
$6/barrel extra cost		21.0	26.8	22.7	24.1
$4/barrel extra cost		14.0	17.9	13.1	16.0
OPEC aid	0	0	0	0	0
Uruguay oil imports	12,081	12,297	12,399	12,670	13,281
at $8/barrel extra cost		98.4	99.2	101.4	106.2
$6/barrel extra cost		73.6	74.4	76.0	79.7
$4/barrel extra cost		49.2	49.6	50.7	53.1
OPEC aid	0	0	0	0	0
Africa					
Oil imports	105,549	104,048	101,064	111,053	110,444
at $8/barrel extra cost		832	809	888	884
$6/barrel extra cost		624	606	666	663
$4/barrel extra cost		416	404	444	442
OPEC aid	699	1,232.9	2,844.5	1,918.8	2,818.7
OPEC aid less Egypt	46.9	373.7	771.8	640.0	697.1

Cameroon oil imports	2,302	2,175	2,455	2,213	2,651
at $8/barrel extra cost		17.4	19.6	17.7	21.2
$6/barrel extra cost		13.1	14.7	13.3	15.9
$4/barrel extra cost		8.7	9.8	8.9	10.6
OPEC aid	0	0	0	0	0
Cape Verde Islands[a] oil imports	1,999	2,120	2,087	n.a.	1,160
at $8/barrel extra cost		17.0	16.7	n.a.	9.3
$6/barrel extra cost		12.7	12.5	n.a.	7.0
$4/barrel extra cost		8.7	8.3	n.a.	4.6
OPEC aid	0	0	0.1	11.8	2.9
Ethiopia[a] oil imports	5,299	5,054	3,801	4,111	3,815
at $8/barrel extra cost		40.4	30.4	32.9	30.5
$6/barrel extra cost		30.3	22.8	24.7	22.9
$4/barrel extra cost		20.2	15.2	16.4	15.3
OPEC aid	0	1.3	15.4	0	2.4
Former West Africa[a] oil imports	14,528[b]	16,122[b]	14,281	16,480[b]	15,521[b]
at $8/barrel extra cost		129.0	114.6	131.8	124.2
$6/barrel extra cost		96.7	85.7	98.9	93.1
$4/barrel extra cost		64.5	57.1	65.9	62.1
OPEC aid	7.7	127.7	88.7	166.0	153.5

Table 6.9 contd.

	1973	1974	1975	1976	1977
Ghana[a] oil imports	6,701	6,614	7,200	7,462	7,392
at $8/barrel extra cost		52.9	57.6	59.7	59.1
$6/barrel extra cost		39.7	43.6	44.8	44.4
$4/barrel extra cost		26.5	28.8	29.8	29.6
OPEC aid	0	0	4.4	0	4.6
Kenya oil imports	8,921	9,141	9,342	12,569	15,702
at $8/barrel extra cost	71.4	73.1	74.7	100.6	125.6
$6/barrel extra cost		54.8	56.1	75.4	94.2
$4/barrel extra cost		36.6	37.4	50.3	62.8
OPEC aid	0	0	3.6	0	5.0
Liberia[a] oil imports	4,399	4,214	4,149	3,819	3,725
at $8/barrel extra cost	35.2	33.7	33.2	30.6	29.8
$6/barrel extra cost		25.3	24.9	22.9	22.4
$4/barrel extra cost		16.9	16.6	15.3	14.9
OPEC aid	0	1.8	1.8	0	0
Malagasy Republic oil imports	5,226	3,486	3,460	3,819	3,446
at $8/barrel extra cost		27.9	27.7	30.6	27.6
$6/barrel extra cost		20.9	20.8	22.9	20.7
$4/barrel extra cost		13.9	13.8	15.3	13.8
OPEC aid	0	0	0	0	0
Morocco oil imports	19,677[b]	19,184[b]	20,763[b]	22,252[b]	25.292[b]
at $8/barrel extra cost		153.5	166.1	178.0	202.3
$6/barrel extra cost		115.1	124.6	133.5	151.8
$4/barrel extra cost		76.7	83.1	89.0	101.2
OPEC aid	0	17.1	99.2	47.4	110.6

Mozambique oil imports	3,414[b]	3,619	3,147	3,266	3,489[b]
at $8/barrel extra cost		29	25.2	26.1	27.9
$6/barrel extra cost		21.7	18.9	19.6	20.9
$4/barrel extra cost		14.5	12.6	13.1	14.0
OPEC aid	0	0	2.1	27.6	3.4
Sierra Leone oil imports	1,701	1,918	1,040	1,068	824
at $8/barrel extra cost		15.3	8.3	8.5	6.6
$6/barrel extra cost		11.5	6.2	6.4	4.9
$4/barrel extra cost		7.7	4.2	4.3	3.3
OPEC aid	0	1.9	1.8	0.2	1.1
Somalia[a] oil imports	834	804	631	1,518	1,892
at $8/barrel extra cost		6.4	5.0	12.1	15.1
$6/barrel extra cost		4.8	3.8	9.1	11.4
$4/barrel extra cost		3.2	2.5	6.1	7.6
OPEC aid	5.5	49.6	80.4	37.5	187.4
Sudan oil imports	6,540	6,436	6,734	7,566	12,972
at $8/barrel extra cost		51.5	53.9	60.5	103.8
$6/barrel extra cost		38.6	40.4	45.4	77.8
$4/barrel extra cost		25.7	26.9	30.3	51.9
OPEC aid	3.3	80.0	188.2	257.0	119.3
Tanzania oil imports	6,685	4,533	5,195	7,919	5,222
at $8/barrel extra cost		36.3	41.6	63.4	41.8
$6/barrel extra cost		27.2	31.2	47.5	31.3
$4/barrel extra cost		18.1	20.8	31.7	20.9
OPEC aid	0	0	0	0	0

Table 6.9 contd.

	1973	1974	1975	1976	1977
Zaire oil imports	5,952	5,296	5,096	e	e
at $8/barrel extra cost		42.4	40.8		
$6/barrel extra cost		31.8	30.6		
$4/barrel extra cost		21.2	20.4		
OPEC aid	0	0	12.4	0	2.2
Zambia oil imports	5,513	6,219	6,219	6,613	5,921
at $8/barrel extra cost		49.8	49.8	52.9	47.4
$6/barrel extra cost		37.3	37.3	39.7	35.5
$4/barrel extra cost		24.9	24.9	26.5	23.7
OPEC aid	0	1.9	12.7	0	0.3

a Bunkers not deducted.
b Estimated from bunkers for other years.
c Bunkers negligible throughout.
d Bunkers in 1977 were negligible, but adjustments for bunkers in other years
   have not been made.
e Zaire became a net exporter in 1976.

Notes
As a part of bunkers will be consumed by flags of developed country fleets, where possible, bunkers have been deducted from the data for domestic consumption including bunkers. If anything, this adjustment will tend to understate the non-oil exporting less developed countries' consumption of oil as a part of bunker is used by flags of these countries.
   Where a non-oil exporting less developed country imports refined petroleum products it is assumed that the whole value of the extra oil cost is passed on to the importing nation.

Sources: Calculations drawn upon data in US Department of Mines, *International Petroleum Annual*, various issues, and UNCTAD (1979b).

increases, having to pay an additional $16 billion for imported oil (at $8 per barrel extra); South America $12 billion; Central America and the Caribbean $6 billion; and Africa $3.4 billion. These outlays are, of course, correspondingly lower if the extra cost of the imported oil is reduced (see Table 6.8).

Country basis. Interesting conclusions on the relationship between the extra cost of imported petroleum products and OPEC aid can be drawn if the balance between the two is presented for individual countries.

Africa actually received more OPEC aid in the 1973–7 period than it had to spend on additional outlays on imported petroleum products, even if the extra cost is taken to be $8 per barrel. However, this observation must be qualified owing to the high proportion of OPEC aid disbursements to Egypt. Setting Egypt aside, in *no* single year did the rest of Africa receive as much OPEC aid as it paid out in additional oil import costs at $8 per barrel extra. This total extra cost of net imported petroleum products minus disbursed OPEC aid in 1974–7 was $930 million. However, if the extra cost of oil is put at $6 per barrel, OPEC aid exceeded the addition to the oil import bill in two of these four years (even so the Africans still paid out $76 million more than they received in OPEC aid). At $4 per barrel extra cost, OPEC aid disbursements to Africa (excluding Egypt) was greater than the additional outlay on imported oil by $777 million.

At the country level, it is even more apparent that the OPEC aid donors have not treated African NOPECs evenly. Table 6.10 shows thirteen of these countries whose additional petroleum products net import bill (at $6 per barrel extra cost) exceeded OPEC aid disbursements by between $26 million and $272 million in the 1974–7 period. However, the reverse was true in the case of Egypt ($7.0 billion in aid with zero net import bill), Somalia ($29 million net gainer) and Sudan ($202 million net gainer).

Of the fourteen Asian NOPECs, ten received no or negligible amounts of disbursed OPEC aid, as Table 6.9 shows. Only Afghanistan, Bangladesh, India and Pakistan were significant OPEC aid recipients. The three Muslim countries among these were net gainers in the OPEC aid – higher oil import bill calculus. India, however, was a large net loser. For example, the extra petroleum products import bill (at $6 per barrel extra) averaged $711 million between 1974 and 1977 while OPEC aid disbursements averaged only $268 million. Of the others, South Korea and Taiwan received no OPEC aid to compensate for very large additional petroleum products import bills. For example, in 1977 in South Korea's case, the additional bill was over $900 million even at $6 per barrel extra cost, and in Taiwan's case nearly $600 million was added to the import bill. On this basis, Thailand and the Philippines also suffered badly.

Finally, of the eight Latin American NOPECs listed in Table 6.9 none except Guyana received any OPEC aid and even in this one case the dis-

Table 6.10   *Additional expenditure on petroleum product net imports and OPEC aid disbursements, 1974–7*

	Additional petroleum products import bill (at $6 per barrel extra) minus OPEC aid $ million
Cameroon	57
Cape Verde Islands	56
Ethiopia	82
Ghana	164
Kenya	272
Liberia	92
Malagasy Republic	85
Morocco	251
Mozambique	48
Sierra Leone	24
Tanzania	137
Zaire	43
Zambia	135

Source: Table 6.9.

bursement was small. Brazil is in the unfortunate position of having the greatest additional petroleum products import bill at $1.8 billion ($6 per barrel extra cost) in 1977. All the other Latin American countries fared much less badly.

Turning now to consider the trade-off between aid and higher oil prices as it has emerged since 1973, Table 6.9 indicates above all the contrasts between three groups of oil importing ldcs. On the other hand there is a set of four ldcs which were more than compensated for their extra outlays on oil (Afghanistan, Bangladesh, Somalia and Sudan). In addition to having fairly clear regional importance to the Arab aid donors, these four countries also share Muslim sympathy. Next is a group of eleven ldcs which received some aid to mitigate the oil price rises, which emerged nonetheless as net losers to OPEC. Among this group[9] are six countries in the below-$300 GNP per capita group as distinguished by the World Bank. Finally, there is a set of twenty ldcs which received no aid in return for the higher price of oil.[10] Of these twenty, six are particularly low-income countries. Using this fairly rough criterion of measured GNP per capita as an indicator of the distributive aspect of OPEC aid, then, Figure 6.1 was drawn up. This shows diagrammatically the relationship between the OPEC aid recipients' GNP per capita and the extent of the aid obtained over 1974–7. Lack of data prevent a fuller account of this relationship to be made: Figure 6.1 does nonetheless reveal a vague tendency for aid to be disbursed in line with this proxy for need. A more sophisticated measure for the same relationship is provided in Figure 6.2.

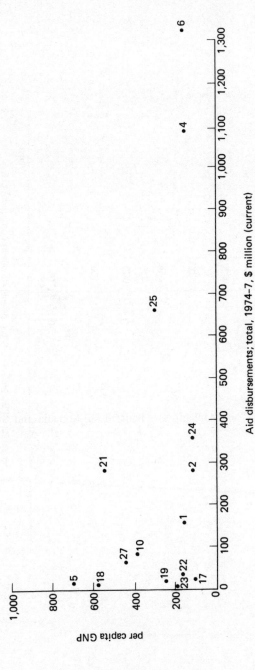

Figure 6.1   *Receipts of OPEC aid and recipients' per capita GNP*

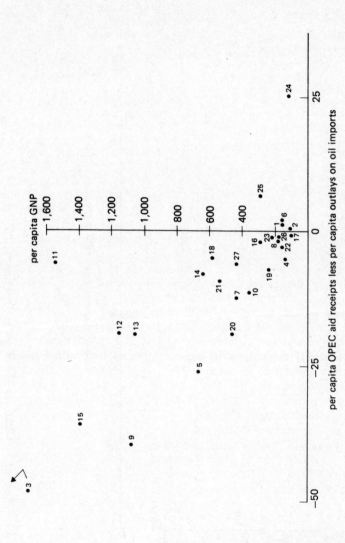

Figure 6.2 Net balance between OPEC aid receipts per capita and extra per capita outlays on oil imports at $8 per barrel

Key to Figures 6.1 and 6.2

Figure 6.1: Countries not shown are those which received no OPEC aid. These are: Hong Kong, Philippines, Sri Lanka, Taiwan, Argentina, Brazil, Chile, Paraguay, Uruguay, Cameroon, Tanzania.

1	Afghanistan	15	Uruguay
2	Bangladesh	16	Cameroon
3	Hong Kong	17	Ethiopia
4	India	18	Ghana
5	South Korea	19	Kenya
6	Pakistan	20	Liberia
7	Philippines	21	Morocco
8	Sri Lanka	22	Mozambique
9	Taiwan (Republic of China)	23	Sierra Leone
10	Thailand	24	Somalia
11	Argentina	25	Sudan
12	Brazil	26	Tanzania
13	Chile	27	Zambia
14	Paraguay		

This shows the difference between the aid received from OPEC and the additional oil outlays paid to OPEC, assuming an extra $8 per barrel is the notional price rise.[11] When this difference, aggregated over the years 1974–7, is divided by the 1976 population and then ranged against the estimated GNP per capita for the same year, Figure 6.2 is obtained. Again a roughly consistent relationship between the poverty of each NOPEC and the net oil/aid welfare effect is observed, with those countries with significantly higher than average GNP per capita (for example, Hong Kong, observation number 3; Uruguay, observation number 15) suffering relatively more from the higher oil prices. Two further points can be made about this relationship. First, to a large extent the countries in Figure 6.2 which are located near the top left of the first quadrant typically received no OPEC aid whatsoever; their position is therefore simply a reflection of their enlarged oil bill. Secondly, far from trying to impute some form of intentional motive of rough distributive justice to the pattern of OPEC aid, it is possible to argue that the results summarised in Figure 6.2 indicate not so much the intended outcome of an aid policy as the inevitable results of ldcs' differing industrial structure. For ldcs with substantial heavy manufacturing and processing capacity naturally use more oil energy in total than those with less sophisticated economies relying more upon indigenous energy like firewood fuel.

Turning finally to appraise the net cost of higher oil prices balanced against aid flows, the extra resource cost imposed by OPEC's price policy can be expressed as a percentage of per capita GNP. Thus, the figures used to draw up Figures 6.1 and 6.2 can be reworked to indicate the implied proportion of GNP per capita that had to be allocated over 1974–7 to OPEC. The average figure for this is 0.18%. If Egypt is excluded from the calculations the figure rises sharply to 0.4%.[12] The greatest per capita gain, that of Somalia, amounts to 5.5%; the greatest cost, that of Liberia, is equivalent to 1.1% of GNP.

Conclusions

It has been argued in this chapter that the main reasons for the impressively rapid growth of OPEC's foreign aid programmes are to be found in the relationship between the high expected returns and the relatively low cost of these aid programmes. OPEC aid is mainly disbursed from burgeoning foreign exchange reserves which would otherwise earn a negative rate of return in inflation-prone Western, mainly American, financial centres. On the other hand, the expected political advantages that the OPEC aid donors expect to obtain from their aid programmes are large. The Persian Gulf states are situated in an area of political instability. Saudi Arabia, growing in awareness of its potential as the main regional power, has used its aid to influence developments in nearby countries such as Somalia, North and South Yemen and Oman. Iran, as another important regional power until 1979, used its aid similarly. Kuwait and the UAE, as small vulnerable states, have used their aid in the interests of 'winning friends'. Moreover, and more important than these factors, Arab aid has been channelled to the front-line states against Israel on a massive scale, with Egypt, Syria and Jordan having been the main beneficiaries. Some Arab aid has also been disbursed to other Muslim countries *qua* Muslim countries. Aid to non-Muslim NOPECs has been on a small scale, presumably because the political benefits are viewed as relatively minor by the OPEC donor countries. None of this latter group of countries has received more OPEC aid disbursements than was paid out in increased oil import bills. Despite the often stated view by OPEC members that they are a part of the Third World, it is becoming clear that they in fact have to a large extent differentiated themselves from the rest of the Third World. And correspondingly it seems to be inevitable that the rest of the Third World will begin more loudly to voice its criticism of high oil prices or to request much higher OPEC aid as the price of its support for OPEC's oil price policy and the Arabs' policy towards Israel.

Notes

1 The data used here has been taken from UNCTAD (1979b). Owing to differences in reporting practices, OPEC aid is not exactly known. However, the disparity between OPEC aid data as reported by UNCTAD and the OECD is relatively small. For a discussion see Shihata and Mabro (1979).
2 The shares of bilateral aid in total OPEC aid disbursements were: 100% in 1973; 90% in 1974: 92% in 1975; 88% in 1976 and 65% in 1977.

3   The members of GODE were Saudi Arabia, Kuwait, United Arab Emirates and Qatar.

4   When the oil has been imported in a refined form it is assumed here that the whole value of the crude oil price increases that occurred in the 1970s have been passed on to the NOPEC importers.

5   In some cases the data for bunkers is unavailable. Accordingly, the data in Table 6.6 will tend to overstate net oil imports for use by NOPEC residents. However, there are two mitigating factors: first, the volume of oil for bunkers in the NOPECs is small in relation to total domestic consumption of oil. (Data for bunkers supplied by such large bunkers suppliers as Panama Canal Zone and Singapore is available and has been deducted.) Secondly, understatement of the volume of bunkers is to some extent offset by the fact that some bunkers sales are to carriers owned by residents of the NOPECs themselves.

6   Arabian light 34° marker crude.

7   The industrial countries export price and consumer price indices are taken from IMF, *International Financial Statistics*, various issues.

8   Reuter's commodity price index.

9   Consisting of: India, Pakistan, Cape Verde Islands, Ethiopia, Ghana, Kenya, Liberia, Morocco, Mozambique, Sierra Leone and Zambia.

10 After 1977 two of them did begin receiving a little aid. These were Burma and South Korea. The links between the latter country and the Middle East are discussed in Chapter 7 on trade relationships.

11 In other words, this is the same procedure as was used for drawing up Table 6.9.

12 The sample of ldcs involved here is twenty-seven.

7

The Growth of Trade between OPEC and the Developing Countries

In December 1973 it seemed that most countries of the developing world had been dealt such a severe body-blow that their prospects were grimmer than ever before. The effects of the quadrupling of the oil price during 1973 — that 'wave of potentially disruptive structural change' (Cohen, 1978), that 'explosion in north—south economic relations' that was to be 'a critical turning point in history' (Gardner *et al.*, 1974) — could hardly be overstated. Yet six years later one finds that the ldcs as a group were exporting close to $10 billion worth *more* goods to the OPEC countries than they were in 1973, and that ten of the biggest ldc trade partners with OPEC *improved* their trade balance with OPEC between 1973 and 1978. Moreover, one finds that ldcs' share of all OPEC imports has risen by 50% since 1972 and nearly doubled over the period 1974—8. Clearly these facts, which reveal a complex evolving pattern of OPEC—ldc trade over the years since the 1973 oil price-rise, deserve some elaboration.

In the Introduction it was suggested that one reason for the success of certain ldcs in selling goods to OPEC was the deliberate effort by OPEC to channel orders that way. Later in this chapter it will be shown that price alone is sufficient to explain the success of the Asian ldcs in selling construction and certain joint venture projects to OPEC clients in the Middle East. But in other cases the price advantage of non-oil ldcs is not so apparent. Here it may be that the commitment by several OPEC spokesmen to fostering intra-ldc solidarity and trade links is more than mere rhetoric.

As Chapter 4 indicated, the overall OPEC—ldc trade gap widened markedly in 1974, fell in 1975, opened again in 1976 and then again tailed off somewhat in 1977—8. Most recently, after the increases in oil prices throughout 1979, the gap has again opened up. Figures 7.1 and 7.2 illustrate these trends and also show how OPEC members increased their imports from both dcs and ldcs after 1973. The latter phenomenon, the concern of this chapter, is examined first in terms of regional ldc trade balances.

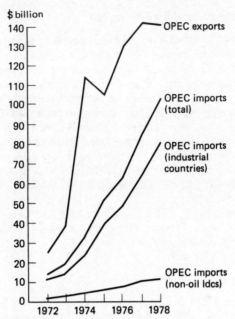

Figure 7.1   *OPEC Foreign Trade* $ billions

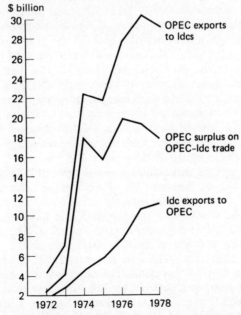

Figure 7.2   *OPEC foreign trade with non-oil exporting ldcs* $ billions

The payments balance considered by region

The increase in ldcs' exports to OPEC countries was, predictably, not shared equally between regions. The two most significant changes which occurred in the 1972–8 period were the halving in importance of the non-oil Middle East countries[1] from 27% of total ldc exports to OPEC in 1972 to 13% by 1978; and the rise in the importance of non-oil Asian countries,[2] from providing 48% of all ldcs' exports to OPEC states to providing 65% six years later. Table 7.1 presents these trends. The greatest rises in export value were those of the Asian group (a 907% rise) and the non-oil Western hemisphere ldcs[3] (a 904% rise). These increases compare with an overall ldc export increase to OPEC of 673%, and an increase in intra-OPEC trade of 1,197%. The smallest rise was that of the non-oil African ldcs,[4] with 253%.

The major rise in exports from non-oil Asian ldcs reflects the extremely rapid build-up in trade between OPEC and a few particularly dynamic countries – chiefly those identified in Chapter 1.

The dynamic exporters

Just as it was explained in Chapter 1 that some ten ldcs between them accounted for nearly 90% of the increase in ldcs' manufacturing value added over 1966–75, so it is true here too that a small set of ldcs dominates the export drive with OPEC. Table 7.2 shows the thirteen ldcs most involved. As might be expected, seven of the thirteen shown here are also among the ten which provided the bulk of the overall manufacturing growth in the prior years. The seven are Argentina, Brazil, Hong Kong, Mexico, Singapore, South Korea and Thailand. The Republic of China (Taiwan), which figures prominently here, would also show in the growth of manufacturing data if she were recognised by the UN and included in its statistics. The most modest increase in export value in this group (in current US $) is that of Mexico, with a 220% increase; the greatest is South Korea's, at 7,558%. For each dollar of exports from South Korea to OPEC in 1972, by 1978 there were $75.5-worth. Together, these thirteen ldcs increased their export earnings from OPEC trade by $8,727 million over 1972–8; this was 90% of the increase achieved by all ldcs together, which totalled $9,706 million.

The extent to which these thirteen were able to cover their imports from OPEC after 1973 is shown next in Table 7.3. This indicates that nine of the thirteen (eight of them in Asia) were able to increase their export/import ratio with OPEC over the years 1973–8; while Brazil was able to keep its more or less stable. The three countries among this dynamic exporting group that suffered a substantial fall in their net payments position with OPEC were Argentina (which in fact ran a net surplus with OPEC except for 1974 and 1978), Columbia (which was still running a

Table 7.1   Ldc regional exports to OPEC, 1972–8 ($ million) and shares of Total by region (percentages)

	1972	%	1973	%	1974	%	1975	%	1976	%	1977	%	1978	%	% increase 1972–1978
All non-oil ldcs	1,694		2,860		4,541		5,970		7,723		10,803		11,400		673
Non-oil West. Hemp.	218	13	465	16	868	19	1,313	22	1,452	19	2,248	21	1,971	17	904
Non-oil Mid. East	456	27	662	23	1,113	25	1,341	22	1,610	21	1,881	17	1,528	13	335
Non-oil Asia	814	48	1,403	49	2,157	48	2,870	48	4,287	56	6,103	56	7,378	65	907
Non-oil Africa	207	12	330	12	403	9	446	7	375	5	572	5	524	5	253
(COMECON)	653	100	1,054	100	1,764	100	2,009	100	1,994	100	2,498	100	2,677	100	410
OPEC intra-trade	149		275		605		863		1,571		1,876		1,783		1,197

Source: Calculated from IMF, Direction of Trade, various issues.

Table 7.2 The ten major ldc trading partners with OPEC, 1972–8 ($ million)

	1972	1973	1974	1975	1976	1977	1978	% of total (1978)	% increase 1972–8
South Korea	19	37	146	215	388	749	1,436	15	7,558
India	146	100	379	701	1,065	1,391	1,498	14	1,026
Taiwan	42	79	208	320	440	763	1,138	11	2,710
Brazil	53	230	461	667	582	874	938	9	1,770
Hong Kong	127	291	307	346	463	622	897	8	706
Singapore	132	202	358	494	795	926	903	8	684
China	165	270	515	552	661	823	865	7	524
Bahrain	31	62	106	113	244	368	482	5	1,555
Thailand	49	100	236	144	322	469	515	5	1,051
Pakistan	72	169	230	201	285	378	432	4	600
Argentina	24	82	181	202	198	378	258	2	1,075
Colombia	17	17	40	96	120	159	175	2	1,029
Mexico	56	45	49	76	79	121	123	1	220
								100	

Source: Calculated from UNCTAD (1978a). Countries selected were those with growth of exports to OPEC exceeding 500%, plus Mexico.

Table 7.3   *Selected ldcs' balance of trade with OPEC; exports to OPEC as a percentage of imports from OPEC members*

	1972	1973	1974	1975	1976	1977	1978
Argentina	56	132	61	115	225	109	77
Brazil	13	29	17	25	16	25	28
Colombia	283	213	235	417	250	123	142
Mexico	140	43	42	106	293	11	439
Bahrain	25	32	15	18	34	39	56
Taiwan	29	41	29	43	36	54	67
Hong Kong	310	582	320	481	609	1,244	1,281
India	64	48	31	58	85	126	142
South Korea	11	12	12	16	24	35	64
Pakistan	111	184	62	59	70	78	95
Singapore	28	25	17	23	33	28	31
Thailand	48	59	49	24	44	62	85
China	917	844	858	1,127	3,005	1,005	1,169
All non-oil ldcs	30	34	22	26	25	31	34

Source: Calculated from UNCTAD (1978a).

healthy surplus with OPEC by 1978) and Pakistan (which has been grad-ually clawing back to balance since 1974).

The question arises as to whether these thirteen ldcs made a special effort to export more to their OPEC trade partners or whether their rapid increase of exports to OPEC is merely part of a wider-spread export effort on their part. Table 7.4 shows the share of exports to OPEC countries as a proportion of these ldcs' total exports, and suggests that while the share of OPEC in total exports rose in each of the thirteen cases except Mexico, it rose by no more than all ldcs' average in five of these cases. The aggregate increase in exports of ldcs to OPEC as a proportion of all exports of ldcs was from 3% in 1972 to 7% in 1978. This increase (233%) was exceeded by Brazil (700%), Singapore (500%), Argentina (400%), Korea (400%), India (280%), Colombia (250%) and Pakistan (245%). The overall ldc effort to export to OPEC countries did, however, outweigh that of all industrial countries in aggregate (with a 225% increase). For India, Korea and Pakistan, then, OPEC by 1978 had obviously come to be an extremely significant trade partner, and the trade between these particular ldcs and OPEC countries is analysed in more detail in a later section.

Some OPEC members were more assiduous in cultivating their ldc trade links than others. Figure 7.3 shows that every OPEC member increased its imports from ldcs in current dollar terms, but the countries which in-creased this value fastest were the United Arab Emirates and Saudi Arabia. They achieved annual average growth rates of imports from ldcs of 68.2% and 54.3% respectively. By so doing they also increased their share of total OPEC imports from ldcs, as Table 7.5 shows. Only three OPEC countries

Table 7.4   *Selected ldcs' exports to OPEC: share of OPEC in their total exports, 1972 and 1978, by value*

	1972	1978
	%	%
Argentina	1	4
Brazil	1	7
Colombia	2	5
Mexico	3	2
Bahrain	14	30
Taiwan	5	8
Hong Kong	5	8
India	5	14
Korea	3	12
Pakistan	11	27
Singapore	1	5
Thailand	5	11
China	6	10
EEC	4	9
All non-oil ldcs	3	7

Source: Calculated from UNCTAD (1979b).

substantially changed their share in all OPEC imports from ldcs: apart from the cases of UAE and Saudi Arabia just mentioned, Iraq showed a sharp drop from 10% to 4% of the total, a reflection of her low rate of increase of imports, 21.7%.

Imputing causality to these trends is extremely difficult. Was it an accident that Saudi Arabia and UAE sharply increased the share of their foreign orders going to ldcs? Was it a reflection of explicit strategy to draw OPEC countries closer to other ldcs? Or was this change contingent upon quite different factors? In the last case, one might expect the product composition of OPEC imports to have been important in dictating the relative weight of trade partners. Given the increasing dominance of manufactured goods in the overall output and export mix of the ldcs listed in Table 7.2, might it be the case that these countries were sought as trade partners not for themselves but simply because they exported a particular mix of goods?

The product structure of OPEC imports from non-OPEC ldcs can as yet only be analysed for the early period 1973–6.[5] The conclusions drawn from these figures can therefore only be tentative. The interesting point which emerges from the 1973–6 data, however, is that manufactured goods (SITC 5 to 8 less 67 and 68) did not play any greater part in OPEC countries' imports from the non-oil ldcs at the end of the period than at the beginning. On the contrary, their share fell steadily. This finding

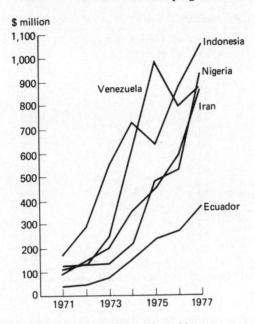

Figure 7.3 (a)   *OPEC members' imports from ldcs*

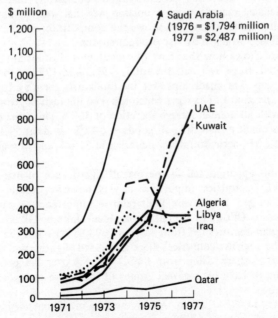

Figure 7.3 (b)   *OPEC members' imports from ldcs*

Table 7.5   *OPEC member countries' imports from ldcs, 1971–7*

	Annual Average Growth Rate of Increase	Share of Total OPEC Imports from ldcs	
	%	1971 %	1977 %
Algeria	40.6	5	4
Indonesia	34.9	16	11
Iran	42.1	10	9
Iraq	21.7	10	4
Kuwait	42.4	9	8
Libya	31.0	7	4
Nigeria	40.9	11	10
Qatar	32.2	1	1
Saudi Arabia	54.3	15	24
UAE	68.2	3	9
Venezuela	44.9	9	9
Ecuador	44.8	4	4
		100	100

Source: Calculated from IMF, *Direction of Trade*, various issues

seems to stand in contrast to the conclusions regarding the country composition of OPEC–ldc trade, which showed conclusively that it was the
fast-industrialising manufactures exporting ldcs that were dominating the
growth of that trade. Figure 7.4 shows the composition of OPEC imports
from non-oil ldcs arranged by five product groups.

This figure shows how the share of manufactured goods in this flow of
trade has fallen from over half the total – 51.2% in 1973 – to 44.4% by
1975. The gap was made up first by foodstuffs then by fuels. Fuels
(SITC 3) is the group of exports which has seen the highest growth rate in
this trade, with an annual average accretion of 360%. The other categories
grew far less quickly than this: all goods at 64.1%; foods at 59.4%; manufactures at 52.8%; agricultural raw materials at 51.0%; and ores and metals
at 43.6%.

Despite this apparent fall in the overall significance of manufactured
goods in OPEC countries' imports from ldcs, however, certain groups of
ldcs have managed to increase their relative importance as suppliers of
manufactures to OPEC. In overall terms, ldcs' share of OPEC countries'
imports of manufactures fell from 8.6% in 1973 to 7.1% in 1975 and 6.5%
in 1976. (The socialist countries' share also eased slightly, with the developed countries' share rising from 84% to 87.8% over the period.) This
overall seems to have hit regional groups of ldcs more or less equally, as
Table 7.6 shows.

The figures in Table 7.6 do reveal the falls in the overall ldcs' manufactures market share in OPEC markets being shared reasonably equally.

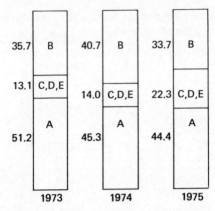

Code
A   manufactures - SITC 5 to 8 less 67 and 68
B   all foods - SITC 0 + 1 + 22 + 4
C   agricultural raw materials - SITC 2 − (22 + 27 + 28)
D   ores and metals - SITC 27 + 28 + 67 + 68
E   fuels - SITC 3

Figure 7.4   *Commodity Structure of OPEC Members' Imports from ldcs*

They also, however, disguise the success of the South and South-East Asian group in increasing the value of its manufactures sales in OPEC markets. Table 7.7 shows these sales over the period 1970–6 and contrasts them with the record of the three other regional groupings used earlier in this chapter. Not only did the South and South-East Asian group's share in the ldcs' total rise, from 58% in 1973 to 71% in 1976, but its absolute increase, as measured in current dollars ($1,405 million f.o.b.), was the largest too.

Interestingly, the emerging patterns of OPEC–ldc trade as just outlined do not, it seems, reflect the wider trends of intra-developing bloc trade. A brief discussion of this is presented here before the chapter turns to look

Table 7.6 *Ldcs' share in OPEC imports of manufactures, total and regional shares, 1973–6*

	All non-oil ldcs' share %	American ldcs %	African ldcs %	West Asia %	S. and SE. Asia %
1973	8.6	1.1	0.6	2.8	5.0
1974	9.0	1.2	0.6	3.2	5.0
1975	7.1	0.9	0.4	2.1	4.1
1976	6.5	0.8	0.2	2.1	4.6

Sources: UNCTAD (1978a), p. 76; UNCTAD (1979b), p. 108.

Table 7.7 *Non-oil ldcs' shares in ldcs' total manufactures exports to OPEC, 1970–6, by region ($ million current, f.o.b.)*

	All ldcs	Developing America	Developing Africa	Developing West Asia	Developing S. and SE. Asia
1970	310	18	17	86	185
1971	380	24	22	105	235
1972	550	40	34	180	340
1973	840	61	55	265	530
1974	1,420	94	88	495	840
1975	1,690	92	83	495	1,170
1976	2,050	120	115	480	1,590

Source: UNCTAD (1979b), pp. 764–6.

at one unmistakably successful trade link – that of construction contracts in OPEC members. In the 1970s the pace of trade between ldcs increased markedly. In the 1950s and 1960s it was consistently the slowest-growing component of aggregate world trade flows but from an 8.3% annual average growth over 1965–70 intra-ldc trade took off and by 1970–6 was rising at 35.9% per year, with 1973/4 alone showing a 107% increase. The oil price rises in 1973 distort these figures, however, but if non-fuel trade is analysed separately it transpires that the annual average growth over 1970–6 was still 24%. Manufactures were the fastest-growing component of this trade flow, with their share in total intra-ldc trade value rising from 25.2% in 1955 to 46.3% in 1975 (UNCTAD, 1978a). Table 7.8 indicates the rising share of manufactures in total intra-ldc trade value over the 1960–75 period, and the fact that the rise in fuel trade values was so great that it pushed the share of manufactures in total intra-ldc trade down between 1970 and 1975.

OPEC work for ldc contractors

The aspect of OPEC members' development effort which has perhaps attracted the greatest comment in the West has been construction projects. In scale, speed of execution and technical daring many of these

Table 7.8 *Intra-ldc Trade, 1960–75*

	1960	1970	1975
Fuels as a percentage of total intra-ldc trade	37	34	54
Manufactures percentage	17	28	21
Manufactures as a percentage of total non-fuel intra-ldc trade	27	42	46

Source: UNCTAD (1978a).

projects have made an enormous impression upon foreign commentators. But a less well known aspect of this development, particularly since 1976 or so, has been the greatly increased resort, on the part of OPEC Middle Eastern states, to ldc partners in these projects. In the period immediately after the 1973 oil price-rises, most OPEC countries looked to developed country firms and consortia to build their infrastructure. A large number of extremely high value contracts were arranged, totalling some $24 billion by 1976. Of this total, $3.2 billion was for housing, $2.2 billion for public buildings, $3.7 billion for highways and bridges and $2 billion for harbours and airports. Relying on long-established links, British, French and American firms were the early winners; but afterwards contracts were distributed more widely. Since 1974 Yugoslavia (buses in Kuwait, bridges in Sudan, and so on), Greece (roads and harbours in Saudi Arabia), Cyprus (joint ventures in Saudi housing) and Australia (cold storages) have won shares. The size of the market in individual countries grew very rapidly. For building materials and construction machinery alone, the market in UAE, Iran, Saudi Arabia, Kuwait, Libya and Iraq doubled between 1973 and 1975, from around $2 billion to $4.2 billion (EIU, 1979).

Quite rapidly, however, disillusion set in. It was increasingly felt by OPEC clients that they were being overcharged, both in international trade consignments and in tenders for projects within the Middle East, and in 1977 the Saudi minister of industry and electricity toured Pakistan, India, South Korea and Japan to appraise how far contractors there could help in the next five year plan. Other OPEC countries reacted by ordering more from ldc-based consortia. Tenders were more frequently re-evaluated and by 1979 the Saudis at least felt that they had put a stop to the days of 'unrealistic and opportunist prices' (*MEED*, 13 July 1979).

The boom year for South Korea was 1978, which yielded $9 billion-worth of contracts. In 1978 contracts totalling $2 billion for housing work were won by South Korean firms, and early in 1979 they obtained a further $636 million-worth of housing work in Saudi Arabia (*Saudi Newsletter*, 18 June 1979). Similarly in Kuwait, South Korean firms obtained nearly half the major construction projects over 1976–9.

A notable aspect of this entry by ldc firms into OPEC tendering is the extent of price competitiveness between ldc companies, and the speed with which the initiative has passed down the chain, as it were, from the relatively high-labour-cost ldcs such as South Korea towards the lower-cost sources such as India, Pakistan and even Mainland China. By early 1979 India was regularly gaining housing contracts in Kuwait, as was Pakistan. Labour costs will clearly differ substantially between these sources, with South Korean labourers in the Middle East earning (in 1979 dollars) some $800 per month, as against a prevailing rate of perhaps $300 for Indians. But the willingness of ldc governments to subsidise their national firms' tenders has also been crucial. South Korean firms have lately enjoyed easy access to credit (9% 'promotion loans', which are considerably cheaper than normal loans), a 50% tax rebate on revenues remitted, and tax exemption for five years on construction materials exports (*MEED*, 16 March 1979). The army in South Korea has also helped to train skilled workers, some 5,000 annually. Men are allowed an early discharge from the South Korean army if they agree to work on overseas projects.

One aspect of the low prices seen at bids for OPEC contracts involving Taiwanese government-owned firms is the overwhelming desire to retain good commercial relations and thence diplomatic recognition. Taiwan has only twenty-one diplomatic partners left following the resumption by the USA of diplomatic relations with China in late 1978, and this makes the retention of official recognition by Saudi Arabia — by far Taiwan's biggest Middle East market — an imperative of commercial diplomacy. The joint committee between the two countries has recently been upgraded, and Saudi Arabian officials have made clear their satisfaction with their tie with Taiwan. But the price has been high: the celebrated Al-Baha power project, which cost $160 million, was referred to by the chairman of Taipower, the contractor, as 'virtual aid' (*MEED*, 27 July 1979). In general Taiwan is not keen to compete with South Korea solely on price terms, but this was a prestige venture and a delicate moment.

As a result of the aggressive entry by lower wage-cost countries, South Korean firms above all are increasingly obliged to look to high technology contracts, where their quickly rising labour costs will not put them at a disadvantage against such competitors as Indian or Pakistani firms. Examples are the £170 million electrification scheme in the southern Asir region of Saudi Arabia built by Hyundai Construction, and Korean firms' supplying 585 bulldozers and other heavy construction equipment to Saudi Arabia in 1979. One form of defence which came to be increasingly used by Western firms is subcontracting parts of their contracts to ldc-based labour agents. UK firms including Bovis and Wimpey have recruited Asians themselves in the hope of suppressing costs to some extent, and Filipinos were hired to labour on the liquid petroleum gas project of Pullman Kellogg in Kuwait (*MEED*, 16 March 1979). But South Korean companies too have hired Bangladeshis to finish off their projects in Kuwait.

Entry to this market has by no means been easy. All firms tendering in the Middle East find that up to two years may elapse between the initial expression of interest in a project and the signing of contracts, and as the level of demand for construction in OECD countries has generally been low in recent years, governments in the Middle East have been able to play firms from the West off against one another. A notable casualty in 1978 was the Yulsan group from South Korea, which grew from inception in 1975 to have an export order-book of $166 million in 1977 and then to bankruptcy just over a year later. Like all South Korean construction companies, this firm was badly hit by the South Korean government's decision to tighten credit and ban the export of cement. Both of these directives were part of an effort to cool South Korea's inflation (22% over 1977/8) and roaring excess demand for labour, causing 33% wage rises in 1977 and again in 1978. Companies in South Korea tend to be highly geared, so the interest rate rise, coupled with companies' tendency in 1976/8 to pursue orders at the expense of margins, caused rapid bankruptcy. The wider topic of the nature of the impulses leading ldc-based firms to expand abroad and become multinationals has as yet received little scrutiny. One exception is the analysis of Lecraw (1977) which found – as if to confirm the experience of the South Korean firms in the Middle East – that the major reason for ldc-based firms' setting up capacity in another ldc (in his case, Thailand) was the small volume of sales possible in the home market, due primarily to the low average per capita income. Certainly in the cases of South Korea and Taiwan the high savings ratios, to the extent that these depress the volume of sales available in the domestic market, coupled with the often high levels of protection confronting sellers to OECD markets, will make expansion elsewhere among ldcs an essential strategy if economies of scale are to be achieved.

The end of the construction boom: the beginning of export competition?

It has been shown that OPEC countries have offered substantial export opportunities for ldcs as well as for industrialised countries. Earlier sections of this chapter referred to the emerging patterns of OPEC–ldc trade and noted the considerable successes of some Asian ldcs, particularly in construction and engineering joint ventures. There is, however, another side to this coin. For once the industrial capacity in these OPEC members has been set up and has satisfied the bulk of domestic demand (or, indeed, possibly even before this has been satisfied), this capacity will be turned to face export markets. In part this likelihood stems from explicit policy decisions to diversify, especially in the Middle East countries, away from reliance upon crude oil as the predominant source of export earnings and GNP. As the Saudi minister of industry put it, when defending his country's ambitious industrialisation push, 'It is no longer acceptable for us to export energy and have it come back to us in manufactured form at an exorbitant price' (*MEED*, 1978). In part, however, the desire to export from new Middle East industries is also a reflection of the cost characteristics of the industries being nurtured there. Oil refining, basic petrochemicals production (ethylene, propylene, benzene and butadeine) and – depending on the reduction system chosen – iron and steel all feature substantial economies of scale and must be run at high levels of capacity utilisation if unit costs are not to exceed wildly prevailing world levels. Again, it is the intention of the Arab states to carry more crude and refined oil in tankers they themselves own. At present Middle East OPEC states own only 1.6% of the hydrocarbon fleet operating in the world despite accounting for 33% of the cargo turnover (1976 figures) (UNCTADa, 1978, p. 28).

Some other OPEC members have, however, been having mixed fortunes with their non-oil efforts, with Nigeria's importance as an agricultural goods exporter having dwindled away since the mid 1960s due largely to a network of policies favouring urban over rural interests. Indonesia's efforts at industrialisation and export diversification have also suffered from mismanagement; in her case the crash of the enormous Pertamina group of public companies which had been steered almost independently of the government set back the country's ambitions by some years and left a foreign debt of some $6 billion. Venezuela, on the other hand, has been building up for decades a relatively sophisticated industrial base, so that oil and oil products contributed only 26% of GNP by 1976.

Although there are at present no serious difficulties — petrochemical production from OPEC, along with iron and steel production, is still some way in the future — the intention of OPEC planners to push forward should be having an impact upon other ldcs' planners already.

The extent to which the Middle Eastern OPEC countries will cause market disruption with their exports in the last two decades of the century is much debated.

In oil refining, the Middle East will certainly be building the bulk of the new capacity in the next ten years, with 120 million tonnes per year of throughput, which will nearly double the region's capacity (Quinlan, 1979). Meanwhile excess capacity in certain OECD countries should lead to refinery closure (*Oil and Gas Journal*, 21 January 1979). The effect that these new refineries will have on those already existing in ldcs is unlikely to be favourable. For one thing, many of these refineries are already run at less than optimal capacity rates, since many of them were in the first place built by multinational oil companies with an eye to market shares for crude oil sales rather than to reap profits from refineries (Herman, 1975). Moreover, now that OPEC states control the depletion and distribution of their crudes more than was typical in the 1960s, they might be able to use the threat of reduced crude oil supplies as a lever to ensure adequate markets for refined products. Concern has been expressed by OPEC industrialisers regarding conditions of market access for their processed goods in the 1980s (*Oil and Gas Journal*, 29 January 1979, p. 82) and the threat of reduced access to crude in retaliation for protecting domestic refining capacity would severely affect ldc refineries.

A further aspect to the surge of industrialisation in OPEC that is paralleling the industrialisation of most of the ldcs is that the former have the wherewithal to subsidise their products to gain entry to established markets if they so wish. It is clear that COMECON oil products are being sold at very low prices to undercut established traders and gain a high market share in the shortest possible time (*The Economist*, 7 April

1979); the same tactics could be open to OPEC. There are reasons for doubting this (chiefly, because OPEC companies require the co-operation of the Western-based oil multinationals in their long-term marketing effort) and industry spokesmen have denied any intention to quote subsidised prices. As an executive of SABIC, the Saudi Basic Industries Corporation, has said, 'SABIC has clear profit objectives' (*Euromoney*, April 1979, p. 99). None the less, energy-intensive processes could conceivably be carried out in OPEC Middle Eastern locations and reduce the possibilities for other ldcs' entry to those industries. Already there are aluminium smelters in operation in Bahrain, Egypt and Iran and others are nearing completion in Dubai, Algeria, Iraq, Kuwait, Libya, Qatar, Saudi Arabia and Syria. The direct reduction of iron ore into sponge iron was developed in Mexico, and is ideal wherever cheap natural gas and iron ore are found together. Thus Mexico and Venezuela, which both have these inputs, should be able to expand in this area, as should those Middle Eastern OPEC countries willing and able to import iron ore cheaply (Roemer, 1976).

Whether or not the Bahraini example of aluminium smelting will be followed elsewhere in the Gulf is unclear. Smelting is a process which even non-bauxite producing ldcs had intended to enter in the next ten years to take advantage of their hydroelectric power possibilities. In the bauxite producing ldcs aluminium production is planned to increase from 0.5 million metric tons in 1976 to 2.3 million metric tons by 1990, while output of non-bauxite ldcs, who will import bauxite simply to add value to it with their energy resources, are projected to increase their aluminium output from 0.4 million metric tons to 4.7 million metric tons over 1976–90. The extra value added generated by the latter group of ldcs is estimated at $20 billion, at 1975 prices.

The worldwide implications of this Middle Eastern industrialisation effort remain opaque. Although a number of ldcs have unquestionably gained by boosting their exports to OPEC countries since 1973, it is conceivable that the energy-intensive processing industries to be established by those OPEC states will in turn come to constrain some of the non-oil ldcs' development ambitions in the next decade. Looking back, however, a number of OPEC countries seem to have made an effort to direct more of their import orders to ldc firms or consortia, and in the construction field at least this has yielded impressive benefits for some Asian ldcs. Remittances of savings, as Chapter 8 discusses in greater depths, represent an important element in the gains from OPEC's boom. By underwriting the rapid industrialisation and export growth of certain ldcs these imports of goods and services by OPEC members unquestionably assist the ldcs' development effort. But how far these import orders are a placebo for dearer oil, for the felt inadequacy of aid disbursements, or an effort to patch up greater unity in the face of developed country criticism, the figures alone cannot tell. Chapter 10 therefore attempts to appraise the wider dimensions of the OPEC–ldc nexus.

Notes

1 IMF category 405.
2 IMF category 505.
3 IMF category 205.
4 IMF category 605.
5 The statistics as compiled in UNCTAD, *Handbook of International Trade and Development Statistics, 1977 Supplement* (New York, 1978) are three years behind. The later edition, published in 1979 (Doc. E/F.79.II.D.2, TD/STAT.8), provides only some 1976 figures.

8

Labour, Migration and Remittances

The enlarged expenditures with OPEC on oil by oil importing developing countries have, as Chapter 6 indicated, sometimes been offset by substantial OPEC aid transfers. Another channel through which certain ldcs are gaining resources from OPEC countries is by acting as reservoirs of labour for labour-scarce OPEC members. Great migrations across the Arab world of course predate the foundation of OPEC by many centuries. These movements of people between Arab lands ('inter-Arab migration') have more recently been supplemented by considerable flows from Arab countries into Europe. Beginning in the early 1960s, this second wave of Arab migration has come to have increasing significance, both for the recipient countries (chiefly France and West Germany) and the donor countries (Schiller, 1975). Finally, these two patterns have had a third, the great drift to the towns, superimposed upon them. This last phenomenon, which has been referred to as 'the largest migratory movement in human history' (Koenigsberger, 1976), has affected Arab countries just as much as most other ldcs; it has also had a major impact upon the need for further inter-Arab labour flows. These flows of Arab workers have been both within countries and between countries.

It can readily be seen that untangling these patterns is a difficult undertaking. But since the prime concern of this book is with OPEC—ldc relations rather than with OPEC issues *per se*, this chapter deals only with certain themes within the subject. The chapter deals first with conditions of labour shortage, investigating the inter-Arab and ldc—Arab migration that the boom in OPEC countries has given rise to. This leads to a discussion of remittances and an assessment of the net gains to those eleven or twelve ldcs that are currently involved in supplying labour to OPEC members. Then the chapter turns to consider the labour-surplus OPEC countries (Indonesia, Iran, Nigeria and Venezuela), and briefly discusses conditions there. The ways in which the provision of labour to OPEC affects other elements of the foreign affairs relationship that ldcs enjoy are then discussed. It begins, however, by considering the non-OPEC Arab countries that have labour supplies excess to their requirements, and the ways in which mainly internal migration takes place to bring about greater equilibrium there.

Inter-Arab labour migration

The countries which are the chief importers of labour are Bahrain, Kuwait, Libya, Qatar, Saudi Arabia and UAE. Table 8.1 shows the composition of the immigrant labour forces in each of these countries, and indicates that Saudi Arabia is by far the biggest absorber of foreign workers. In 1975 it alone accounted for nearly half of all immigration. Table 8.2 shows the proportion of the labour force that these inflows represent. Here it is apparent that despite Saudi Arabia's dominance as an importer of labour in absolute terms, the relative weight of foreign workers is far greater in Kuwait, Qatar and UAE. Bahrain is the most self-sufficient, with roughly six out of ten workers in 1975 being nationals.

Ranged against these recipient countries are those Middle Eastern states which are unable to absorb usefully all their rural population in agriculture. These include Egypt, Jordan, Morocco, Oman, Syria and Tunisia.

In the case of Jordan, fragmented land-holdings ('the curse which accompanies land ownership in the Arab world in general' – Sayigh, 1978, p. 212), typically of less than 10 hectares, tend to propel the younger, more ambitious people outside the country in search of work. In Morocco, too, underemployment in rural areas tends to be considerable. While agricultural pursuits, loosely defined, occupy 68% or so of the population, it has been estimated that the same output could be gleaned from one-quarter of that number of people if techniques used in towns were available (Sayigh, 1978, p. 609). Reference has already been made to the characteristic use made of labour in Egyptian agriculture, which allows absence from the farm seasonally and also permanently if there is a gross excess of workers on a small plot.

Table 8.3 shows data for the main labour—exporting countries of the area. It is clear from this that in three cases, Jordan, Oman and North Yemen, the proportion of the workforce that is abroad is considerable. Indeed, in the case of Jordan the proportion of its potential labour supply that has been temporarily 'exported' is so great that shortages have developed in some areas, with some Asian workers being hired to fill the gap. Ultimately one would expect relative wage differentials to adjust to restore equilibrium by mediating the excessive outflow of labour from such an area, but the consequent rise in wages might, under certain monetary circumstances, generate a more widespread inflation.

The involvement of migrants from Asian ldcs in Middle East construction and other sectors is relatively recent. From occupying just over one-quarter of all foreigners' jobs in Kuwait, Bahrain, Qatar and UAE in 1970

Table 8.1 *Migrant workers by ethnic origin and country of employment, 1975*

Country	Arab		Asian		European		Iranian, Turkish, African and others		All migrant workers	
	no.	% of total	no.	% of total	no.	% of total	no.	% of total	no.	% of total
Saudi Arabia	669,900	90.5	38,000	4.9	15,000	1.9	20,500	2.6	773,400	46.9
Libyan Arab Jamahiriya	310,400	93.4	5,500	1.7	7,000	2.1	9,500	2.9	332,400	20.2
Kuwait	143,300	68.9	33,600	16.1	2,000	1.0	29,100	14.0	208,000	12.6
Bahrain	6,200	20.7	16,600	55.3	4,400	14.7	2,800	9.3	30,000	1.8
United Arab Emirates	62,000	24.6	163,500	65.0	5,000	2.0	21,000	8.4	251,500	15.2
Qatar	15,000	27.9	34,000	63.2	800	1.5	4,000	7.4	53,800	3.3
Total	1,236,800	75.0	291,200	17.6	34,200	2.1	86,900	5.3	1,649,100	100.0

Source: Birks and Sinclair (1979).

Table 8.2 *Employment by nationality in capital-rich Arab states, 1975*

Country	Nationals' employment	% of total	Non-nationals' employment	% of total	Total employment
Saudi Arabia	1,026,500	57.0	733,400	43.0	1,799,900
Libyan Arab Jamahiriya	449,200	57.5	332,400	42.5	781,600
Kuwait	91,800	30.6	208,000	69.4	299,800
Bahrain	45,800	60.4	30,000	39.6	75,800
United Arab Emirates	45,000	15.2	251,500	84.8	296,500
Qatar	12,500	18.9	53,800	81.1	66,300
Total	1,670,800	50.3	1,649,100	49.7	3,319,900

Source: Birks and Sinclair (1979).

Table 8.3 *Migrant workers and domestic workforce of labour sending countries, 1975*

Country	Size of Workforce	Number of workers abroad	% workforce abroad
Jordan (East Bank)	532,800	150,000	28.1
Oman	137,000	38,413	28.0
North Yemen	1,070,000	290,128	27.1
Syria	1,838,948	70,415	3.8
Egypt	10,756,000	397,545	3.7
Sudan	3,700,000	45,873	1.2
Palestine	–	114,717	–
South Yemen	550,000	500,000	91.0
Lebanon	570,000	49,661	8.7
Tunisia	1,730,000	38,649	2.2
Iraq	2,858,000	20,625	1.0
Somalia	–	6,547	–
Total		1,295,750	

Sources: Birks and Sinclair (1979); Sayigh (1978); *UN World Statistical Pocketbook*; IMF (1978) own estimates.

(83,869 jobs), their share grew quickly to reach 45% by 1975, with nearly a quarter of a million involved (Birks and Sinclair, 1979).

When this data on immigrants is arranged to show their importance in subsectors of the economy, it transpires that the bulk of migrants to OPEC countries in the Middle East are unskilled or semi-skilled. They tend to work in agriculture, manufacturing and construction. At the same time, non-nationals tend to predominate in the professions, however, with nationals usually filling most of the country's clerical jobs. Table 8.4 shows the share of non-nationals in occupations in the four countries for which data are available. (Bahrain is not an OPEC member, but as an oil exporting labour-shortage country is included in the table.) The table suggests that, except for Qatar, where the average of non-nationals in each skill category is exceptionally high, clerical jobs are those most often filled by domestic labour, with the professional category showing the highest shares of non-nationals.

The exceptionally small shares of nationals in agriculture is significant. Qatari agriculture is confined almost completely to a few oases; in general there is too little water to support cereal field crops. Efforts by the Department of Agriculture since 1961 to establish forestry and to experiment with the most suitable plants have been successful, as have experiments with improving water provision (Fenelon, 1976, p. 47). In total only around 0.52% of the land area is cultivated but the constantly rising price of imported foods provides an incentive to boost domestic production.

Fully 95% of those active in agriculture in Qatar are foreign; in turn these represent only 4% of the total population. Thus only eighty-six

Table 8.4   *Share of non-nationals in labour forces, 1976*

	UAE	Qatar	Saudi Arabia	Kuwait (1)	Kuwait (2)	Libya	Bahrain
	%	%	%	%	%	%	%
Professional	–	81	–	70.2	15.2	55.9	60
Administrative	–	52	–	44.1	21.6	–	–
Clerical	–	72	–	47.6	11.7	13.8	14.8
Sales	–	81	–	50.3	18.7	–	
Farming, fishing	–	95	–	–	–	$(20.2)^a$	$(35.5)^a$
Transport and communications	53	66	51	42.7	17.0	$(18.8)^b$	$(41.0)^b$
Craftsmen	–	87	–	–	–	–	–
Agriculture	7	95	96	56.2	21.1	–	–
Services	63	86	61	–	–	–	–
Total	84	83	43	69		42	37

Notes: (1) Non-Kuwaiti Arab   (2) Non-Arab
[a] Technician   [b] Semi-skilled and skilled
Reprinted from *Economic Development and Cultural Change* by permission of the University of Chicago Press
Sources: Farrag (1975). Hassan (1978).
Copyright 1976, ILO Geneva

Qataris are actually employed on the land! (Hassan, 1978) Those who are successfully recruited to the country tend to return home very quickly or move off to the city, and a constant recruiting effort is required. Productivity – in so far as it can ever be satisfactorily measured in agricultural pursuits – appears to be high. Data collected for the US Department of State in 1976 show that output per person engaged in agriculture in Qatar was above that in services and not far below that in non-oil industries (El Mallakh, 1979, p. 27).

Regarding the skills lost by the ldcs that contribute this labour to the Middle East, it has been found in a number of surveys that a very high proportion of certain professions migrate. In Sri Lanka, over 35% of doctors, 73% of accountants and 50% of engineers who migrated during the period 1971–4 went to other ldcs (UNCTAD, 1979c). In the case of Pakistan, up to 45% of the labourers in certain skill categories were absent from the country at the end of 1977, and the fact that 60% of recorded remittances in that year came from OPEC countries provides a clue as to their whereabouts.

Recruitment channels differ according to the level of skills being sought, as would be expected. Some recruitment by OPEC states is managed at government level. For example, each year the Egyptian government gathers requests for teachers and supplies up to 10% of the country's stock to OPEC countries (Farrag, 1975, p. 104). Similarly, the Saudi Arabian Public Transport Co. has hired 1,000 drivers and 1,000 other transport workers from Thailand, Indonesia, the Philippines and the Sudan to operate a new fleet of West German buses (*MEED*, 13 July 1979). This type of block hiring is likely to have entailed an element of government supervision. In lower skill categories, the nature of the screening process differs according to the country of origin. In the Yemens, physical proximity to the centres of demand allows labourers to move fairly freely and to locate jobs that become vacant from day to day. Those coming from further afield naturally require more structured information and selection. In Asian labour exporting countries agencies which administer skill proficiency tests are common, though little is known about these procedures. In this respect international migration between ldcs is akin to internal migration, in that the channels through which information flows between town and country have not been properly documented. While the pre-arrangement of jobs before migrants begin their move is typical in some countries (Berry, 1975; Perlman, 1976; Joshi and Joshi, 1976), elsewhere the tendency is for certain villages or towns habitually to provide applicants for certain occupations elsewhere in the ldc; and for this to operate as a screening mechanism (Joshi and Joshi, 1976). Whether or not similar systems have sprung up to mediate migration from Asian ldcs to the Middle East is simply not known yet.

The costs and benefits assessed

Large-scale emigration has in the last twenty years been favoured by certain Arab governments as a palliative to fast-growing populations. The Fourth National plan of Tunisia for 1973–6, for instance, required that a continuing flow of emigrants should absorb 60% of the country's labour supply accretion (Bouhdiba, 1979, p. 166). There are, however, many critics of these substantial labour flows. Both in recipient developed economies and in the countries where these emigrants originate, there are many commentators who believe the costs outweigh the benefits in national terms. That there may be such hidden costs, sufficient to counteract the gains, both private (that is, to the individual) and social (that is, to the community), was recognised at the 1974 session of the International Labour Conference, which suggested that the links between Afro-Arab emigration and development be investigated more fully. The type of drawback they had in mind was as follows. There are three sets of objections commonly voiced to the type of migration described in this chapter. The first concerns labour shortages which may arise in the labour-donor regions. This seems paradoxical at first, since the entire rationale for emigration is posed in terms of labour surplus and hidden (or, in some cases, overt) unemployment. But demand for labour varies markedly through the seasons in agriculture-based countries, and labour is sufficiently heterogenous for specific skills to be in shortage even when labour in general is available in abundance.

The intensity with which people need to work on farms in the rural areas of ldcs tends to vary considerably according to the season. This affects migration in two ways. First, in certain regions it means that during spells of slack the able-bodied will go off to a nearby town or perhaps a city to earn extra cash, returning in time for the resumption of work on their home farm, or in the part of the countryside where there are landless labourers. This type of behaviour has been amply documented for Egypt. Egypt has a dualist farm structure, with some 84% of the farms with an area under five feddans each using roughly 96% family labour, contrasted with a smaller number of much larger farms which between them use 60% or more of all wage labour.

A well-known study there by Hanson found that, contrary to popular belief, rural labourers did not spend much of their time in idleness but used the hours when they were not engaged on their own farm working for cash on neighbouring farms. Moreover, for about 10% of their time these people would work outside agriculture altogether. The important conclusion was that 'by ignoring non-field work and non-agricultural work, earlier labour requirement calculations systematically and grossly underestimated actual employment' (Hansen, 1969). Seasonal fluctuations in labour-time needed on the typically small farms in Egypt are equally large for women and children. This is since their efforts tend to be geared closely to certain tasks, such as cotton harvesting in September (Mohie-Eldin, 1977).

In other countries, however, suitable off-farm work is not always available. This demands that those rural workers who cannot find sufficient work locally must migrate on a more permanent basis, possibly to a different region of the country, possibly to a different Arab country or indeed possibly outside the Arab world entirely, for instance to Europe.

Remittances may be sufficient to allow hired labour to come in for certain periods to supplement the depleted local supply. In many parts of Africa this practice of hiring seasonal help is widespread: apart from the Egyptian case already referred to, clear relationships have been observed in southern Nigeria between local rates of labour outflow and expenditure by the remaining family members (using remittances) on seasonal hired labourers (Waters, 1973; Johnson and Whitelaw, 1976; Essang and Mabawonku, 1975). Remittances may in some cases not be sufficient, however, and there the consequences will be decay and atrophy in the agricultural sector. An instance of this is the Yemen Arab Republic which, although gaining perhaps $1 billion in foreign exchange from remittances in 1977, suffered deterioration since most able-bodied adults were absent at critical times of the year. Food output has suffered and reliance upon imported grains has increased (Swanson, 1979). At present over half North Yemen's import bill consists of foods (Central Bank of Yemen, 1974). Rural wages have also been pulled sharply upwards by the shortage of workers due to emigration (IBRD, 1979c, p. 101).

Given the seriousness of the overall food supply position in the Middle

East, this is grave. It has been estimated that by the year 2000 food output in the Middle East will have to have risen by 225% from its 1975 level to allow a moderate improvement in per capita food intake and to cope with the growing population (Askari and Cummings, 1978). Food exports from the region sank steadily from a peak in 1969, while imports of food have risen from $1.07 billion in 1967 to $4.504 billion by 1976. A peak of imports at $5.7 billion was reached in 1974, when imports rose by a staggering 217% over 1973 levels, but since then the position has stabilised somewhat (National Bank of Egypt, 1978).

Unfortunately there is little evidence available on the pattern of re-mittances. One obvious problem with monitoring them is that a prop-ortion will not be channelled through official agencies but will be retained and transmitted in cash or through other means which evade detection. Some funds will be remitted only through the 'grey' market, at a better exchange rate than that officially prevailing. Research on remittances from France to North Africa, for example, suggests that around 20% of re-mittances are not transmitted by money order but through less formal channels.

Detailed data on savings patterns by emigrant Arab workers is only available for Europe, and this shows the proportions of income that is saved contrasted with length of residence abroad. The French statistics show a slight tendency for the ratio of savings to gross income to fall as the duration of residence lengthens, from 18.65% of gross income for residence of less than three years to 10.31% for residence of over twenty-four years (Granier and Marciano, 1975, p. 161). But since the average immigrant worker's income is below that of the average indigenous French worker, the immigrant is managing to save perhaps 50% more than average at his level of income. The data also show a tendency for North Africans to save a higher proportion of their incomes (around 19%) than workers from any other region.

The volume of remittances (at least, of those remittances made known to governments and recorded by the IMF) is shown in Table 8.5. Remittances have risen steadily from $834 million-worth in 1973 to $5,368 million by 1977. In every country, the value of recorded remitt-ances in 1977 was higher than that in 1973; in some cases (notably Egypt, Jordan and Yemen Arab Republic) the increases were extremely large.

How significant are these foreign currency inflows for the recipient countries? In purely monetary terms, an attempt has been made here to show their importance by comparing them to each country's imports of goods and services in the appropriate year. (This method of presentation was selected because 'net unrequited transfers', which may seem a more appropriate indicator against which to gauge remittances, is likely to include some element of remittance payments and thus distort the cal-culations.) Table 8.6 shows the result of these calculations. It is clear, first, that in each case the contribution of remittances towards the foreign

Table 8.5   *Emigrant remittances to selected countries (US $ million)*

Source	1973	1974	1975	1976	1977	1978
Afghanistan	–	–	–	–	200	–
Bangladesh	–	18	43	53	75	–
Egypt	87	189	340	615	1,025	1,700
India	235	297	535	713	1,000	–
Jordan[a]	45	75	167	411	425	–
South Korea	154	154	158	195	172	–
Pakistan	151	230	353	590	1,110	–
Philippines	–	104	128	112	130	–
Sri Lanka	–	–	3	7	12	–
Sudan	–	–	–	12	40	–
Yemen Arab Republic	129	156	307	796	1,000	–
Yemen People's Democratic Republic	33	41	56	115	179	–
Total	834	1,264	2,090	3,619	5,368	1,700

Sources: IMF (1978); *MEED*, various issues.
a   IBRD estimates are significantly lower, at $21.7 million in 1973; $18.6 million, $15.5 million, $24.8 million and $46.6 million in the following years.

exchange costs of importing goods and services has risen since 1973. There are, however, a few ambiguous results, with the Sri Lankan figures being particularly difficult to interpret. This is due to the large revaluation of the currency against the US dollar in 1974–5, which reduced the dollar value of imports at the same time as the value expressed in domestic currency was rising. When converting import values into dollars and comparing these with remittance values in current dollar equivalents of third countries' currencies, it is only to be expected that anomalies will arise. The second point to note here is that Jordan, Pakistan and the two Yemens are the countries whose relative gain from remittances is the greatest, with remittances in the case of Yemen Arab Republic actually exceeding the value of merchandise and service imports in most years.

Remittances to Pakistan are projected to increase by 250% between 1977 and 1983. By 1977 they were already equivalent in value to all the country's exports of raw cotton and cotton textiles, or to one-third the value of all exports. In 1970 three-quarters of these remittances came from the UK, but by 1976 this share had fallen to 15%, with the share of OPEC rising strongly (IBRD, 1977b).

Similarly, remittances are the item in the balance of payments that have improved most rapidly since 1973 in Jordan. They are steadily approaching the earnings obtained from manufactures exports: in 1973 they were equivalent only to 63% of these (IBRD, 1978b). In Algeria, remittances amounted to $368 million in 1973, $405 million in 1974 and $450 million

Table 8.6 *Migrant remittances as a proportion of imports of goods and services*

Country	1973 %	1974 %	1975 %	1976 %
Afghanistan[a]	–	–	–	▸ –
Bangladesh[a]	–	2	4	6
Egypt	5	5	7	12
India	6	6	–	–
Jordan	11	12	18	32
South Korea	3	2	2	2
Pakistan	11	9	13	21
Philippines[a]	–	4	4	3
Sri Lanka[a]	–	–	4	1
Sudan	–	–	–	1
Yemen Arab Republic	126	83	104	193
Yemen People's Democratic Republic	19	10	18	–

a Imports, cif (IMF line 71d).
Sources: Calculated from IMF, *International Financial Statistics*, various issues; Table 8.5.

in 1975, equivalent to 19%, 9% and 10% of f.o.b. exports in those three years. And in Morocco, remittances grew to be equivalent to 32% of f.o.b. exports by 1976, at $548 million (IBRD, 1977c).

Egypt has gained particularly significantly. In 1978 remittances of $1,650 million were the biggest contributor to the invisibles account, and over twice as important as tourism, worth $750 million (IBRD, 1978). In 1977 they covered 13% of the c.i.f. imports of traded goods and were equivalent to 45% of the balance of payments deficit.

Two monetary consequences from these remittances must be mentioned. First is the fact that by relieving the intensity of the foreign exchange constraint, which so frequently requires that developing country governments try to constrain growth to preserve external equilibrium, these remittances underwrite a higher domestic growth rate. Since development projects require a mixture of foreign and domestic resources be mobilised, the more foreign exchange available to the ldc government, the more domestic resources it is able to bring into use. This 'foreign trade multiplier' effect can be very strong in ldcs and yield disproportionate internal benefits.

The second monetary consequence of remittances that receives widespread attention is their inflationary potential. Inflation can be a consequence of emigration and concomitant remittance flows for several reasons. First, the absence of certain types of labour may induce labour shortages (seasonal, regional or both) and force up prevailing wage rates. There is no lack of evidence to illustrate the rapidity with which the rural earnings structure in ldcs can change to reflect pockets of labour shortage. In his case study of Egyptian villages, Hansen found that 'there is no doubt that the variation of the differentials is related to the seasonal fluctuations of the demand for various types of labour' (Hansen, 1969). Moreover, once this has taken grip, a second type of problem might arise: 'the labour-exporting countries are faced with the possibility that the inflationary repercussions of a cost-push type of inflation could be aggravated by a heavy inflow of remittances leading to a demand pull' (IMF, 1978). The problem envisaged here is that money sent back to the ldcs will be used to acquire general items of consumption which, in the short term at least, are not in adequate supply. Their price will therefore rise in response to this new surge in demand and generalised inflation be initiated. An alternative to this in countries where consumer durables are not available is for workers to spend their savings on such items before setting off for home. In the case of South Yemen, workers bringing home consumer goods were, however, obliged to pay heavy import duties on their acquisitions (Wilson, 1979, p. 129).

This type of effect has been documented in Pakistan, which by 1977 had lost some 115,000 workers to OPEC states. A disproportionate number of these were highly educated. In the case of medical school graduates only 50% were remaining in Pakistan each year, the others immediately moving off to practise elsewhere (IBRD, 1977b). In Jordan too an excess of migration had, by 1975, temporarily led to agricultural earnings being forced up towards the level of urban earnings. So severe had local shortages become, especially in the farming areas of the Jordan valley, that some unskilled Asian labour was having to be hired to supplement those left behind (IBRD, 1978b).

Further disquiet has been expressed about the use to which remittances are put. It has just been explained how those remaining in some areas need remittances to allow supplementation of their depleted labour supplies. This is an entirely suitable use of the cash inflow and few criticisms have been made of it. But the money has also been put to less desirable uses. Evidence from some countries shows that some small farmers, on returning with savings, have bought inappropriate items for mechanised agriculture — for instance, tractors in cases where their plots of land do not warrant such capital outlays (Böhning, 1975). Such overabundance of farming machinery merely leads subsequently to imports of spare parts, or — more likely — to the equipment lying idle because the parts cannot be obtained. Similar results may follow when cash is sent home and labour supplies are inadequate; here, permanent mechanisation is the price paid for the absence of key workers.

Finally, a series of problems concerning the upsetting of established mores arises. Returning from a large city in an alien culture is likely to demand considerable flexibility in readjusting, just as similar flexibility was needed to adapt to the new city in the first place. While *associations d'originaires* may exist in the latter case, they are less available in the former. Modern consumption patterns, different attitudes to investment, savings, family and authority are all side effects that have been analysed at length in the sociological literature.

The urbanisation that is frequently the precursor of emigration for the more educated Arabs can in itself exacerbate tension. Although there were many contributing factors to the crisis in Iran in 1978–9, one major element was undoubtedly unbridled urbanisation and concomitant food shortages in rural areas, coupled with earlier unsatisfactory and partial land reforms. The report of the International Labour Office in 1973 made just this point in referring to the fact that the urban population of Iran was increasing three times as quickly as the rural population. This headlong urbanisation was 'perhaps more rapid than was economically necessary and socially desirable' (ILO, 1973, p. 24). Summing up the development impact of emigration to the EEC from North Africa, Böhning's conclusion is that 'the return migrant as a bearer of development and modernisation is a myth . . . the innovative return migrant would appear to be in a tiny minority' (Böhning, 1975, p. 265). Yet others disagree completely; Griffin believes the benefits substantially outweigh the costs (Griffin, 1976).

A big problem with influxes of this sort, and on this scale, lies in arranging suitable conditions for workers. Migrants to the OPEC states tend for the most part to accept whatever living conditions and style of employment they are offered: they know that expulsion will follow from any overt dissent. None of the OPEC states permit their gastarbeiter to acquire property, but medical treatment is free. Accommodation costs in the Middle East are legendary, and this, combined with the need to pay for whatever education is required for accompanying children, tends to discourage families from coming too (Wilson, 1979, p. 85). The fact that social security infrastructure is normally not available to alien workers in OPEC states also encourages rapid turnover. The Yemenis in Saudi Arabia have no access to the (contributory) insurance scheme; immigrant workers in Kuwait cannot buy property but are entitled to free medical treatment: education must be paid for. In 1976 many Egyptian and Tunisian workers were expelled from Libya and Moroccans from Algeria, and there have been disturbances arising from dissatisfaction with conditions. Four thousand Koreans rioted in Jubail in 1978 on account of allegedly poor work conditions and a number of Kenyan labourers were reported to have returned home after finding conditions unattractive in the summer of 1977.

Thus the provision of housing for a transient workforce from a foreign country provides ample opportunity for exploitation, and there is indeed evidence of unscrupulous middlemen and agents getting involved. In the case of migrations between regions of ldcs, surprisingly sophisticated urban reception networks have evolved, which help the new arrival

cope with finding housing, employment and social contacts. Across continents the patterns differ but the principles are similar: always *associations
d' originaires* exist 'to fill the gap created by the migrant who leaves his
homogenous primary group of kinsmen and relatives to settle in this
heterogenous urban community' (Imoagene, 1967; Sinclair, 1978).

The norm is different in migration to Middle East countries. There
many of the migrants are on contract assignments, and their arrival,
reception and departure are handled by the company on whose contracts
they work. South Koreans typify this pattern: their numbers rose from
4,000 to 40,000 over the period 1974—9 in Saudi Arabia alone following
the award of several major contracts to South Korean firms (see Chapter 8).
Few Koreans stay longer than a year: for one thing they stand to earn not
much more than they would at home (perhaps $800 per month).

The influx of migrants is controlled ever more carefully. The Gulf
governments are concerned about possible loss of control over some
areas of the country, about the possible resentment between locals and
migrants, and about the impact of newcomers' attitudes upon traditional
values. Visitors to Mecca in Saudi Arabia (they numbered 830,000 in
1978) are tightly monitored, and have in recent years been shepherded
quickly from their point of arrival in the country towards Mecca. The
Hajj is Saudi Arabia's second biggest source of foreign exchange after oil
and so is much valued but evidence of a Saudi crackdown on illegal residents
comes from the results of the declared tough policy early in 1979. By mid
year 38,000 aliens had been deported.

The labour-surplus OPEC members

For the three highly populated OPEC members, their experiences with
labour matters have been in complete contrast. These countries are,
however, of much less interest here, since the migration and inter-regional
flow of remittances they have witnessed have been almost entirely within
each country. There has been no massive influx of guest workers from
other ldcs to man the oil-funded developments. It is, not, therefore,
appropriate to spend much time with these countries, and a quick glance
at demographic and labour patterns will suffice.

As was found to be the case with the labour-scarce and capital-abundant
Arab states, migration has played a crucial part in recent economic
development. But migration in the non-Arab states has been quite different:
it has not been between countries across borders, but almost exclusively
within each country, and for the most part rural-to-urban. Secondly, it
follows from this that the flow of cash remittances that have been saved
by the migrating workers has not made its way into other countries but
has gone to small towns, villages or farms outside the cities. And finally,
the component of this migration which is accounted for by circular or
return migration is much smaller. Although cases were noted in the Arab

context of workers from (say) the Yemens or India attempting to settle in their new place of work, the majority of these people plan to return home. In the labour-surplus OPEC countries, however, it is typical to find that rural-to-urban migration is undertaken as a lifelong commitment.

In common with virtually all ldcs in the last three decades, Indonesia, Nigeria and Venezuela have experienced a massive rural exodus and a drift to the cities. Each of these countries has a much larger population than the OPEC Arab states: Indonesia has 132 million people, Nigeria between 70 and 100 million and Venezuela 12 million (or 10.7 million at the last official census, in 1971). As regards urban drift, the type of linkages (monetary and sociological) which persist between new townspeople and their rural relatives and the permanence of this migration, Indonesia may be regarded as typical of the three.

Unquestionably, one of Indonesia's most pressing problems is rapid population growth: by the year 2000 the country may have to support a population of 250 million, or nearly twice its present level. This rapid accretion of the labour force naturally means that employment problems will intensify unless more income is generated, yet already by 1976 it was estimated that between 5 and 8 million people were totally without work. In fact this is likely to be an overstatement since, ironically, most people in the cities of ldcs are too poor to be wholly without work, and there will always be some task to be performed, for friends, family or in other casual ways (Berry, 1975; Chossudovsky, 1978). Not much of this income, be it in cash or in kind, will be gained through permanent wage employment, usually called 'formal sector employment'. Instead, for urban newcomers at least, subsistence will be achieved through irregular and fitful activities, sometimes working on one's own account and sometimes in groups. This type of unorganised work is known as 'informal sector' employment (Sinclair, 1978). In Djakarta much of it takes the form of sidewalk vending (perhaps 45,000 people in this city of 5 million), prostitution (10,000), shoeshiners, cigarette butt collectors and others (Papanek, 1975). Scavengers such as cigarette butt collectors are among the poorest inhabitants of the city: in 1975 their average daily earnings were estimated to be less than 150 rupees, or 37 US cents.

Like most towns and cities in Indonesia, Djakarta has swollen terribly in the last decade. One major project which has been mounted to relieve the pressure is a $70 million plan to resettle 1.25 million people out of Java and Bali, and into the less crowded Outer Islands such as Sumatra.

Despite appalling living conditions in such cities (20,000 families were living in cardboard shacks by the railway lines in Djakarta in 1977), most people go there because they believe they will be better off. The extent to which the accretion of oil revenues since 1973 has powered this migration is hard to assess. The range of jobs available in the city is greater; the availability of food usually more certain and there is the much discussed influence of education upon the desire to leave rural areas in ldcs to consider as well (IBRD, 1975).

Conclusions

This chapter has attempted to illustrate the diversity of experience found in labour movements towards, between and within OPEC countries. Certain OPEC states are found still to be suffering from chronic excess labour supplies which lead to fast-growing cities choked with hopeful job seekers, considerable disruption of urban development initiatives, but some useful urban—rural flows of information, money, technology and attitudes. Elsewhere among OPEC members are countries which require massive inflows of labour to help realise ambitious development programmes. By 1975 nearly 1.3 million people were working in countries other than their own in the Middle East. This movement of people naturally gives rise to costs as well as benefits. While the assistance given to the balance of payments of the ldcs involved through the high and rising inflows of emigrant workers' remittances is considerable, certain costs, less manifest than the benefits, also arise. Chiefly these involve the generation of rising prices wherever certain skill categories or regional labour stocks are over-depleted, of if food production falls because of the absence of critical farm workers. The arrival of cash can itself confront an inelastic supply of consumer goods, or food for that matter, and again precipitate rising prices. Whether or not those left behind by migrants are tempted to over-mechanise their farm work is another problem that has been raised. The balance of welfare can never be finally assessed; instead, it can only be observed that changing earnings differentials should in the long run compensate for any vicissitudes produced in neighbouring countries by over-reliance upon migration to OPEC states.

9

Interrupted Growth Patterns?

Previous chapters have dealt with the changes in ldcs' trade flows brought about by the rise of OPEC's import demand, with ldcs' augmented petroleum import bills, with their aid experience and − in a few cases − their temporary export of labour to OPEC states. This chapter now assesses the changes at the macroeconomic level wrought upon ldcs during the 1970s, identifying and, wherever possible, quantifying those components of their experience that are attributable to the actions of OPEC.

Demand for oil products after 1973

Although, as Chapter 3 indicated, a chief reason for the success of OPEC lies in the short-term inelasticity of demand for oil and oil products, it is clear by now that demand did fall off eventually after 1973. In ldcs demand for refined oil products ceased growing at its accustomed 5% − 13% annual rate and fell back to a 1% − 6% growth rate. Table 9.1 shows the average growth rates of oil products consumption during the two periods 1967−73 and 1974−77, and indicates how, against a halving of total world growth in demand, ldcs by regional grouping had very varied experiences. The sharpest fall is clearly that of Asia, which recorded a reduction in its annual growth of consumption from 13.27% per year to 2.91% per year.

   Further investigation of this oil consumption data shows how individual ldcs fared after the 1973 oil price rise. The eighteen ldcs which exhibited the greatest reductions in their growth of oil product consumption after 1973 were picked out from the US Department of Mines statistics. Their 1976 estimated GNP per capita were then compared, to see whether those countries with the lowest GNP per capita had suffered the greatest falls in demand. The results, which are somewhat inconclusive, do not support a strong version of the hypothesis that the poorest ldcs were in this respect relatively more affected by the rise in oil prices than any other set of ldcs. Of the eighteen ldcs considered, ten had GNP per capita of under

Table 9.1 *Apparent consumption of refined oil products, 1967–73 and 1974–7, volume terms*

	Annual average growth rate	
	1967–73	1974–7
	%	%
World[a]	7.83	3.97
Central America and Caribbean	7.46	1.15
South America	5.35	3.22
Africa	7.84	6.24
Asia	13.27	2.91

a Includes COMECON

Source: Calculated from US Department of Mines, Table 13, various issues. No allowance is made for changes in stocks.

$520; six were below $265. On the other hand, almost as many (eight) had GNP per capita over $521, and four had over $2,000. One of the latter group, Gabon, was even a member of OPEC! One might have expected the poorest ldcs, given their normal critical foreign exchange constraint, to have had the biggest and fastest reduction in their oil imports forced upon them, yet no clear outcome of this kind can be discerned. Performing a similar exercise with the fast-growing industrialising ldcs, it transpires that they too all experienced a fall in their growth of refined products demand. The fall in South Korea was the largest, with a 25.8% annual growth over 1967–73 being transformed into 13.0% over 1974–7. Singapore too showed a sharp fall, but the early period in this case only covered the years 1969–73.

The question arises as to how certain ldcs were able to reduce sharply their apparent consumption of refined oil products while simultaneously increasing their national output. For instance, it has been seen that South Korean oil consumption grew by 25.8% annually over 1967–73 but at 13% for the next four years. Yet South Korea's industrial output grew at an average of 19%, over 1974–7, apparently unconstrained by the relative drop in oil imports.

Two possibilities exist. The first is that waste was eliminated and the same level of national output obtained with smaller inputs of oil resources. The second possibility is that after 1973 the output mix of some ldcs changed so that the output of industries using oil inputs relatively intensively fell back while that from industries not so geared to oil inputs rose. One reason for anticipating such a change in the output mix is that demand patterns will be affected by the higher prices charged by oil using sectors for their output. Unfortunately, a detailed assessment of the relative weights of these factors cannot readily be carried out. Even with

Table 9.2   *Changes in real GDP, NOPECs 1967–77*

	Annual average 1967–72 %	Change on preceding year				
		1973 %	1974 %	1975 %	1976 %	1977 %
All NOPECs	6.1	7.3	5.3	4.1	4.8	4.9
Africa	5.0	2.2	5.6	2.3	4.2	2.2
Asia	4.8	7.9	2.7	6.1	5.8	6.4
Latin America and Caribbean	6.8	8.1	7.7	2.6	4.5	4.3
Middle East	8.8	4.8	-1.0	8.4	2.1	6.7

Note: Annual average growth rates are compound.

Source: IMF (1978), Table 2, p. 11.

access to sub-process level input—output tables, compiled over a reasonable length of time, the calculations would be arduous. Turning now from the effect of the oil price rises on oil demand, the next section looks at the extent to which national growth rates differed after 1973.

Macroeconomic performances, 1973–9

In aggregate terms the NOPECs experienced a fall in GDP growth from a 7.3% increase in 1973 to 5.3% the following year, then 4.1% in 1975. In these last two years their real growth rate was significantly down on the 1967–72 average of 6.1% per annum (IMF, 1978, p. 11). By continent, there were again marked differences in experience, as Table 9.2 shows.

When individual country data is examined, using UN *National Accounts Statistics* yearbooks, again it becomes evident that most ldcs' growth rates were substantially different after 1973 from the prior years. There are, however, a number of provisos which must be raised before the results can be discussed in more detail. First, to some extent the sample of ldcs in the UN yearbooks is self-selecting. Only forty-five ldcs provide GDP data for a sufficiently long period for analysis to be carried out; moreover, those ldcs not reporting are likely, *ceteris paribus*, to be among the poorer ones, so that the reported sample is biased towards the middle-income ldcs. To the extent that the latter possess more sophisticated industrial sectors, their ability to respond to the 1973 oil price rises will be different from the average of all ldcs. Secondly, the selection of the first time period — in this case 1964–73 — also tends to affect the results in that different spans in the 1960s and 1970s were associated with different economic circumstances. In some of these years primary product exporting ldcs enjoyed favourable prices; in others very low prices. The impact of such factors as these on GDP, possibly after a complex series of lags, cannot be overlooked.

The results of the exercise indicate a general deceleration in growth after 1973. Seventeen ldcs experienced a faster growth rate after 1973; twenty-eight ldcs saw a fall. Among those with increased GDP growth, however, were three OPEC members (Iraq, Venezuela, Indonesia) and Syria, a country much affected by OPEC aid. But certain countries' appearances amongst those with higher post-1973 growth rates cannot easily be explained. There is no obvious reason, for instance, why Haiti's annual average growth should have risen from 2.1% in 1964—73 to 6.3% in 1974—6, the highest proportionate increase discovered. Similarly, the result for Saudi Arabia (a fall from 12.2% to 5.5%) would seem to owe more to an infelicitous choice of price deflator than to any faltering in the real growth in the Saudi economy.

Further investigation based on a sample of twenty-four ldcs' log-linear real growth rates of GDP and GNP over the period 1967—78 allowed deviations from the trend of each country's growth to be measured and plotted. (Trend growth rates are shown in Table 9.3.) These were expressed as percentage deviations. The results of the percentage deviation analysis are summarised in Figure 9.1, which shows the sample of twenty-four ldcs, selected chiefly on grounds of data availability.[1] The prime objective borne in mind in selecting and manipulating the data was to assess the extent to which the OPEC price rises of 1973 had been associated with greater subsequent volatility in the ldcs' growth experience. At this stage no attempt was made to establish lines of causality; rather, two sub-periods (1967—73 and 1974—8) were merely compared.

Five results stand out. First, more ldcs experienced their greatest deviations from trend *before* 1973 than *after* it. While the longer period can be expected to account for some of this difference (seven years as opposed to five), it is significant that there was no clear bunching of major deviations after 1973 (see Table 9.4).

Second, the year in which the largest number of negative deviations took place was also prior to 1973: it was 1967. Following 1967 in order of largest number of negative deviations from trend were 1976 and 1977. It is notable that 1973 and 1974 had among the fewest negative deviations from trend, a factor most likely associated with the world economic boom and commodities price surge of those years. Next, the year in which the largest number of peak negative deviations occurred was 1977. This result, which perhaps accords better with the popular image of the 1973 oil price rises having had a serious deleterious impact upon most ldcs, is buttressed by another: of the twenty-four less developed countries in the sample, fifteen had their worst slump after 1973, while only nine experienced this prior to 1973. Of those nine ldcs, four of them found their greatest negative deviation occurring in 1967. While the reasons for this are

Table 9.3   *Trend of real GDP growth rates; twenty-four NOPECs, 1967–78*

	Trend growth rate %	't' value of trend	R^2	Durbin-Watson
Argentina[b]	3.31	7.76	0.86	0.67
Brazil[c]	9.76	31.4	0.99	0.75
Burma[d]	3.37	11.0	0.94	1.09
Chile[c]	1.32	2.7	0.44	1.37
Columbia[c]	5.83	40.6	0.99	0.60
Costa Rica[b]	6.21	39.1	0.99	0.99
Dominican Republic[c]	9.91	13.9	0.96	0.56
Ghana[e]	3.90	14.2	0.97	2.01
Egypt[d]	4.59	17.5	0.97	1.78
Guatemala[c]	5.86	46.2	0.99	1.96
India[d]	3.26	11.2	0.94	1.56
Jamaica[c]	1.90	2.4	0.39	0.48
South Korea[b]	9.78	54.3	0.99	1.80
Pakistan[b]	3.72	20.9	0.98	1.77
Philippines[a,b]	6.00	48.9	0.99	0.84
Salvador[b]	4.69	38.9	0.99	0.56
Singapore[b]	9.58	20.2	0.98	0.31
Taiwan[a,b]	8.31	24.5	0.98	0.97
Tanzania[c]	4.38	41.9	0.99	1.96
Sri Lanka[c]	4.37	20.3	0.98	1.57
Thailand[b]	7.06	85.8	0.99	2.39
Turkey[a,b]	6.24	42.7	0.99	1.04
Zaire[c]	3.26	4.4	0.69	0.53
Zambia[b]	3.28	8.9	0.89	1.36

a   GNP, not GDP
b   1967–78 period
c   1967–77 period
d   1967–76 period
e   1967–75 period

Source: Calculated from International Monetary Fund statistics.

not immediately relevant here, it could be noted that 1966 and 1967 witnessed falls in the general level of commodity prices after a peak for the decade had been attained in 1964. A further reason for the cluster of poor results around 1967 is likely to have been the bad economic circumstances of the major OECD countries then. The same time series analysis was carried out for a sample of five such countries (France, Japan, UK, USA, West Germany) and found that all five experienced negative deviations from their growth trend in 1967 (see Table 9.5). This poor record was equalled only by 1975 and 1976, when all again recorded negative deviations. Since the growth rate of OECD countries has a demonstrable

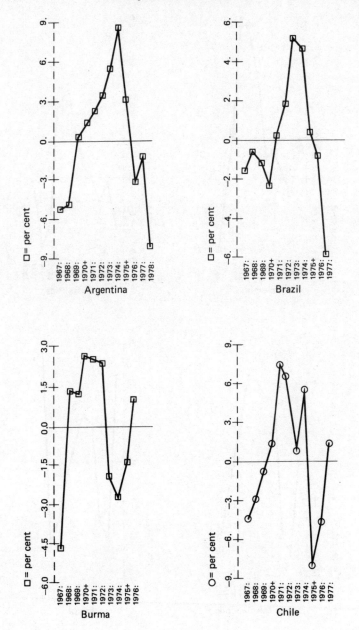

Figure 9.1 *Deviations from GDP growth trends: twenty-four selected NOPECS*

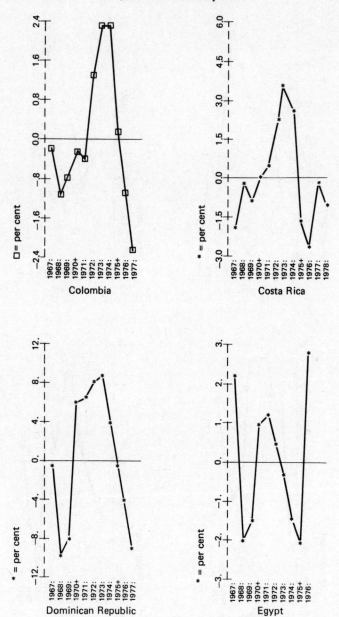

Figure 9.1 (*cont.*)

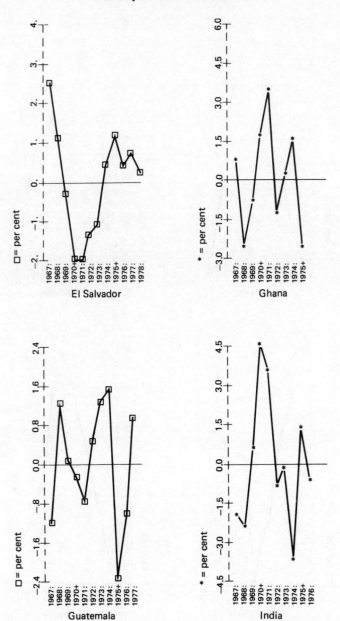

Figure 9.1 (*cont.*)

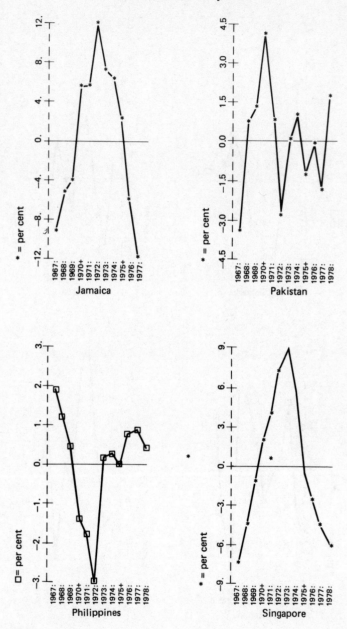

Figure 9.1 (*cont.*)

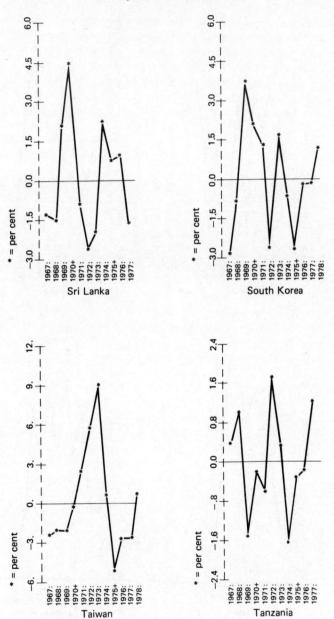

Figure 9.1 (*cont.*)

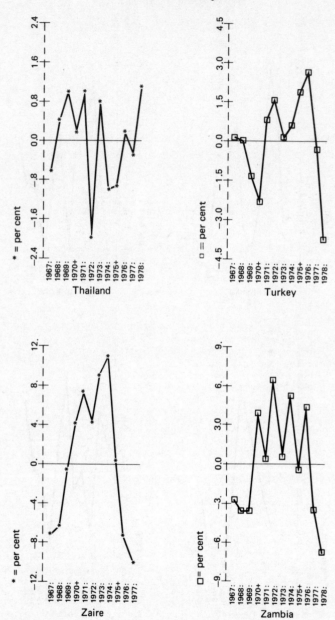

Figure 9.1 (*cont.*)

Table 9.4 Summary of log-linear GDP growth rate deviations, sample of twenty-four ldcs over 1967–78, in percentage terms

	1967	1968	1969	1970	1971	1972	1973	1974	1975	1976[a]	1977[b]	1978[c]
No. of negative deviations in year	18	16	15	8	6	8	5	6	14	15	15	5
No. of countries having maximum negative deviation in year	4	1	0	1	0	3	0	2	4	1	5	3
No. of countries having maximum deviation in year	2	0	1	3	1	3	3	4	2	1	2	2
Biggest % deviation in year	-7.63	-9.41	-7.15	6.11	7.45	12.1	9.13	10.64	-7.67	-7.79	-11.8	-8.24
Mean absolute deviation of year	2.78	2.38	1.66	2.22	2.41	3.37	2.95	3.13	1.67	2.23	2.99	2.81
Standard deviation of year	2.43	2.26	1.70	1.80	2.24	2.28	3.28	2.75	1.73	2.12	3.49	2.83
Coefficient of variation of year	0.872	0.949	1.025	0.809	0.931	0.854	1.108	0.881	1.038	0.948	1.164	1.004

a 23 country sample
b 20 country sample
c 11 country sample

Table 9.5 *Summary of log-linear GDP growth rate deviations, sample of five OECD countries over 1967–78, in percentage terms*

	1967	1968	1969	1970	1971	1972	1973	1974	1975	1976	1977	1978
Number of countries reporting negative deviations in year	5	4	2	2	2	1	0	1	5	5	4	4
Number of countries reporting biggest deviation in year	2	0	0	0	0	0	3	0	0	0	0	0
Mean absolute deviation of year	4.122	2.29	0.806	2.42	2.21	2.98	5.77	1.99	2.638	1.41	2.106	2.514
Standard deviation of year	4.030	1.618	0.295	2.089	1.604	2.59	2.538	0.969	1.211	0.827	1.096	1.586

impact upon that in ldcs (the precise closeness of which naturally depends on the nature and extent of a particular ldcs' involvement in the international economy) one would expect to find a relationship between OECD and ldc growth in this way.

The fourth point brought out by the data is that only two ldcs (El Salvador and the Philippines) experienced no negative deviations after 1974. No ldcs were free of negative deviations in the 1967–73 period. Only a further two ldcs experienced a single year of negative deviations after 1973: the mode number of below-trend years during 1974–8 was two, with ten ldcs. A further seven ldcs experienced three below-trend years and three more experienced four below-trend years.

Fifth, only five ldcs between them accounted for all of the biggest deviations from trend. Persistently, Zaire, Argentina, Dominican Republic, Chile and Jamaica recorded the greatest negative movements away from trend. No other ldc ever recorded the biggest deviation (either positive or negative) in a year.

Examination of the standard deviations of the sample countries in each year further indicates no greater dispersion of experience after 1973. Indeed, the 1975 figure (1.73) was the second lowest recorded over the twelve year period. The standard deviations, when charted, trace a volatile pattern with lows in 1969 and 1975 and peaks in 1973 and 1977. While 1977 was the highest value (3.49) this greater dispersion was not typical of the 1974–8 spell: the average standard deviation of those years (at 2.58) was not significantly higher than that during the 1967–73 period (at 2.37). No obvious reason for the cyclical pattern of the standard deviations appears to exist. It may be, however, that, to the extent that ldcs' own growth experience is linked to dcs' growth (perhaps with a lag of one year or so), the dispersion of a representative sample of ldcs' GDP or GNP about their growth trends should be less when economic activity in dcs is slow. By contrast, when growth in dcs is rapid, one might expect a widening of growth between those ldcs engaged in supplying dcs with imports, reflecting in turn ldcs' varying successes in overcoming supply bottlenecks.

Finally, examination of the coefficient of variation of the sample indicates an extremely volatile time series, with every change being in the opposite direction to the previous change. Five of the observations are in excess of unity; six are below.

For three of the ldcs in this sample (Argentina, India and the Philippines) the time series was extended back to 1958, to assess the extent to which the selection of 1967 as the starting-point of the trends had given a misleading impression of the importance of the 1973–4 deviations. It transpired that for all three countries there had been worse years than 1967. For Argentina, 1963 was a year of extremely large negative deviation unparalleled until 1978. For India, 1966 was a worse year than 1967 and again was not paralleled until 1974. For the Philippines, the negative deviation of 1967 was merely the culmination of a sequence of four bad years: it was thus not an untypically bad year, and the following five years were without exception worse. There seems little reason to believe, therefore, that the negative deviations reported in 1967 were abnormally bad and would thus serve to understate the extent to which the ldcs sampled were thrown off course after 1974.

The overall view obtained from these five results is that few ldcs found their post-1973 performance significantly more volatile than it had been prior to 1973. Although there were nearly twice as many maximum negatives after 1973 as before, the total number of negative deviations in any year was no higher, on average, after 1973. Over the entire 1967–78 period there were on average 11.5 negative deviations in any year. Given the sample size of twenty-four this suggests that the years examined were no more than averagely turbulent. A few ldcs experienced particularly severe upsets: the five ldcs mentioned above were notable for their volatility. Overall, however, the data examined here provide little evidence to support a hypothesis that economic instability in the ldcs, especially the extent to which they were knocked off their growth paths, was substantially and deleteriously affected by the events of 1973.

Conclusions

The various tests carried out to assess the growth patterns of two samples of ldcs before and after the 1973 oil price rises do not show that the post-1973 period was more than normally turbulent. This is true whether the percentage deviation from the 1967–78 growth of GDP trend or the absolute deviation in domestic currency terms is used. It also transpires that there was no greater dispersion of experience within the ldcs sampled after 1973 than before; indeed, the standard deviation recorded in 1975 – the year when one might have expected the lagged impact of the oil price rises to have been greatest – was the second lowest of the period measured. Growth rates over a much longer time period were also examined in the case of three ldcs to see whether by selecting the year 1967 as the starting-point of the analysis any disturbances during or after 1973 had been understated. This was found not to have been the case, and the 1967–78 spell therefore appears to be a legitimate time period for this type of work. However, rates of economic growth in the NOPEC area do seem to have slowed down somewhat after 1973 compared to before that year.

Notes

1 The data used here were from the IMF *International Financial Statistics* disks. In each case a curve of the form $Y = a (\exp bX)$ was fitted to the GNP time series. Table 9.3 shows the R^2, t-test and Durbin-Watson results for each of the twenty-four in the sample.

10

Oil, Debt and Development: An Assessment

The task of this final chapter is to draw together the elements of the relationship between OPEC and the ldcs that have been assessed piece by piece in the preceding chapters. In so doing it is concerned in particular to assess the extent of the 'solidarity' that is alleged to exist between OPEC and the rest of the 'Group of 77' in the developing world. While the topic of relations between members of the Third World is intrinsically interesting, it particularly invites study because of the frequency with which the congruence of interests between OPEC and ldcs is asserted. The introduction began by suggesting that the matrix of relationships fashioned over the 1970s was perceived differently by different members of both groups, was accorded different priorities as time passed, and came to be seen both as an asset and as a liability. Moreover, since the two sets of countries mentioned above can only be dichotomised and treated as coherent, mutually exclusive sets for the crudest analysis, any deeper assessment requires that the relevant tensions *within* each group also be taken into consideration. The following sections therefore present a *tour d'horizon* of the major political issues in the OPEC–ldc relationship.

So far the evidence from the chapters dealing with the terms of trade (Chapter 4), aid (Chapter 6) and debt (Chapter 5) has suggested that initially OPEC countries were reluctant to admit that their action in swiftly increasing the price of oil had seriously affected the welfare of ldcs. Latterly, while remaining reluctant to admit this, and attempting instead to draw the ldcs' fire on to dcs instead, OPEC members have made serious efforts to assist, by aid, many of those countries most badly affected. The same cannot be said of trade trends, however, which indicate, if anything, a desire on the part of the OPEC trading nations to deal with the most successful and the proven deliverers. While several individual ldcs have succeeded in substantially increasing their exports to OPEC, the emerging patterns support (wherever data permits) the proposition that success in industrial exports has been the prerogative of only a handful of ldcs. In principle, of course, there is no reason why the impulses leading to closer political or aid links with certain NOPECs should also lead to trade links with the same countries. There is no attempt here to construct — or, indeed, to search for — a universal theory of OPEC international relations. For there is clearly no reason why such a theory should exist, any more than should a ubiquitous theory of urbanisation, for instance. The chapter begins by tracing the history of Arab involvement in African diplomacy, beginning with the initiatives following from President Nasser's new relationship with the Soviet Union. It then discusses the tensions which this involvement underwent in the 1960s and then in the 1970s as a result of the higher oil prices set by OPEC and goes on to assess the differences between OPEC members' interests. The importance, within OPEC, of Saudi Arabian strategy is assessed, then the overall relationship between OPEC and the NOPECs is examined. Throughout, the differences between the increasingly active diplomatic apparatus of OPEC as an entity and as a collection of states are contrasted with the economic assessments made in the earlier chapters.

The political shrinking of the Saharah

The chemistry of the Arab—Africa relationship after the 1950s led to increasingly close ties, shared experiences and common aspirations. As is well known, by 1972–3 most African countries had defected to the Arab diplomatic camp and away from that of Israel. Yet no sooner had this relationship been forged than it came under pressure. Writers and statesmen in both continents had long foreseen or advocated an Afro-Arab nexus. Gamal Nasser's book *Philosophy of the Revolution* foresaw much greater co-operation and moves towards what Mazrui has termed 'the political shrinking of the Saharah' (1977, p. 138). Nkrumah of Ghana symbolically married an Egyptian girl, partly from a desire to demonstrate the lines of his own thinking, and along with Nyerere of Tanzania, Sekou Toure of Guinea, Modibo Keita of Mali, a number of black African statesmen turned to the north for inspiration. Some years previously, Ghana and the Sudan had been among those attending the first conference of the non-aligned movement in 1955. The weight of the Asian countries in its founding (India, Pakistan, Ceylon, Burma and Indonesia) tended to diminish the sense of African unity there, however, and neither the following Accra Conference (1958) nor the Addis Ababa Conference (1963) brought much more sense of unity to the African continent.

Meanwhile, Nasser had by 1960 become a charismatic figure of enormous appeal to the Arab masses. While remaining independent of the communist apparatus as it operated in the USSR, Nasser came to embrace what he saw as a form of modified socialism which, he felt, allowed Arab culture (which remained more firmly atuned to Western language, literature and thought than to Soviet culture) to coexist with judicious elements of Soviet technology and modernism. In three important respects

Egypt from 1955 onwards came to possess important attractions for other leaders on the Continent. First, by his breaking with the traditional Western arms supply monopoly, and openly ordering Russian matériel through Czechoslovakia, Nasser effectively signalled to the rest of the continent that alternative policy was available. Despite their almost total unpreparedness and lack of strategic vision — failures which, most critics would agree, characterised the entirety of their Arab involvement — the Soviet leadership were keen to be drawn into the region. Secondly, by thinking out and even writing a set of guidelines by which African statesmen could best deal with the Soviets, Nasser played the part of intermediary or fixer between the two, again requiring that Egypt be the focus of this new foreign policy departure for others in Africa. As late as 1968, the new Sudanese president el-Nimeiry was consulting Nasser about how to make his first overtures to Moscow (Heikel, 1978, p. 208). And thirdly, by his skilful use of stage management Nasser was able to bolster the prestige both of his government and his country in such displays as the opening of the Aswan Dam in 1961. Built by the Soviets after Western agencies had backed out after years of prevarication, the dam symbolised the daring and skill of the Egyptians in extracting assistance from Moscow, the possibilities open for other African countries if they followed suit and played by Nasser's rules, and, to Khruschev and his attendant colleagues, the likelihood of greater industrial development in the Nile valley and the consequent creation of an industrial proletariat.

However, the hesitancy which most African statesmen brought to the Egyptian precedent was increased by the fact that Israel had become an important source of aid, particularly technical assistance. African statesmen were moreover impressed by Israeli success in fostering development in their own inauspicious circumstances. At the same time, however, there were doubts over Israel's ties with South Africa, with Rhodesia, with the USA above all; and with the suspicion that entry to Israel was circumscribed for Jews who happened to be black. Finally, the belief that much Israeli aid was directly compensated by the CIA rather tarnished its attraction.

Bolstering the suspicion that there might be a case for breaking with the Israelis, the more diplomatically adventurous statesmen in Africa were also inclined to think that in extent, if not in effectiveness, Arab aid might conceivably contribute more to their countries' economic development.

By 1973 more African countries were ready to side with the Arabs. At the November Algiers summit the Arabs were able to offer their abandoning of relations with South Africa in return for African support against Israel, the catalyst in this final break having been South African aid (both sending Mirage jets and money) to Israel during the 1973 Arab-Israeli war. While in 1967 a few African states had broken their links with Israel, in 1973 twenty-seven others followed within weeks.

Tensions in the 1970s

Almost as soon as these links were forged, however, they came under strain. In the judgement of Mazrui what had been achieved through a mixture of Arab enticement and African willingness amounted to something special: 'Never in modern history did there seem to be as much solidarity between Arab Africans and black Africans as there emerged, however inconclusively, in the course of 1972 and 1973' (Mazrui, 1977, p. 145). Yet even before the end of 1973 at an extraordinary meeting of the Organisation of African Unity (OAU), hurriedly convened to debate the oil price rises announced days before, several African heads of state had voiced disquiet. Statesmen from Tanzania, Ghana and Kenya, among other countries, requested reduced oil prices or direct oil sales outside the multinational companies' distribution apparatus. OPEC rejected these requests on the ground that they were too complex and instead began, with a $200 million offering, the flow of Arab aid to Africa. In the same month the Arab summit held in Algeria established three new aid agencies, the Arab Fund, the Arab Bank for Economic Development in Africa (headquarters in Khartoum) and the Arab Fund for Technical Aid to Africa.

While the full cost of the higher oil prices introduced in 1973 had yet to become apparent, the African states were shortly made aware of a second set of costs attaching to their new diplomatic alignment — the loss of much US sympathy and the loss even of US food aid. The latter point was seized upon by the new and ebullient United States representation (orchestrated by their Ambassador, Daniel P. Moynihan) at the UN as an illustration of the lack of forethought that some of the African states had shown in their recent manoeuvring, and lent some sting to the Africans' difficulties. For at the insistence of the Algerians, then in the ascendant at the 1974 Sixth Special Session of the UN, the non-aligned ldcs were obliged to turn down the $4 billion-worth of additional food aid offered by the USA in respect of food shortages and fertiliser price rises. By the spring of 1974, then, those African heads of state who had envisaged a more comfortable passage with the Arab bloc had had several unexpected costs revealed to them.

The further 10% oil price rise of September 1975 prompted the Tanzanian minister of commerce and industries to observe that OPEC were 'appearing to turn their backs on the developing countries, particularly the least developed' (*New African Development*, February 1977, p. 117). (By 1975, OPEC's various multilaterial aid agencies had yet to begin proper functioning. As explained in Chapter 6, non-Muslim ldcs were in the second wave of recipients, after the initial phase during which OPEC aid was almost exclusively channelled to Islamic states.) In the same year President Mobutu of Zaire was quoted by *Al-Ahram* as being willing in principle to restore relations with Israel, so little did he feel his country had gained from the Arabs. Indeed, the vote at the UN in November 1975 on the notorious resolution equating Zionism with racism showed the extent to which growing awareness of the costs attaching to diplomatic distancing from the West coupled with reluctance wholly to commit themselves to the Arabs' struggle with Israel had led African ldcs within two years to retrench. The Third Committee vote on the draft resolution did not result in a solidly anti-Israel vote from the ldcs: twenty-six abstained and a further fifteen were 'absent' from the chamber; this included sixteen in Africa. The suspicion that the loss of Israeli aid had not yet met with a *quid pro quo* — that the Arabs had still not made any sacrifices — was clearly not being allayed. True, Arab states had never accorded diplomatic recognition to South Africa and Rhodesia, countries which the OPEC statesmen involved were concerned to represent as the enemies of black Africa. But this principle had cost them nothing. At least one OPEC member (Iran) was continuing to sell oil to these countries, either directly in the case of exports of crude to South Africa, or through 'swap' arrangements in the case of Rhodesia.

President Siad Barre of Somalia had suggested to the Seventh Arab Summit of October 1974 that there should be an Afro-Arab summit in March 1977. This, the first such gathering of heads of state, was held in Cairo and was attended by thirty-nine African and twenty-one Arab representatives. Those representing states which were only in the OAU came conscious of the weaknesses revealed at their own summit in Mauritius six months before, which only seven presidents had bothered to attend. In OPEC, the Saudis came now as regional peacemakers (in the Lebanese civil war, in the Syrian-Iraqi tension, in the South Yemen—Oman war and elsewhere); this 'busy new policy'[1] had contained just sufficient substance for them to retain authority in the eyes of the OPEC radicals.

The diplomatic activity which was a prelude to this summit turned up many hopeful references to unity. President Senghor of Senegal spoke of the 'Afro-Arab continent', but the central issue of the meeting was best posed by an Egyptian journalist who judged that 'the two sides are still searching for a suitable form for their mutual interests' (*New African Development*, February 1977, p. 117). More recently, friction arose at the fifth UNCTAD conference at Manila in May 1979. Energy matters had deliberately been kept off the agenda, with OPEC maintaining that as far as UNCTAD was concerned they were not an oil cartel but simply members of the African group. Despite this stage-management the matter inevitably entered discussions. Significantly, it was those Latin American ldcs not in receipt of much OPEC aid that took the initiative in the months before UNCTAD V by pressing Venezuela to offer lower oil prices. Venezuela, keen to defuse these tensions and especially keen to be perceived as its region's natural leader rather than Mexico or Brazil, had expended a lot of effort prior to the conference, with a two week tour by the energy minister in North Africa and the Middle East. The creation of OPIC, as mentioned in the Introduction, was a further embarrassment if only a minor diversion. So too was the renewed request, at the OAU meeting in Monrovia in July 1979, from Mali and Sierra Leone, that another oil fund be established to help the poorest among the black African states. As OPEC members, Gabon and Nigeria opposed the suggestion,[2] and managed to have a full discussion postponed until the OAU ministerial council at the end of the year. The question posed by this persistent series of requests for and denials of concessional oil, then, is whether or not it raises, in OPEC members' eyes, fundamental diplomatic problems or merely minor annoyances. To answer this the configuration of interests within OPEC must be examined in some detail.

OPEC interests: unity and fragmentation

The view is often expressed that the OPEC states, and Saudi Arabia in particular, are victims of their own success. For the more they are able to dictate the terms at which crude oil is traded internationally, the worse the payments problems of the NOPECs become, and, correspondingly, the weaker their support for OPEC in international forums. While certain members of OPEC can mitigate the effects of higher oil prices with a screen of radical rhetoric the Saudis are significantly less willing to do so. (All available evidence underlines the profound conservatism of the centralised Saudi decision making apparatus.) But these simpler versions of the argument that OPEC states must tread a tightrope between income maintenance and political alienation are not particularly convincing. To begin with, by no means all of the black African states which were wooed away from Israel in 1972–3 were convinced of the intrinsic merits of the Arabs' case; some, certainly (Guinea, Congo), made the change primarily for ideological reasons; Niger for religious motives, and Uganda for its own reasons to do with its Israeli-trained army. But the others (Kenya, Ethiopia, the small West African states) did so more for fear of being 'isolated from continental African diplomatic trends' (Mazrui, 1977, p. 145). Given this bundle of motives for making the break, it follows that the receipt of sufficient Arab aid as *quid pro quo* need be neither necessary nor sufficient to sustain this realignment. Moreover, there are reasons to believe that in addition to the heterogeneity of motives behind the Africans' shift of allegiance, there was a fundamental difference of intent. While the Arab partners anticipated a political alliance of some form (and presumably a less intimate one than that presaged by Nasser and Nkrumah years before), the Africans preferred to instigate what Mazrui has termed an 'economic partnership', whereby oil might have been sold or bartered advantageously for (say) African exports to OPEC states.

Ranged against this somewhat fragile coalition of interests stood a definite uneasiness on the part of several of the OPEC partners to entertain plans of anything stronger, deeper or longer. Above all in the OPEC camp, Saudi Arabia had a difficult foreign policy task deriving from being a conservative monarchy in an apparently radical cartel, and from having a lot to lose from undermining the confidence and backing of the United States. Saudi interests in the OPEC–ldcs nexus were thus even less plain than those of its other OPEC partners.[3] On the other hand Saudi Arabia could not be said to 'need' the alliance with the ldc camp, either financially or militarily. The loss of ldc support in the UN or at the various specialised agencies' international conferences could hardly have begun a precipitate decline in the price of oil, for that price had by the late 1970s acquired a momentum of its own. Indeed, in the opinion of the *Petroleum Economist* the task of OPEC as an oil cartel had long been accomplished: 'As far as price-maintenance is concerned, the Organisation might almost as well be disbanded tomorrow' (*Petroleum Economist*, August 1979, p. 311). And as for the diplomatic dangers of leaving OPEC, the USA could reasonably be counted upon as an active ally, even if its manifest paralysis in the early months of the Iran crisis had called the strength of this support into question. Since 1973 the Saudis came to hold some $35 billion in US government securities and a further $25 billion in other American assets (Dawisha, 1979). They had also acted in defence of American interests by attempting on occasion to suppress oil price rises, even though this incurred the anger of Iran, Iraq, Syria and Libya. Thus, the notion (which is still frequently seen in press reports) that 'Saudi Arabia and Kuwait, whose regimes live in fear of overthrow, will be eager to seek political allies among the poor' is a complete misperception of the issue. Quite apart from the questionable assessment of the security of the 'regimes' in these countries, there is absolutely no reason to believe that these regimes are any more stable if they forge fractured and fragile accords with NOPECs.

At the same time Saudi Arabia was in the early 1970s by no means keen to assume the role of a regional power. Naturally the kingdom had taken an active interest in the affairs of neighbouring states but in the case of radical-leaning governments initiatives from Riyadh had typically taken the form of discreet grants in return for quiescence. While there had unquestionably been failures, as Chapter 6 indicated, this low-profile stance could be expected to continue as the main form of foreign policy, in part because of the absence of a reliably trained army. As for the content of policy, Saudi Arabia again had a lot to lose from assuming too overt a part in foreign policy in the area, since all of her policies or desires could be seen as falling into much the same line as US policy in the area. And the last thing Saudi policy makers wanted was a clear division to emerge in the Middle East between two camps: those pro-Western and those not (Ramazani, 1979, p. 824). Particularly over the Egypt-Israel conflict (as Chapter 6 again discusses, in the light of Egyptian aid receipts) Saudi Arabia stood to lose far more from Egyptian reversion to radical or closer USSR alignment than she had to gain by sharper public identification with Libya, Iraq or her more impetuous OPEC colleagues (Abir, 1974).

It might appear that the chief cost to the Saudis of becoming identified with the ldcs (say in their 'Group of 77' form) would be a corresponding distancing from the USA (Issawi, 1974). Yet too close an association with the US in the public eye was also to be avoided. A full assessment of Saudi foreign policy is beyond the scope of this book, but there is one element which more than any other conditions Saudi regional relations and thence Saudi–ldc relations. This is the perennial topic of Soviet interest in the region. There are analysts in the West that are convinced of continued Soviet military ambitions in the Middle East. These would have two reasons: the geo-political advantage to be obtained from greater influence in 'the last major region of the Free World directly adjacent to the Soviet Union' (Lenczowski, 1979, p. 796), and the fact that control over Middle East oil would give the USSR an edge over the Western economies that virtually nothing else could (Foreign Affairs Research Institute, 1979). Yet motive does not prove intent, and many of the events over 1973–8 which appear to support a Soviet influence interpretation can also be marshalled to suggest the opposite.[4]

The proposition that the USSR will increasingly be drawn to the region for another reason – the likely transition in the early 1980s from a net exporter to a net importer of crude oil – complicates the picture, as does the counterpoint that Soviet aggression on this count, even if intended, must be delayed until sufficient Western oil technology has been acquired to allow full use to be made of the region's resources (*Petroleum Review*, August 1979, p. 4; Willrich, 1975; Park, 1979; *FT*, 3 September 1979; *Petroleum Economist*, September 1979, p. 356; Hoffman, 1979). No resolution of this complex topic is possible here. What can be observed is, briefly, that by 1977 Soviet interest in the Middle East, which had begun almost by surprise in 1955 in Egypt, was ruined. The Palestinians alone remained faithful, but they of course possessed no land and their motives were in any case hard for Soviet strategists to comprehend. Most of the African countries which had passed through the phase of flirtation with the USSR had amassed substantial debts and were unwilling to pay them back; Ghana, along with Syria and Egypt, were threatening to default (Heikel, 1978, p. 172). The Soviets were in any case uncertain of the reasons for their being invited into the continent: were they intrinsically valuable or merely substitutes for a US presence? Cultural differences abounded. Moreover, Nasser's death removed the closest tie to the continent the Soviets possessed. They had never been able adequately to diversify from this link and their summary expulsion by Sadat two years later convinced them of the precarious nature of their African adventure.

The Yom Kippur war provided another opportunity to extract gains from the Middle East. By encouraging the Arabs to persist with their oil boycott of the USA (in the face of opposition both from Egypt and Saudi

Arabia) Moscow hoped to intensify American interest in Siberian oil and thus obtain improved access to the US technology so desperately needed there (Golan, 1977, p. 150). This naturally brought tensions between the Saudis and the Soviets, and the propaganda of the latter, presenting King Feisal as a puppet of a US effort to fragment the Middle East and sell arms, hardly mollified relations (Golan, 1977, p. 201). In the event the failure of the Kremlin to prolong the embargo on the USA was fairly widely seen as 'a defeat for the Soviet leadership' (Freedman, 1976, p. 308).

What this delicate foreign policy posture of Saudi Arabia within OPEC points to is a reluctance to have OPEC appear as overly hostile to the interests of the developed West; as plainly unhappy about the negotiations between the fragmented yet moderate leadership in Egypt over the Palestine and Israeli questions; but none the less as unequivocally behind the ldcs' positions on such 'soft' matters as the common fund for primary product price stabilisation, debt rescheduling, and the larger questions of the north–south dialogue. While Saudi Arabia had initially seen it as being entirely in her interests to press for the extension of the original American plan for an oil producer–consumer dialogue (there having unquestionably been a marked change in US foreign policy after the impact of an oil boycott had been demonstrated), the resulting Paris Conference on International Economic Co-operation which began in December 1975 subsequently spawned forums and pressures which were less attractive (Quandt, 1976, pp. 288–90). From taking explicit lines on the cluster of issues just listed Saudi Arabia stood to gain little and jeopardise a lot.

With the assassination of King Feisal in 1975, however, and the ascendancy of Crown Prince Fahd among Saudi decision makers, initiatives have been somewhat bolder. By 1976, Iranian regional defence expenditure had become substantial and 'Saudi Arabia's increasingly active diplomacy, added to Iran's security policy, poured concrete meaning into the hitherto empty rhetoric of an American "twin-pillar policy"' (Ramazani, 1979, p. 822). A preference remained, however, for unobtrusive policies, preferably those with a moral or religious veneer. Aid to NOPECs fulfilled these needs and grew very rapidly. Before this is discussed, however, OPEC policy in Latin America is examined.

OPEC in Latin America

One of the most significant points revealed in Chapter 7 dealing with trade between OPEC states and ldcs was the dominance of a dozen or so exporting countries in this relationship. Of necessity, these tended to be ldcs which had, prior to the influx of imports to OPEC members after 1973, already set up fairly sophisticated pockets of industry; also they were, predictably, those ldcs with considerable export experience already accumulated from trade in manufactures with dcs. (Chapter 1 indicated the extent of this trade and its recent rapid growth.) But the point of particular interest here concerns the dominance of Mexico and Brazil among the OPEC trading partners. For Latin America tended initially to be of little concern to OPEC aid agencies and indeed to OPEC states' foreign relations. Yet managing OPEC interests in Latin America (that is, presenting the cartel's point of view and dispensing its largesse) quickly came to be too big a task for Venezuela, which was anyway caught up with its own preoccupations in the form of general elections (in 1974 and 1978), virtually uncontrolled public expenditure and its ambitions as spokesman for Central America. The tensions at UNCTAD V, with some small Latin American countries led by Costa Rica making a gesture of defiance in the form of OPIC (the Organisation of Petroleum Importing Countries), encouraged the spread of OPEC aid to that continent. While, in terms of income per head or need for infrastructure, several of the countries there cannot be said to need OPEC aid as desperately as most African states, the more extensive industrial structures of these countries has reduced their ability quickly to cut down their oil products consumption. As Chapter 9 showed, many of the biggest interruptions to growth (and as Chapter 5 showed, many of the biggest debts built up) were in Latin American ldcs. In partial recognition of this, OPEC Special Fund loans in 1979 were awarded to Honduras ($3.5 million for a hydroelectric project); Haiti ($4 million for storm damage); and Bolivia ($5 million for urban sewerage).

The likelihood of there being greater interest in Latin American affairs by the Arab OPEC countries is difficult to assess at present. Within OPEC, there are certain tensions that would prevent Venezuela from wishing to be seen as too committed a member of the Organisation. First, Venezuela's decline as a major oil producer (from the late 1940s until 1960 Venezuela was the major source of US crude imports) can be traced to the increasing competition suffered from lower-cost Middle Eastern oil sources. While in the 1960s the existence of OPEC did not materially affect Venezuela's oil prospects — her oil exports were largely supply-constrained — the same members of OPEC came by 1973 to have obtained far greater benefits than Venezuela. The fact that Venezuela was the founder member of OPEC, under the guidance of Juan Pablo Perez Alfonzo, ensured that this was an irony not lost on dissatisfied voters in that country. As Vallenilla, the historian of Venezuelan involvement in OPEC, has put it: 'the production growth in the Middle East — Venezuela's main competitor — has negatively affected the development of Venezuela's oil industry' (Vallenilla, 1975, p. 76). Although even its diminished petroleum revenues have generated substantial growth of GNP in Venezuela — by 1976 GNP per capita stood at $2,540, easily the highest in South America and twice that of Brazil — the existence of democratic pluralism requires that statesmen there stress only the benefits and not the lost opportunities of the country's oil. Secondly, Venezuela has long had regional interests which sit uneasily with overt alignment with OPEC. Through its membership of

ARPEL, the Latin American State Association for Reciprocal Oil Assistance,[5] Venezuela is made well aware of the costs imposed by oil price rises on neighbouring Latin American ldcs. Thirdly, Venezuela has not always kept ranks with the other OPEC members over some important policy questions. Notable were Venezuela's actions as the first OPEC country to lend to the World Bank, and as the initiator of a $500 million trust fund, to be administered by the Inter-American Development Bank (IADB), to assist the payments problems of its region's ldcs. There was also a scheme to sell oil to Central America and Jamaica at $6 per barrel, with the difference in price being treated as a twenty-five year 8% loan to be repaid in local currency. This 1975–80 'Central American Agreement' began in 1974 (*FT*, 6 April 1979).

The aid programme since 1973

An arena in which foreign policy objectives could be pursued without such intense interest from the press, the Soviet Union and dissenters within the OPEC camp was aid. For differences of opinion over religious matters – their substance or their weight – and strategy could all be submerged in the glow of good intent that aid engenders. Chapter 6 indicated the rapid growth of OPEC aid, its volume and institutions, and discussed the relaxation of its initial regional concentration.

While it is still far from a global programme, the use of co-financing with longer-established aid agencies has allowed diversification by type of project and recipient to flourish quickly. But what of the motives of this aid? Chapter 6 commented upon the coincidence of geo-political and ethnic interests and the extent to which these were consistent with the relative urgency of different recipient countries' needs. What did these figures indicate in political terms? Is it possible to adduce a variety of 'spheres of influence' interpretation of the spread of OPEC aid? Was there, for instance, an explicit policy to help those countries of greatest geo-political 'use' to the donors, or was this a secondary objective coinciding with an overriding aim to allocate most aid for the poorest? The intention of concentrating aid disbursements on the poorest ldcs, and – wherever possible – on the poorest groups within those ldcs, has been enshrined by all major national and multilateral aid donors in the 1970s. Since they are normally mindful of the need to be perceived as members of the Third World, it is perhaps to be expected that OPEC agencies would apply broadly similar criteria in drawing up their own aid plans. Judging from Table 6.4, however, it is apparent that the weight of Muslim countries is considerable: eighteen of these twenty main aid recipients are Muslim, with per capita GNP (in 1976 prices) in four cases exceeding $750. Moreover, of the twenty-five least developed countries identified by the UN, only six appear in this list. It is very difficult, therefore, to conclude that

OPEC bilateral aid planners have had distributional criteria high on their list.

As it happens, Chapter 6 did adduce evidence to show that after the estimated net effect of aid transfers and higher oil bills had been taken into account there was a vaguely equitable allocation of aid according to need. But this analysis presupposes that there was an *ex ante* interest in the distributive impact, and there are reasons for believing that aid flows were not seen in this light at all by the OPEC donors. Efforts have however been made by OPEC to present aid as distributionally fair as well as big in volume. An assessment of OPEC aid by the OPEC secretariat in mid 1979 concluded that a greater proportion of OPEC multilateral aid (87%) has been channelled to ldcs with GNP per capita below $800 than was the case with OECD aid (*OPEC Review*, vol. 3, no. 2, Summer 1979). In essence the OPEC position is that the world is not of their making and that poverty is largely the result of the nature of the relationship that the presently developed countries have had with the ldcs. At the Sixth Special Session of the UN General Assembly, convened at the instigation of President Boumedienne when Algeria's foreign policy was in its active phase, Sheikh Yamani rehearsed the basic OPEC view. The greater part of the aid needed by the ldcs should, he proposed, come from 'the advanced industrial countries, which receive from the developing countries prices for the manufactured goods they export to them that greatly exceed, in relative terms, the prices that oil producers realize for their oil'. Boumedienne himself gave a rather wider account of the OPEC–ldcs relationship when he proposed to the non-aligned conference in Colombo in 1976 that 'the field of international economic relations has become the main ground for confrontation between the holders of the out-dated order inherited from colonial domination, and the peoples who are aspiring to build their own road to progress' (cited in Younger, 1978, p. 113).

The OPEC stance provided a lot of contentious economic debate. Yet there was little substance to it. The OPEC Secretary General Rene G. Ortiz told UNCTAD V that the energy 'problem' could indeed be recognised, but that it could only be considered 'as an integral part of all the other problems'. Again, he insisted that OPEC stood ready to discuss oil and energy problems, 'provided there was also a readiness to include such questions as technology, raw materials and development' (*OPEC Bulletin*, 11 June 1979, p. 32). This desire constantly to be shifting the ground of the debate reveals two things. First, it suggests that OPEC prefers that the consequences for ldcs of its actions are submerged in a long and much vaguer list of economic injustices perpetrated by dcs on all ldcs including OPEC. In other words OPEC is concerned to give the appearance of closed ranks to dcs. Yet, secondly, the leisurely pace at which discussions on any of the problems caused for ldcs by the higher oil prices have proceeded strongly suggests that the substance of this sought-after solidarity is of comparatively less importance. If there were a genuine interest in identifying and mitigating the ldcs' energy problems this could have been done long before 1979. Indeed, far from there being an effort to elucidate and deal satisfactorily with the real grievances voiced by ldcs, OPEC has persistently preferred to obscure the issue. As late as 1979, for instance, an assessment of OPEC's relations with the ldcs put forward the view that 'ldcs are far more dependent for growth on the economies of [the dcs] than they are on the price of oil' (*OPEC Review*, p. vii). This point – and other similar points – seem to reveal above all a reluctance to deal seriously with the ldcs' point of view. First, the nature of the 'dependence' spoken of is clearly different in the two cases which are contrasted. While ldcs' growth prospects manifestly do depend on – among other things – dcs' growth prospects, to suggest that dc policy makers might deliberately restrain their countries' growth in order to damage ldc interests, as is implied in the sentence, is untenable. Moreover, the attempt to brush aside the impact of oil price rises which, as Chapter 2 showed, did have a significant effect upon the ldcs independent of the slower growth in exports to the depressed dcs, is unworthy. A further example of an attempt to achieve both objectives at once in the OPEC press release of 28 June 1979 which began: 'the conference expressed concern for the problems being faced by developing countries', and added, 'especially in the light of the continued lack of readiness on the part of the industrialised countries to face up to their responsibilities towards the problems of the Third World'. And once again: 'For their part, OPEC member countries have in the past proved their strong solidarity with the Third World'. This precisely echoed the speech of the Secretary General of OPEC to UNCTAD V a month earlier, which had begun by observing that OPEC spoke 'as members of the Third World Community', and, later, as 'full members of the Third World'.

Conclusions

If these attitudes adopted by OPEC appear to be disingenuous, it should be borne in mind that efforts have, as previous chapters have shown, in fact been made to ensure that the worst effects of the oil price rises have been mitigated. One of the themes which has recurred in several of the foregoing chapters has been the concentration of the impact of OPEC's price policy upon the ldcs. Not only has the growth of debt in ldcs been concentrated in relatively few countries in the 1970s, but also the OPEC multilateral and bilateral aid effort (initially at least), OPEC–ldc trade flows and labour transfers to OPEC countries have similarly been restricted to a handful of partners. In the case of both debt and trade the countries most intensively affected have tended to be the fast-industrialising group of manufactures exporting ldcs, with the addition of India and Pakistan. This finding raises the question of the distributive impact of the OPEC price policy: if the compensating gains to non-oil ldcs through extra trade, labour remittances and aid have been concentrated but the effect on their balance of payments more or less shared proportionately, does this imply that the actions of OPEC since 1973 have in any way exacerbated the differences between groups of ldcs? This is a far wider question than any which this book has set out to answer, and to confront it fully would require further research. But in so far as the distributive effect of OPEC aid programmes can be judged by the criteria of the recipient countries' income per head, or against net flows of 'extra' oil out-payments and augmented aid in-payments, the effect has been broadly equitable. Figures 6.1 and 6.2 confirm this impression. While this auspicious outcome seems to owe as much to luck as to judgement, in that the geo-political dimension of aid was normally the dominant imperative over concern for 'aid for the poorest', there seem to have been some genuine efforts to assist the least developed ldcs.

Another finding, in Chapter 9, was that for the least developed and the developing world, it would be quite wrong to conceive of 1973–4 as a watershed in growth patterns. While most of the non-oil countries experienced negative deviations from their long-run growth trends immediately after 1973, by no means all of them did. Nor were these deviations in all cases worse than preceding troughs in growth. In addition, there have been other years (1967, for instance) in which it was far more common to find ldcs being seriously deflected from their growth paths.

In conclusion, then, it can be seen that while the succession of oil price rises engineered by OPEC members during the 1970s undeniably had an impact upon the nature and direction of the non-oil ldcs' economies, it had by no means the disastrous consequences that were widely foreseen. There were no 'explosions in north–south relations'; nor was there any 'unmitigated disaster'. The overall picture which has emerged is by no means one of a clearly identifiable change in the nature of the Third World's economic structure or performance. Rather, the impact of the OPEC price rises appears to have been as diffuse and lagged and above all as disparate as the ldcs that have encountered them.

Notes

1 *The Economist*, 2 April 1977, p. 15.
2 It is, however, significant that Nigeria had proposed oil discounts for NOPECs to an OPEC meeting in 1974. One reason for the change in attitude is likely to be the great pressure on government expenditure in Nigeria after the swollen budgets of 1974–8.
3 Splits within OPEC of course predated the 1973 oil price rise. For instance, Hirst observed as early as 1966 that 'Iran's membership in OPEC has always been potentially awkward for the Arab producers, both for political reasons and because . . . Iran has always been . . . prone to attitudes of embarrassing moderation' (Hirst, 1966, p. 112). Similarly, 'the ideological split between the Socialist-style and monarchist regimes . . . prevented the conferences from advancing any closer to a unified or coordinated oil policy' (*Petroleum Intelligence Weekly*,

20 March 1967). A more recent analysis of economic interests as they differ between OPEC members is presented in Willett (1979). See also Noreng (1978), pp. 70–1. Later in this book Noreng does tend to overstate the cohesion within OPEC with respect to the importing countries interests, and refers to a 'trend towards polarization between OPEC and the International Energy Agency' (p. 156).

4 Dealing with the related question of the ability of the USA to influence this supposed Soviet threat, Campbell (1979, p. 630) has warned that 'to see the problem as primarily one of American weakness . . . is to apply a theory based on a fixed view of Soviet global strategy'.

5 This was formed in September 1966, with Argentina, Bolivia, Brazil, Colombia, Mexico, Peru, Uruguay and Venezuela as members.

Bibliography

M. Abir, *Oil Power and Politics* (London: Frank Cass, 1974).

I. Adelman and C.T. Morris, *Economic Growth and Social Equity in Developing Countries* (Stanford, Calif.: Stanford University Press, 1973).

M. A. Adelman, *The World Petroleum Market* (Baltimore, Md: Johns Hopkins Press, 1972).

M. A. Adelman, 'Politics, economics and world oil', *American Economic Review*, Papers and Proceedings, vol. 64, no. 2 (1974), pp.58–67.

M. Ahluwalia, 'Income inequality: some dimensions of the problem', in Chenery *et al.*, *Redistribution with Growth*, pp. 3–37.

R. J. Alexander, 'The import substitution strategy of economic development', *Journal of Economic Issues*, vol. 1, no.4 (1967), pp. 297–308.

S. S. Alexander, 'Devaluation versus import restrictions as a means of improving foreign trade balances', *IMF Staff Papers*, April 1951.

A. al-Janabi, 'Production and depletion policies in OPEC', *OPEC Review*, vol. III, no. 1 (March 1979), pp. 34–44.

S. Amin, 'NIEO: how to put Third World surpluses to effective use', *Third World Quarterly*, vol. 1, no. 1 (January 1979), pp. 65–72.

Arab Bank of Economic Development in Africa, *Annual Report: 1978*.

H. Askari and J. T. Cummings, *Oil, OECD and the Third World: A Vicious Triangle*, Middle East Monograph no. 5, Centre for Middle East Studies, University of Texas, Austin, 1978.

J. Baker, 'Oil and African development', *Journal of Modern African Studies*, vol. 15, no. 2 (1977), pp. 172–212.

Bank of England, *Quarterly Bulletin*, vol. 19, no.3 (September 1979), p. 250.

Bank for International Settlements, *Annual Report*, various years (Basle: BIS).

N. Baster, *Measuring Development* (London: Frank Cass, 1972).

R. A. Berry, 'Open unemployment as a social problem in urban Columbia: myth and reality', *Economic Development and Cultural Change*, vol. 23, no. 2 (January 1975).

J. S. Birks and C. A. Sinclair, 'International labour migration in the Arab Middle East', *Third World Quarterly*, vol. 1, no. 2 (April 1979), pp. 87–99.

W. R. Böhning, 'Some thoughts on emigration from the Mediterranean basin', *International Labour Review*, vol. III, no. 3 (March 1975), pp. 251–77.

A. Bouhdiba, 'Arab migration', in R. Aliboni (ed.), *Arab Industrialisation and Economic Integration* (London: Croom Helm, 1979), pp. 134–88.

E. M. Brook and E. R. Grilli, 'Commodity price stabilisation and the developing world', *Finance and Development*, vol. 14, no. 1 (1977), pp. 8–11.

Cambridge Economic Policy Review, no. 5 (April 1979).

J. C. Campbell, 'The Middle East: the burdens of empire', *Foreign Affairs*, vol. 57, no. 3, special issue (1979), pp. 613–32.

Central Bank of Yemen, *Annual Report 1974/75* (Sana).

Charles River Associates, *Policy Implications of Producer Country Supply Restrictions*, Report no. 220 (Cambridge, Mass., 1976).

H. B. Chenery, 'Introduction' in Chenery *et al.*, *Redistribution with Growth*, London: (OUP for IBRD, 1974).

H. B. Chenery and M. Syrquin, *Patterns of Development, 1950–1970* (London: OUP for IBRD, 1975).

H. B. Chenery *et al.*, *Redistribution with Growth* (London: OUP for IBRD, 1974).

M. Chossudovsky, 'Capital accumulation and unemployment in Venezuela', *Manpower and Unemployment Research*, vol. II, no. 2 (November 1978), pp. 29–51.

N. Choucri, *International Politics of Energy Interdependence* (Lexington, Mass.: Lexington Books, 1976).

CIA, *The World Oil Market in the Years Ahead* (Washington, DC: CIA, doc. ER 79 – 10327U, 1979).

H. van Cleveland and W. H. Bruce Brittain, 'Are the LDCs in over their heads?', *Foreign Affairs*, 1977.

S. D. Cohen, 'Changes in the international economy – old realities and new myths', *Journal of World Trade Law*, vol. 12, no. 4, (July 1978), pp. 273–88.

R. N. Cooper and R.S. Lawrence, 'The 1972–5 commodity boom', *Brookings Papers on Economic Activity*, no. 3 (1975), pp. 671–715.

G. Corea, 'The debt problem of developing countries', *Journal of Development Planning*, no. 9 (1976).

A. I. Dawisha, 'Internal values and external threats: the making of Saudi's foreign policy', *Orbis*, vol. 23 (Spring 1979), pp. 129–43.

Development Assistance Committee (OECD), *Development Assistance Efforts and Policies*, 1978.

J. Donges, 'A comparative survey of industrialisation policies in 15 semi-industrial countries', *Weltwirtschafts-Archiv*, vol. 113 (1977).

R. M. Dunn, 'The less developed countries', in Z. A. Yager and E. B. Steinberg (eds), *Energy and US Foreign Policy* (Mass.: Ballinger, 1974), pp. 163–81.

Economist Intelligence Unit, *Construction in the Middle East* (London: EIU Special Report no. 55, 1979).

O. Emminger, 'The exchange rate as an instrument of policy', *Lloyds Bank Review*, no. 133 (July 1979), pp. 1–22.

S. M. Essang and A. F. Mabawonku, 'The impact of urban migration on rural development: theoretical considerations, and empirical evidence from Southern Nigeria', *The Developing Economies*, vol. 13, no. 2 (June 1975), pp. 137–49.

M. A. M. Farrag, 'Migration between Arab countries', paper for seminar on unemployment in Arab countries, Beirut, 13–14 May 1975.

K. G. Fenelon, *The United Arab Emirates* (London: Longman, 1976).

D. Fischer, D. Gately and J. F. Kyle, 'The prospects for OPEC: a critical survey of models of the world oil market', *Journal of Development Economics*, vol. 2, no. 4 (1975), pp. 363–86.

Foreign Affairs Research Institute, *Soviet Strategy in the Middle East* (London, June 1979).

M. Frankena, 'Devaluation, recession and non-traditional manufactured exports from India', *Economic Development and Cultural Change*, vol. 24, no. 1 (October 1975), pp. 109–38.

E. R. Fried, 'World market trends and bargaining leverage', in J. A. Yager and E. B. Steinberg (eds.), *Energy and US Foreign Policy* (Mass.: Ballinger, 1974), pp. 231–75.

E. Freedman, 'Financing energy in developing countries', *Energy Policy*, March 1976, pp. 37–49.

R. N. Gardner, S. Okita and B. J. Udink, 'A turning point in North–South economic relations', in Trilateral Commission, 1977, pp. 57–74.

D. Gately, 'The prospects for OPEC five years after', *European Economic Review*, vol. 12, no. 4 (1979), pp. 369–79.

G. Golan, *Yom Kippur and After: The Soviet Union and the Middle East Crisis* (Cambridge: CUP, 1977).

R. Graham, *Iran – The Illusion of Power* (London: Croom Helm, 1978).

R. Granier and J.P. Marciano, 'The earnings of immigrant workers in France', *International Labour Review*, vol. III, no. 2 (February 1975), pp. 143–66.

K. Griffin, *The Political Economy Agrarian Change* (Cambridge, Mass.: Harvard University Press, 1974).

K. Griffin, 'On the emigration of the peasantry', *World Development*, vol. 4, no. 5 (1976), pp. 353–61.

K. Griffin and A. K. Ghose, 'Growth and impoverishment in the rural areas of Asia', *World Development*, vol. 7, nos. 4–5 (April–May 1979), pp. 361–83.

C. P. Hallwood, *Stabilization of International Commodity Markets* (Greenwich, Conn.: JAI Press, 1979).

B. Hansen, 'Employment and wages in rural Egypt', *American Economic Review*, vol. 59, no. 3 (1969), pp. 298–313.

F. H. Harbison, *Human Resources as the Wealth of Nations* (London: OUP, 1974).

M. F. Hassan, 'Agricultural development in a petroleum based economy: Qatar', *Economic Development and Cultural Change*, vol. 27, no.1 (October 1978), pp. 145–68.

M. Heikel, *Sphinx and Commissar: The Rise and Fall of Soviet Influence in the Middle East* (London: Collins, 1978).

B. Herman, 'A case of multinational oligopoly in poor countries: oil refinery investment in East Africa', *Journal of Development Economics*, vol. 2, no. 2 (1975), pp. 121–43.

D. Hirst, *Oil and Public Opinion in the Middle East* (New York: Praeger, 1966).

G. W. Hoffman, 'Energy projection – oil, national gas and coal in the USSR and Eastern Europe', *Energy Policy*, vol. 7, no. 3 (September 1979), pp. 232–41.

H. Hughes, 'The external debt of developing countries', *Finance and Development*, vol. 14, no. 4 (December 1977).

H. Hughes, 'Industrialisation and development: a stocktaking', *Industry and Development*, no. 2 (1979), pp. 1–27.

IBRD, *Investment in Education: National Strategy Options for Developing Countries* (Washington, DC: IBRD, 1975).

IBRD, *World Bank Atlas* (Washington, DC: IBRD, 1977a).

IBRD, *Pakistan: Current Developments and Issues* (Report 1423 – PAK, Washington, DC, 1977b).

IBRD, *Country Economic Memorandum on Morocco* (Washington, DC: IBRD, 1977c).

IBRD, 'Arab Republic of Egypt' (IBRD Internal Paper, no. 2071–EGT, 1978a).

IBRD, *Country Economic Memorandum on Jordan* (Washington, DC: IBRD, 1978b).

IBRD, *World Trade and Output of Manufactures: Structural Trends and Developing Countries' Exports* (IBRD Staff Working Paper no. 316, 1979a).

IBRD, *The Changing Composition of Developing Country Exports* (IBRD, Staff Working Paper no. 314, 1979b).

IBRD, *Yemen Arab Republic: Development of a Traditional Economy* (Washington, DC: World Bank Country Study, 1979c).

IBRD, *World Bank Atlas*, various years (Washington, DC: IBRD).

IBRD, *World Debt Tables*, various issues (Washington, DC: IBRD).

ILO, *Employment and Incomes Policies for Iran* (Geneva: ILO, 1973).

ILO, *Manpower and Employment in Arab Countries: Some Critical Issues* (Geneva: ILO, 1977).

IMF, 'Wave of Middle East migration raises questions of policy in many countries', *IMF Survey*, 4 September 1978.

IMF, *Annual Report*, various years (Washington, DC: IMF).

IMF, *Direction of Trade*, various years (Washington, DC: IMF).

IMF, *International Financial Statistics*, various years (Washington, DC: IMF).

IMF, *National Accounts Statistics Yearbook*, various years (Washington, DC: IMF).

S. O. Imoagene, 'Mechanisms of immigrant adjustment in West African urban community', *Nigerian Journal of Economic and Social Studies*, vol. 9, no. 1 (March 1967).

Islamic Council of Europe, *The Muslim World and Future Economic Order* (London: Islamic Council of Europe, 1979).

C. Issawi, 'Oil and Middle East politics', in R. H. Connery and R.S. Gilmour (eds), *The National Energy Problem* (Lexington, Mass.: Lexington Books, 1974), pp. 111–22).

A. Al-Janabi, *OPEC Review*, vol. 3, no. 1 (March 1979).

G. E. Johnson and W. E. Whitelaw, 'Urban–rural income transfers in Kenya' an estimated remittances function', *Economic Development and Cultural Change*, vol. 22, no. 3 (April 1976).

M. Joshi and V. Joshi, *Surplus Labour and the City: A Study of Bombay* (London: OUP, 1976).

B. A. Kalymon, 'Economic incentives in OPEC oil pricing policy', *Journal of Development Economics*, vol. 12, no. 4 (1975), pp. 337–62.

C. P. Kindleberger, *International Economics* (Homewood, Ill.: Irwin, 1973).

O. Koenigsberger, 'The absorption of newcomers in the cities of the Third World', *ODI Review*, no. 1 (1976), pp. 57–79.

N. D. Kondratieff, 'Long waves of economic life', *Lloyds Bank Review*, no. 129 (July 1978), pp. 41–60.

R. E. Kuenne, 'Rivalrous consonnance and the power structure of OPEC', *Kyklos*, vol. 32, fasc. 4 (1979), pp. 695–717.

A. A. Kubbah, *OPEC Past and Present* (Vienna: Petro-Economic Research Centre, 1974).

A. Lambertini, *Energy and Petroleum in Non-OPEC Developing Countries, 1974–1980* (IBRD Staff Working Paper no. 229, 1976).

D. Lecraw, 'Direct investment by firms from LDCs', *Oxford Economic Papers*, vol. 29 (1977), pp. 442–57.

G. Lenczowski, 'The arc of crisis: its central sector', *Foreign Affairs*, Spring 1979, pp. 796–820.

M. Lipton, *Why Poor People Stay Poor* (London: Temple Smith, 1977).

I. M. D. Little, T. Scitovsky and M. F. G. Scott, *Industry and Trade in Some Developing Countries* (London: OUP for OECD, 1970).

R. El Mallakh, *Qatar: Development of an Oil Economy* (London: Croom Helm, 1979).

R. C. O. Matthews, 'Why has Britain had full employment?', *Economic Journal*, September 1968, pp. 555–64.

Ali A. Mazrui, *Africa's International Relations* (London: Heinemann, 1977).

J. E. Meade, *A Geometry of International Trade* (London: Allen & Unwin, 1952).

M. S. Mendelson, 'That sinking feeling', *The Banker*, January 1979.

Middle East Economic Digest, various issues (London).

F. Modigliani and E. Tarantelli, 'Market forces, trade union action and the Philips curve in Italy', *Banco Nazionale del Lavoro Quarterly Review*, 1977.

A. Mohie-Eldin, 'Underemployment in Egyptian agriculture', in ILO, 1977, pp. 110–39.

Morgan Guaranty Trust, *World Financial Markets* (New York, various issues).

National Bank of Egypt, 'The Arab food gap, 1967–1976', *Economic Bulletin,* Cairo, vol. 31, no. 3 (1978), pp. 235–51.

O. Noreng, *Oil Politics in the 1980s: Patterns of International Cooperation* (New York: McGraw-Hill, 1978).

P. R. Odell, *Oil and World Power* (Harmondsworth: Penguin, 1979).

OECD, *Economic Outlook*, no. 25 (July 1979), pp. 6, 148.

Oil and Gas Journal, 'Oil in the 1980s', 12 November 1979.

OPEC BULLETIN, Journal of OPEC Secretariat, various years.

OPEC Press Release, '54th Meeting of the Conference' (OPEC: Vienna, 28 June 1979).

OPEC Secretariat, 'A review of OPEC aid', *OPEC Review*, vol. III, no. 2 (Summer 1979).

M. S. al-Otaiba, *OPEC and the Petroleum Industry* (London: Croom Helm, 1975).

G. Papanek, 'The poor of Djakarta', *Economic Development and Cultural Change*, vol. 24, no. 1 (October 1975).

D. Park, *Oil and Gas in Comecon Countries* (London: Kogan Page, 1979).

Y. S. Park, *Oil, Money and the World Economy* (London: Wilton House, 1976).

A. Parker, 'Western energy policy after Carter', *Lloyds Bank Review*, no. 127 (January 1978), pp. 28–43.

Pearson Commission, *Partners in Development* (London: Pall Mall Press, 1969).

E. Penrose, 'OPEC's importance in the world oil industry', *International Affairs*, vol. 55, no. 1 (1979), pp. 18–22.

J. E. Perlman, *The Myth of Marginality* (Berkeley: University of California Press, 1976).

R. Prebisch, 'Commercial policy in underdeveloped countries', *American Economic Review*, 1967, Papers and Proceedings.

W. B. Quandt, 'US energy policy and the Arab Israeli conflict', in Sherbiny and Tessler (eds), 1976, pp. 279–94.

M. Quinlan, 'Gloom in Western Europe', *Petroleum Economist*, vol. XLVI, no.6 (June 1979), pp. 233–5.

R. K. Ramazani, 'Security in the Persian Gulf', *Foreign Affairs*, Spring 1979, pp. 821–35.

M. Roemer, 'Resource-based industrialisation in the developing countries', Harvard Institute for International Relations paper, October 1976.

A. Sampson, *The Seven Sisters* (London: Coronet, 1976).

P. Samuelson, 'International trade and the equalisation of factor prices', *Economic Journal*, June 1948.

N. Sargen, 'Use of economic indicators in country risk appraisal', Reserve Bank of San Francisco, *Economic Review*, Fall 1977.

Saudi Newsletter, various issues (Riyadh: Saudi Arabian Government).

J. S. Saul and R. Woods, 'African peasantries', in T. Shanin (ed.), *Peasants and Peasant Societies* (Harmondsworth; Penguin, 1971).

Y. A. Sayigh, *The Economies of the Arab World* (London: Croom Helm, 1978).

F. Shehab, 'Kuwait: a super-affluent society', *Foreign Affairs*, April 1964.

N. A. Sherbiny and M. A. Tessler (eds), *Arab Oil: Impact on the Arab Countries and Global Implications* (New York: Praeger, 1976).

I. F. I. Shihata and R. Mabro, 'The OPEC aid record', *World Development*, vol. 7, no. 1 (February 1979).

G. Schiller, 'Channelling migration: a review of policy', *International Labour Review*, vol. III, no. 4 (April 1975).

S. W. Sinclair, *Urbanization and Labour Markets in Developing Countries* (London: Croom Helm/New York St Martins Press, 1978).

A. Z. Sofia, 'How to rationalise country risk ratios', *Euromoney*, September 1979.

R. M. Solow, 'The economics of natural resources', *American Economic Review*, Papers and Proceedings, 1974, pp. 1–14.

S. Strange, 'Debts, defaulters and development', *International Affairs*, July 1967.

J. C. Swanson, 'Some consequences of emigration for rural economic development in the Yemen Arab Republic', *Middle East Journal*, 1979.

D. E. Syvrud, *Foundations of Brazilian Economic Growth* (Stanford Calif.: American Enterprise Institute, 1974).

K. Takeuchi, 'CIPEC and the copper export earnings of member countries', *The Developing Economies*, 1972, pp. 3–29.

Trilateral Commission, 'A turning point in North–South economic relations', in *Trilateral Commission Task Force Report* (New York: New York University Press, 1977).

J. Tumlir, 'Oil payments and oil debt in the world economy', *Lloyds Bank Review*, no. 113 (July 1974), pp. 1–14.

UN, 'The United Nations Development Decade, proposals for action', *Report of the Secretary General* (New York, 1962), pp. 7–13.

UN, 'Review of international trade and development' (New York: TD/5/Rev. 1, 1967).

UN, *Transnational Corporations in World Development: A Re-Examination*, UN Economic and Social Council Commission on Transnational Corporations, 4th Session, 15–26 May 1978, Item 7(a) of Agenda (Doc. E/C. 10/38).

UN, *World Statistical Pocketbook* (New York: UN, 1978).

UNCTAD, *The Cost of Tying Aid to Recipient Countries* (Doc. TD/7/ Supp. 8, 1968).

UNCTAD, *Trade Among Developing Countries by Main SITC Groups and by Regions* (TD/B/C.7/21; 20 September 1978a).

UNCTAD, *Energy Supplies for Developing Countries: Issues in Transfer and Development of Technology* (Doc. TD/B/C.6/31, 17 October 1978b).

UNCTAD, *Basic Data on the Least Developed Countries* (Manila, May 1979a).

UNCTAD, *Handbook of International Trade and Development Statistics* (Doc. E/F.79.II.D.2, TD/STAT.8, 1979b).

UNCTAD, *Cooperative Exchange of Skills among Developing Countries* (Doc. TD/B/C6/AC4/Rev 1, New York, 1979c).

UNIDO, *Industrial Development Survey* (UNIDO, Vienna, 1979a).

UNIDO, *The Impact of Trade With Developing Countries On Employment in Developed Countries: Empirical Evidence from Recent Research* (UNIDO Working Papers on Structural Change, Vienna, 1979b).

US Department of Mines, *International Petroleum Annual*, various years (Washington, DC: US Government Printer).

L. Vallenilla, *Oil: The Making of a New Economic Order: Venezuelan Oil and OPEC* (New York: McGraw Hill, 1975).

A. R. Waters, 'Migration, remittances and the cash constraint in African smallholder economic development', *Oxford Economic Papers*, vol. 25 (1973), pp. 437–54.

T. D. Willet, 'Structure of OPEC and the outlook for international oil prices', *The World Economy*, vol. 2, no.1 (January 1979), pp. 51–64.

M. Willrich, *Energy and World Politics* (New York: Free Press for American Society of International Law, 1975).

R. Wilson, *The Economies of the Middle East* (London: Macmillan, 1979).

Worldview, various issues.

P. A. Yotopoulos and J. Nugent, 'A balanced growth version of the linkage hypothesis: a test', *Quarterly Journal of Economics*, vol. 87, no. 2 (May 1973), pp. 157–71.

S. Younger, 'Ideology and pragmatism in Algerian foreign policy', *The World Today*, March 1978, pp. 107–14.

Index

References in italics refer to tables and figures and those in bold refer to chapters.

Author Index